Tales from Wonderland

volume three

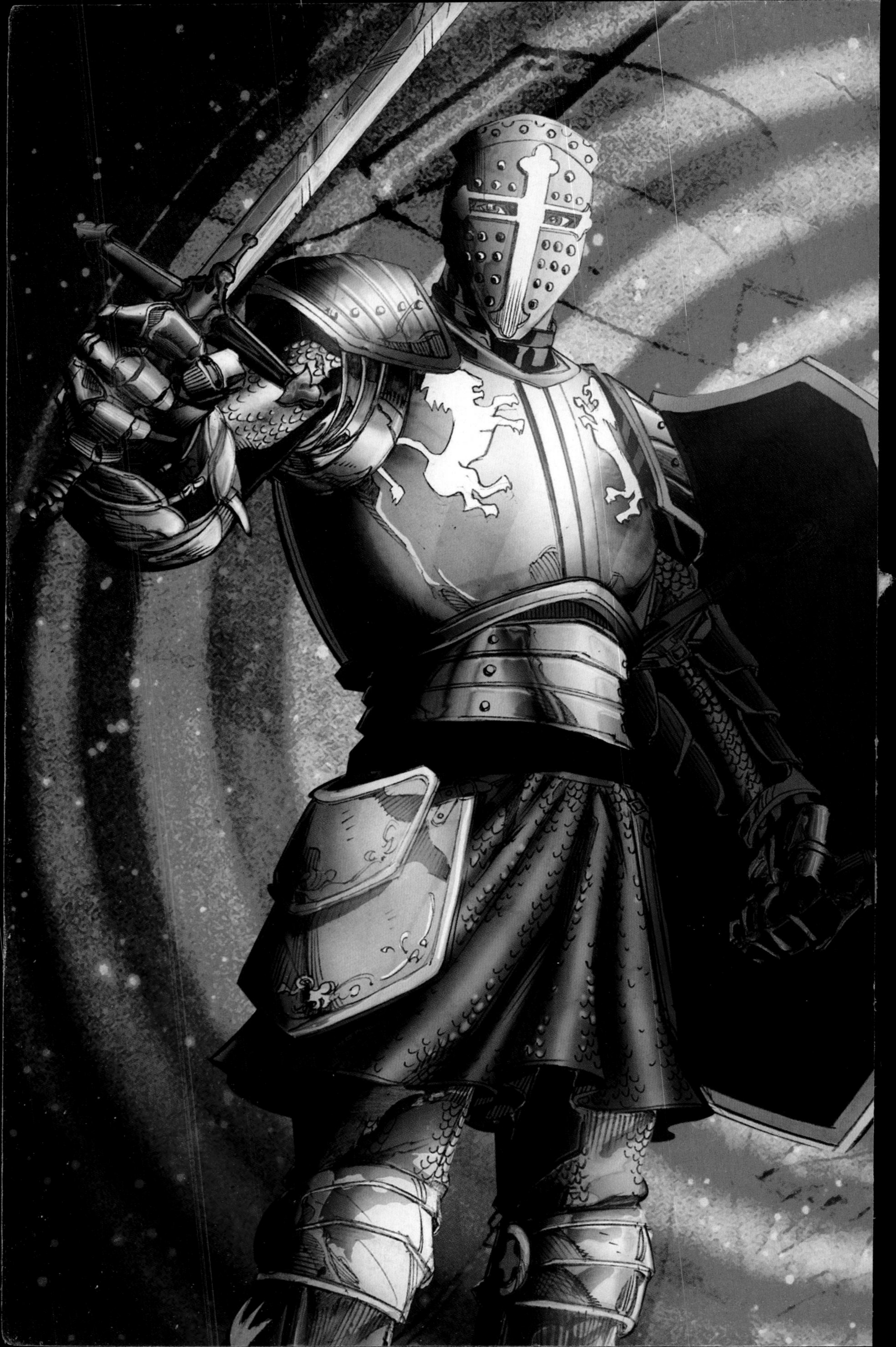

CREATED BY
RAVEN GREGORY
JOE BRUSHA
RALPH TEDESCO

WRITTEN BY
RAVEN GREGORY
TROY BROWNFIELD

ARTWORK BY
TOMMY PATTERSON
MIKE DEBALFO
MARTIN MONTIEL
IAN SNYDER

COLORS BY
WES DZIOBA
MICHAEL GARCIA
MILEN PARVANOV
JEFF BALKE
ALEX OWENS
JASON EMBURY

LETTERS BY
CRANK!

TRADE DESIGN BY
CHRISTOPHER COTE
DAVID SEIDMAN

TRADE EDITED BY
RALPH TEDESCO

THIS VOLUME REPRINTS THE
"TALES FROM WONDERLAND"
VOLUME THREE ONE-SHOTS

WWW.ZENESCOPE.COM

FIRST EDITION, DECEMBER 2010
ISBN: 978-0-9825826-5-7

zenescope

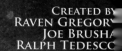

ZENESCOPE ENTERTAINMENT, INC.

JOE BRUSHA - PRESIDENT
RALPH TEDESCO - V.P./ EDITOR-IN-CHIEF
CHRISTOPHER COTE - ART DIRECTOR
RAVEN GREGORY - EXECUTIVE EDITOR

Tales From Wonderland Trade paperback Volume 3, December 2010, First Printing. Published by Zenescope Entertainment Inc., 501 Office Center Drive, Ste. 8, Fort Washington, Pennsylvania 19034.

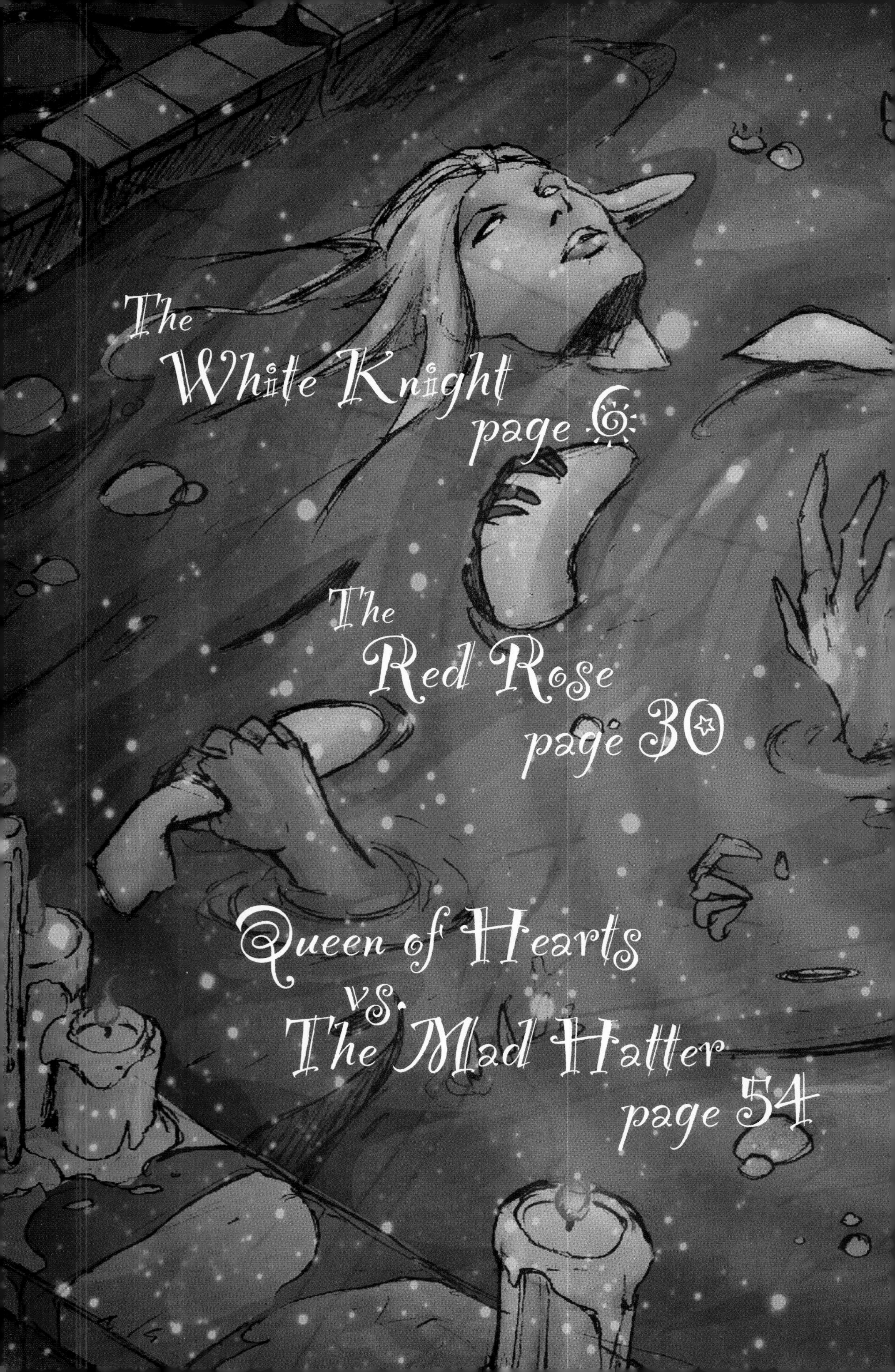

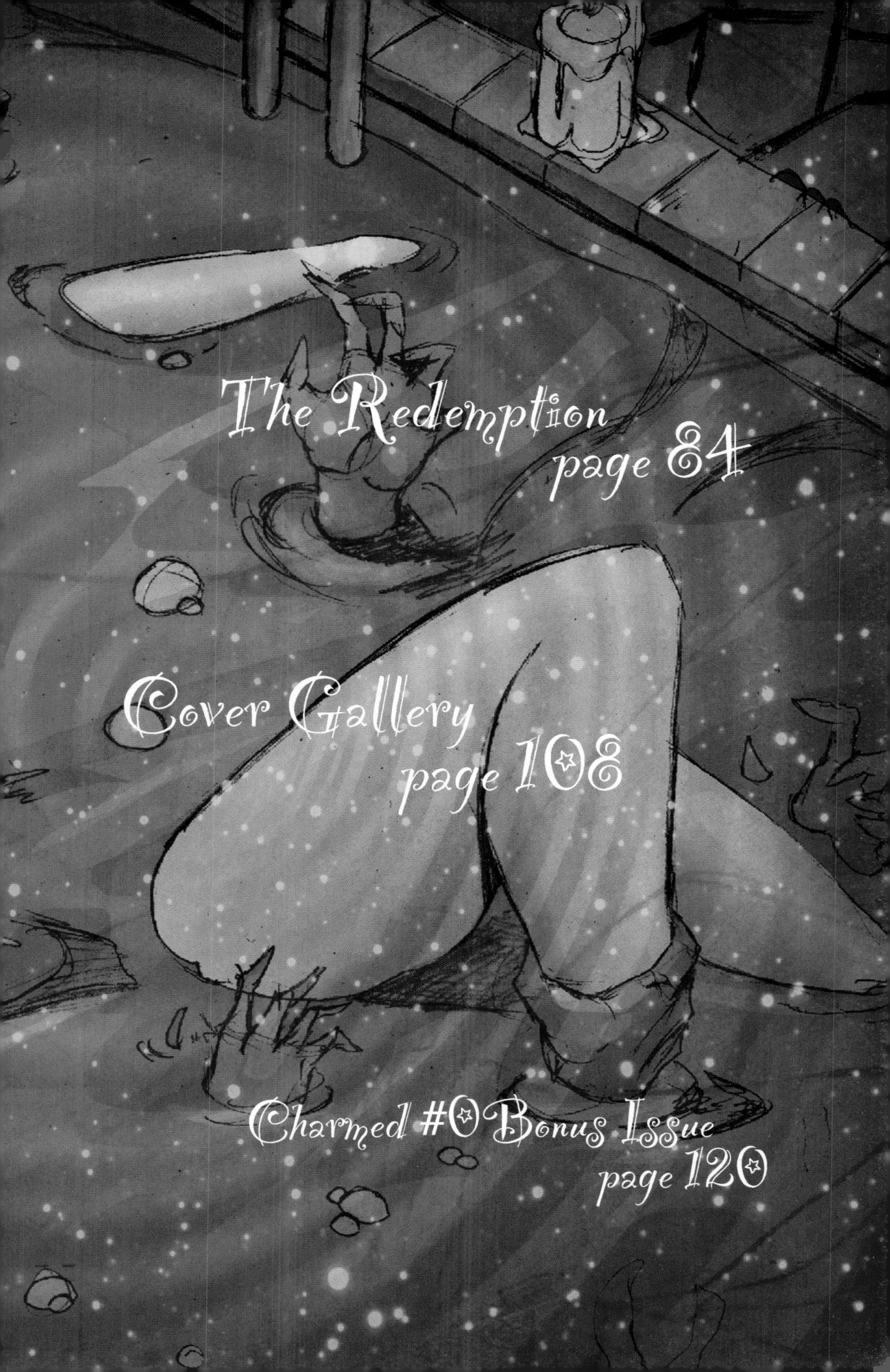

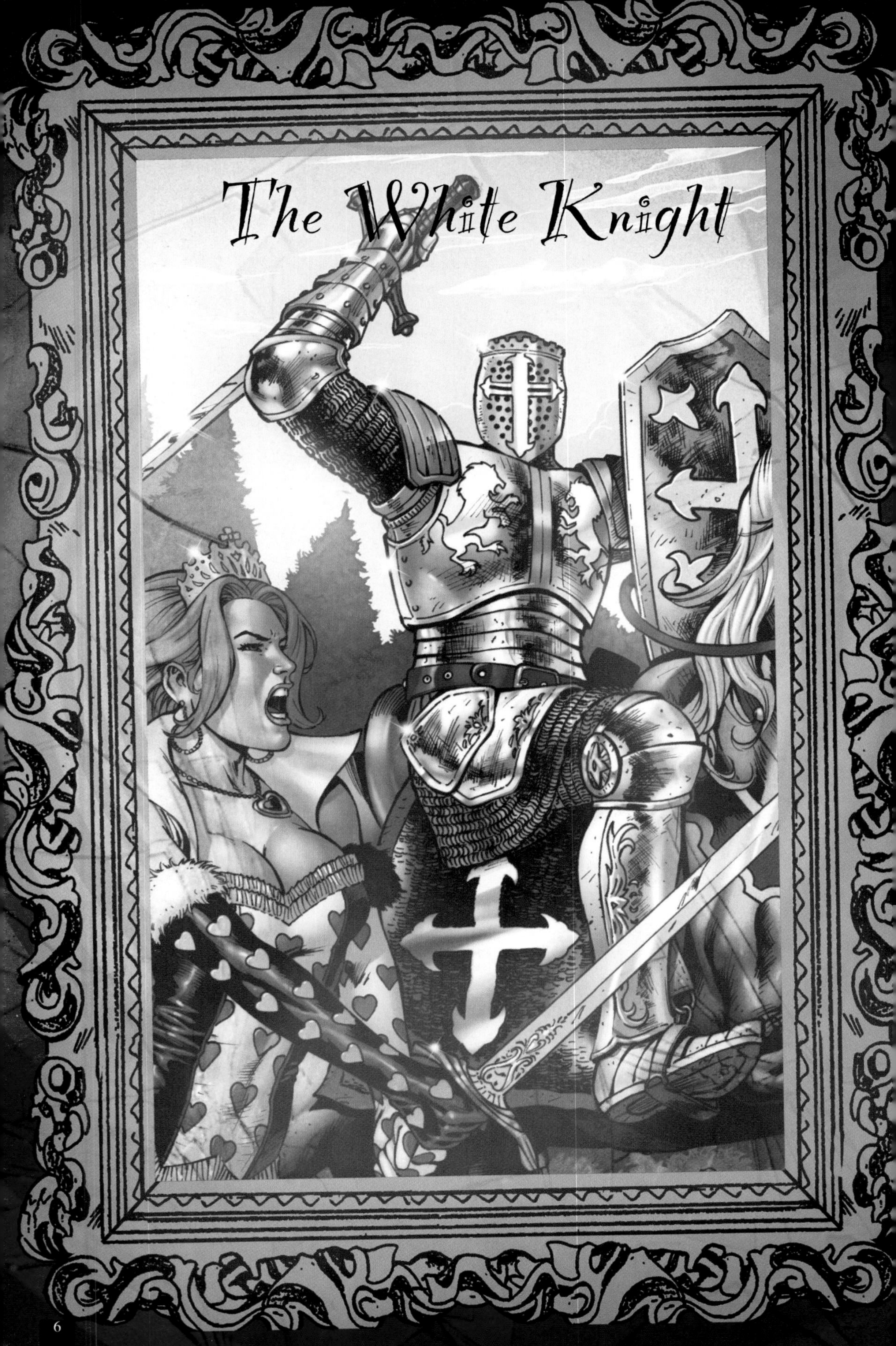
The White Knight

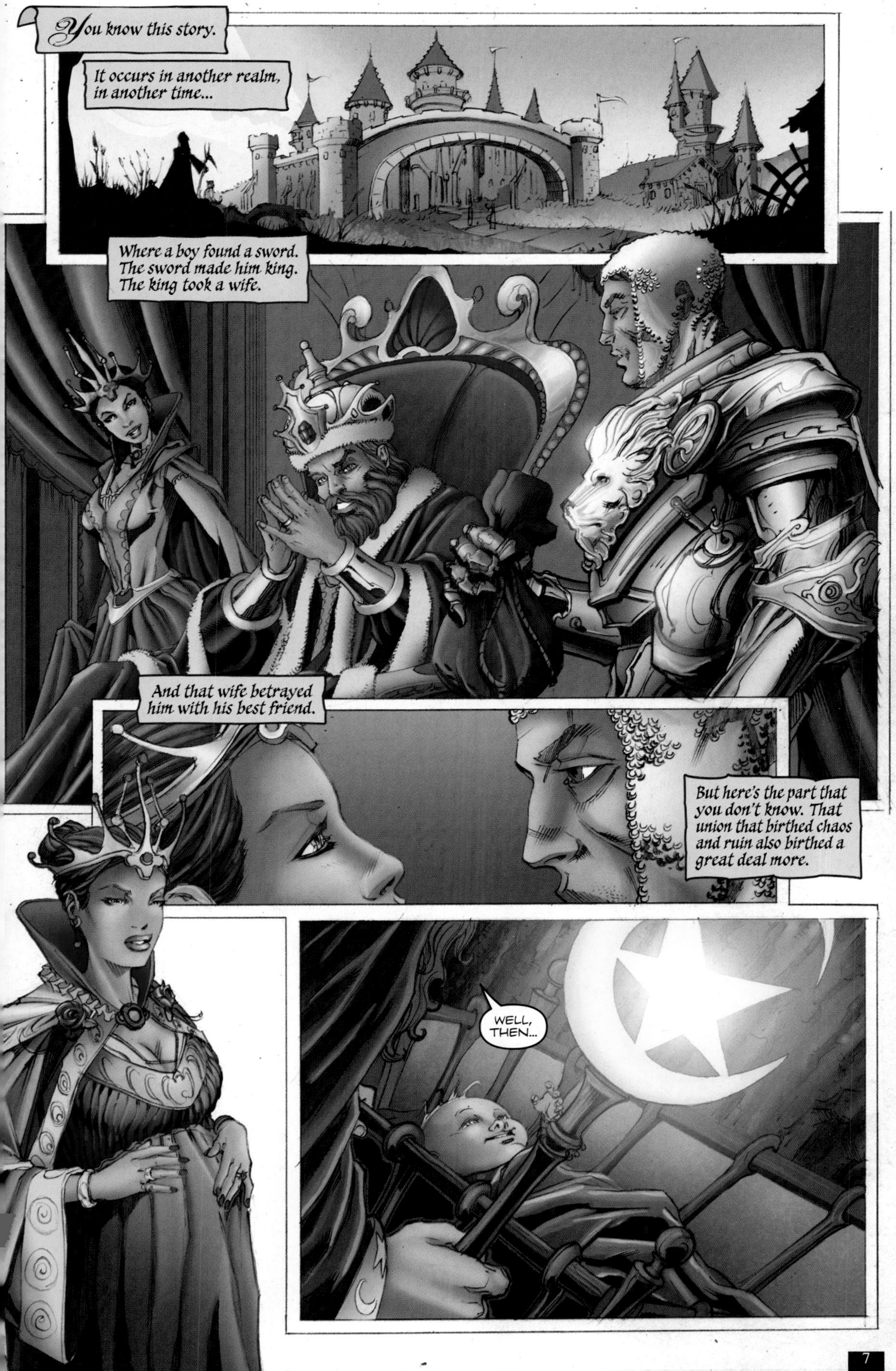
You know this story.
It occurs in another realm, in another time...
Where a boy found a sword. The sword made him king. The king took a wife.
And that wife betrayed him with his best friend.
But here's the part that you don't know. That union that birthed chaos and ruin also birthed a great deal more.
WELL, THEN...

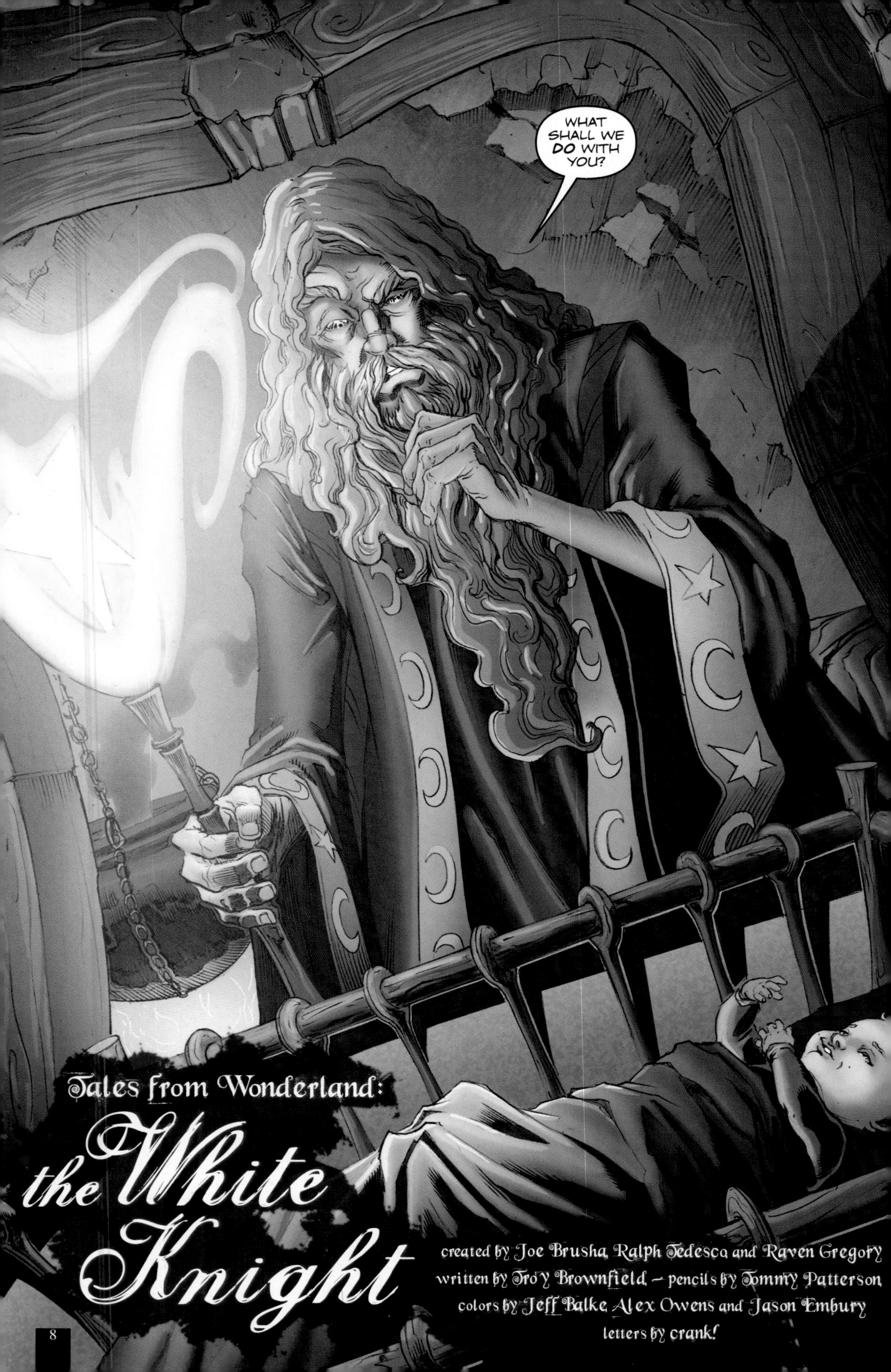
WHAT SHALL WE DO WITH YOU?
Tales from Wonderland:
the White Knight
created by Joe Brusha, Ralph Tedesco and Raven Gregory
written by Troy Brownfield – pencils by Tommy Patterson
colors by Jeff Balke, Alex Owens and Jason Embury
letters by crank!

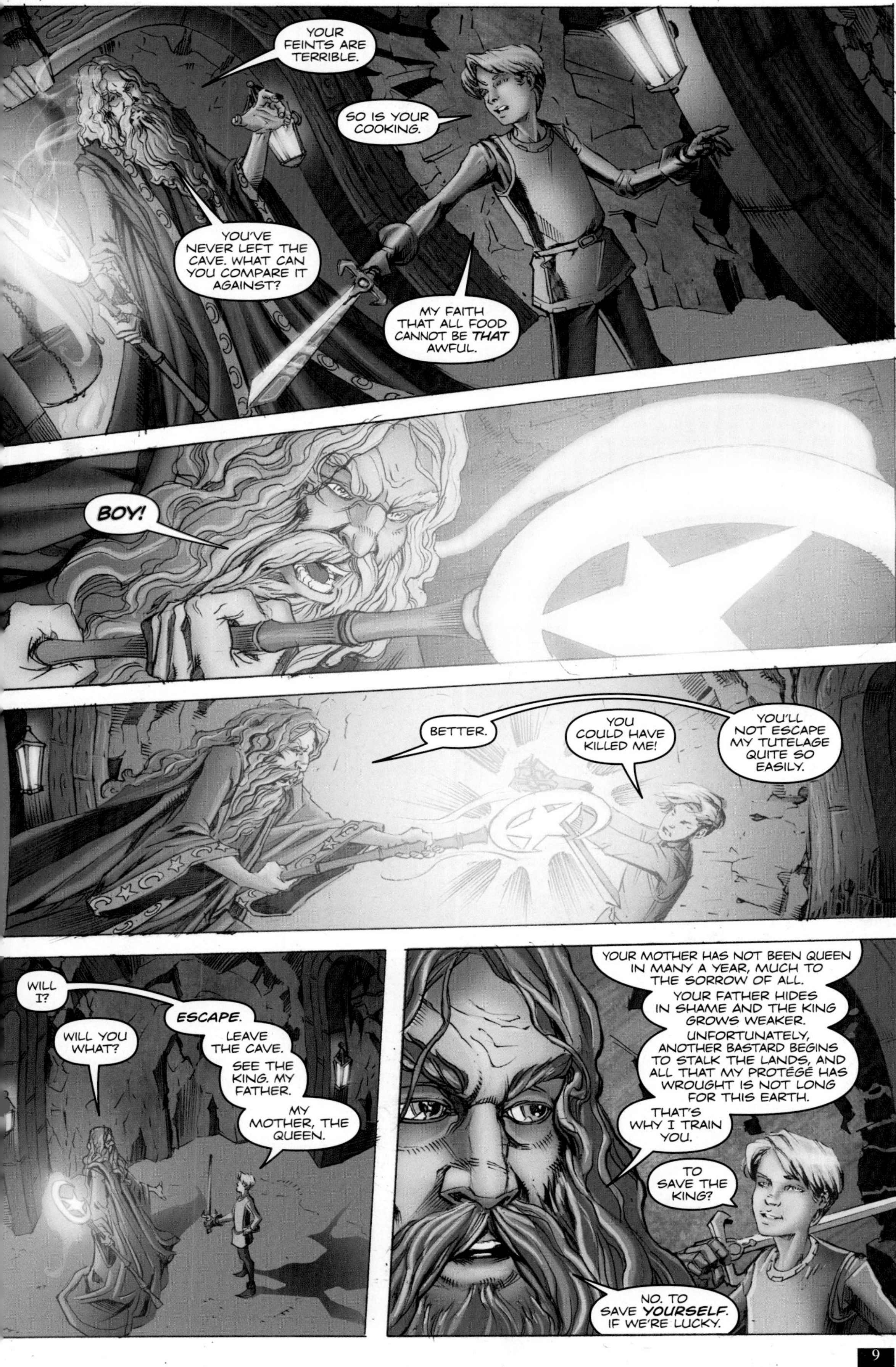
YOUR FEINTS ARE TERRIBLE.
SO IS YOUR COOKING.
YOU'VE NEVER LEFT THE CAVE. WHAT CAN YOU COMPARE IT AGAINST?
MY FAITH THAT ALL FOOD CANNOT BE *THAT* AWFUL.
BOY!
BETTER.
YOU COULD HAVE KILLED ME!
YOU'LL NOT ESCAPE MY TUTELAGE QUITE SO EASILY.
WILL I?
WILL YOU WHAT?
ESCAPE.
LEAVE THE CAVE.
SEE THE KING. MY FATHER.
MY MOTHER, THE QUEEN.
YOUR MOTHER HAS NOT BEEN QUEEN IN MANY A YEAR, MUCH TO THE SORROW OF ALL.
YOUR FATHER HIDES IN SHAME AND THE KING GROWS WEAKER.
UNFORTUNATELY, ANOTHER BASTARD BEGINS TO STALK THE LANDS, AND ALL THAT MY PROTÉGÉ HAS WROUGHT IS NOT LONG FOR THIS EARTH.
THAT'S WHY I TRAIN YOU.
TO SAVE THE KING?
NO. TO SAVE *YOURSELF*. IF WE'RE LUCKY.

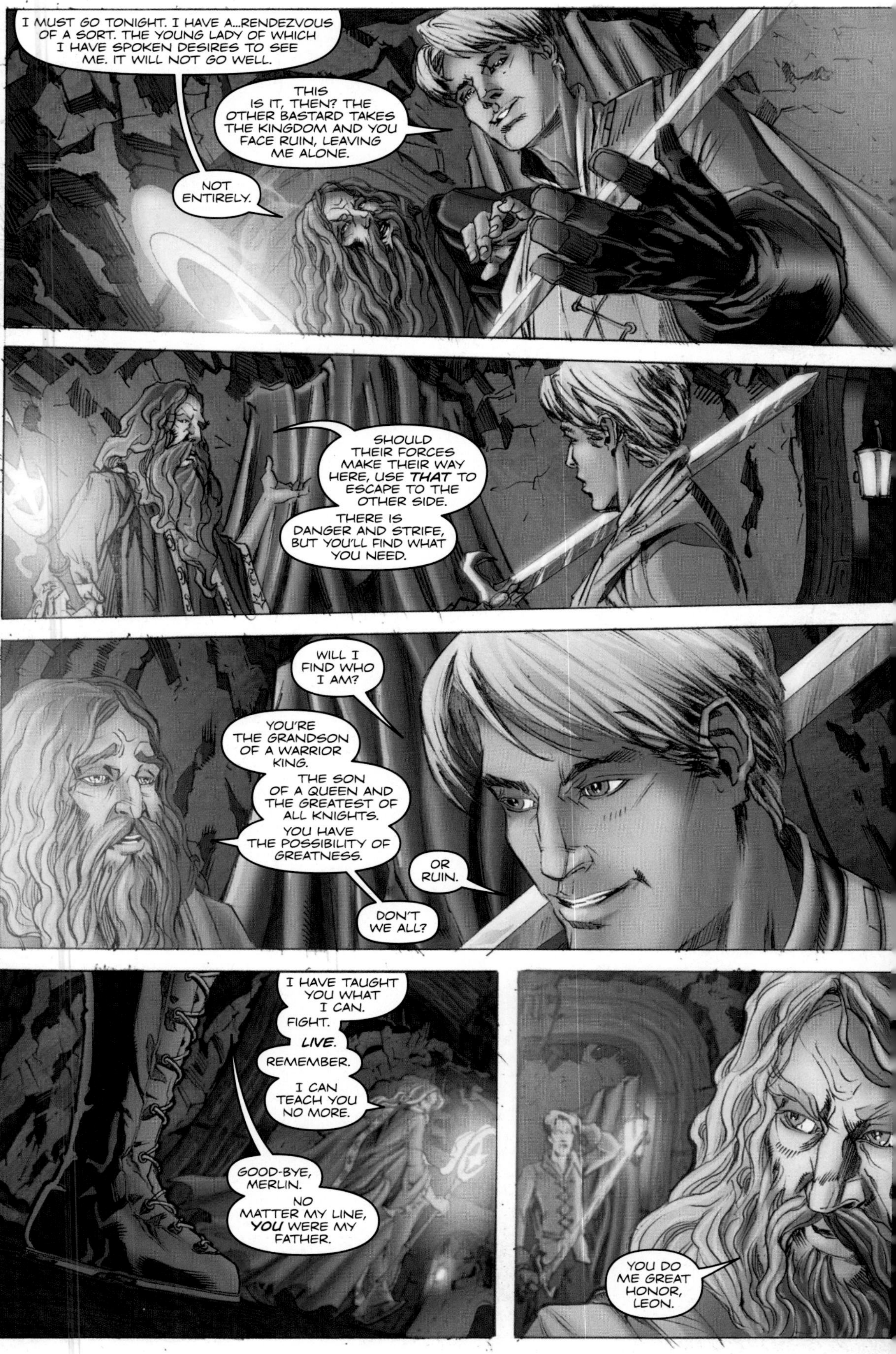
I MUST GO TONIGHT. I HAVE A...RENDEZVOUS OF A SORT. THE YOUNG LADY OF WHICH I HAVE SPOKEN DESIRES TO SEE ME. IT WILL NOT GO WELL.
THIS IS IT, THEN? THE OTHER BASTARD TAKES THE KINGDOM AND YOU FACE RUIN, LEAVING ME ALONE.
NOT ENTIRELY.
SHOULD THEIR FORCES MAKE THEIR WAY HERE, USE *THAT* TO ESCAPE TO THE OTHER SIDE.
THERE IS DANGER AND STRIFE, BUT YOU'LL FIND WHAT YOU NEED.
WILL I FIND WHO I AM?
YOU'RE THE GRANDSON OF A WARRIOR KING.
THE SON OF A QUEEN AND THE GREATEST OF ALL KNIGHTS.
YOU HAVE THE POSSIBILITY OF GREATNESS.
OR RUIN.
DON'T WE ALL?
I HAVE TAUGHT YOU WHAT I CAN.
FIGHT.
LIVE.
REMEMBER.
I CAN TEACH YOU NO MORE.
GOOD-BYE, MERLIN.
NO MATTER MY LINE, *YOU* WERE MY FATHER.
YOU DO ME GREAT HONOR, LEON.

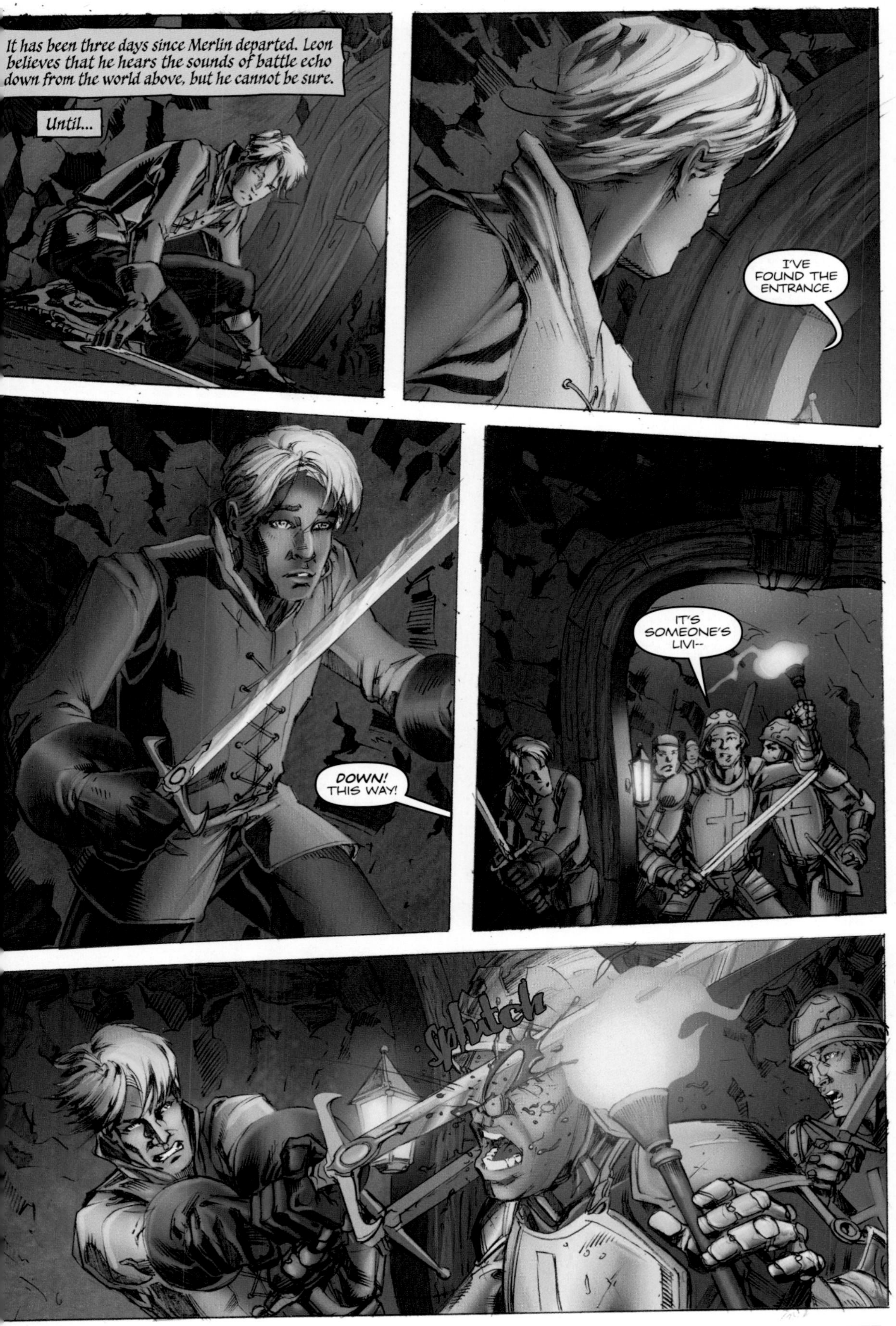
It has been three days since Merlin departed. Leon believes that he hears the sounds of battle echo down from the world above, but he cannot be sure.
Until...
I'VE FOUND THE ENTRANCE.
DOWN! THIS WAY!
IT'S SOMEONE'S LIVI--
Splutch

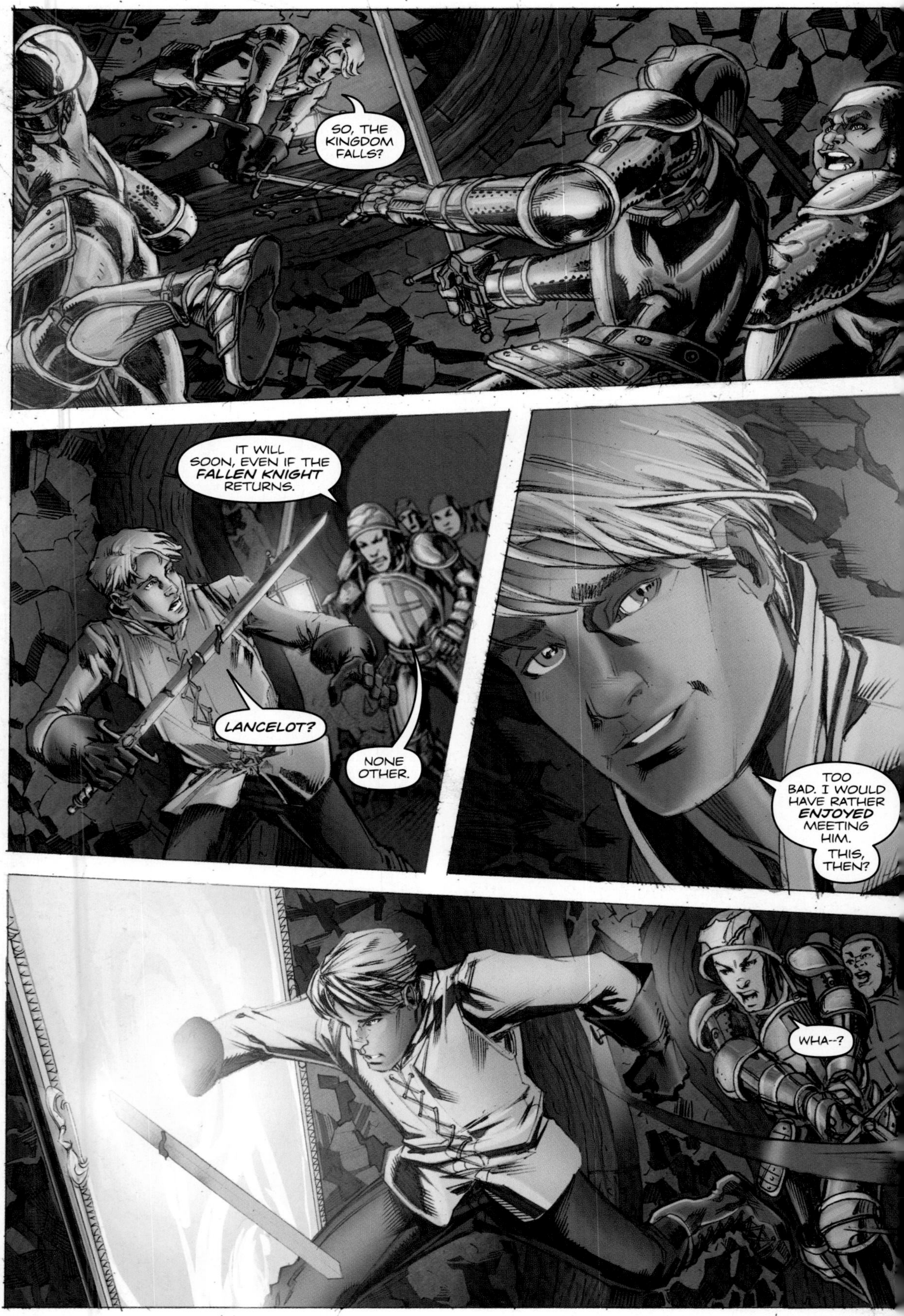
SO, THE KINGDOM FALLS?
IT WILL SOON, EVEN IF THE FALLEN KNIGHT RETURNS.
LANCELOT?
NONE OTHER.
TOO BAD. I WOULD HAVE RATHER ENJOYED MEETING HIM.
THIS, THEN?
WHA--?

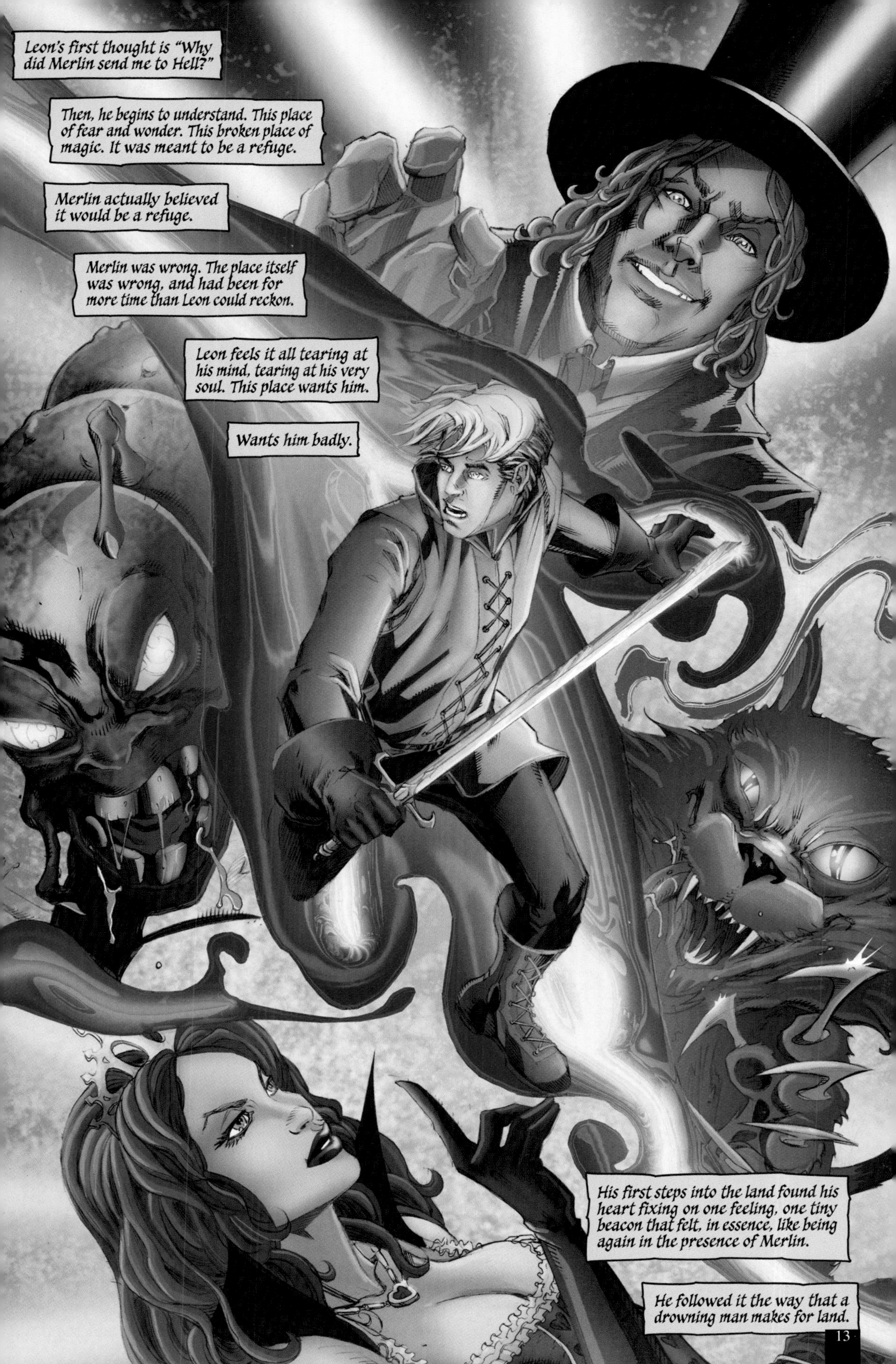
Leon's first thought is "Why did Merlin send me to Hell?"
Then, he begins to understand. This place of fear and wonder. This broken place of magic. It was meant to be a refuge.
Merlin actually believed it would be a refuge.
Merlin was wrong. The place itself was wrong, and had been for more time than Leon could reckon.
Leon feels it all tearing at his mind, tearing at his very soul. This place wants him.
Wants him badly.
His first steps into the land found his heart fixing on one feeling, one tiny beacon that felt, in essence, like being again in the presence of Merlin.
He followed it the way that a drowning man makes for land.

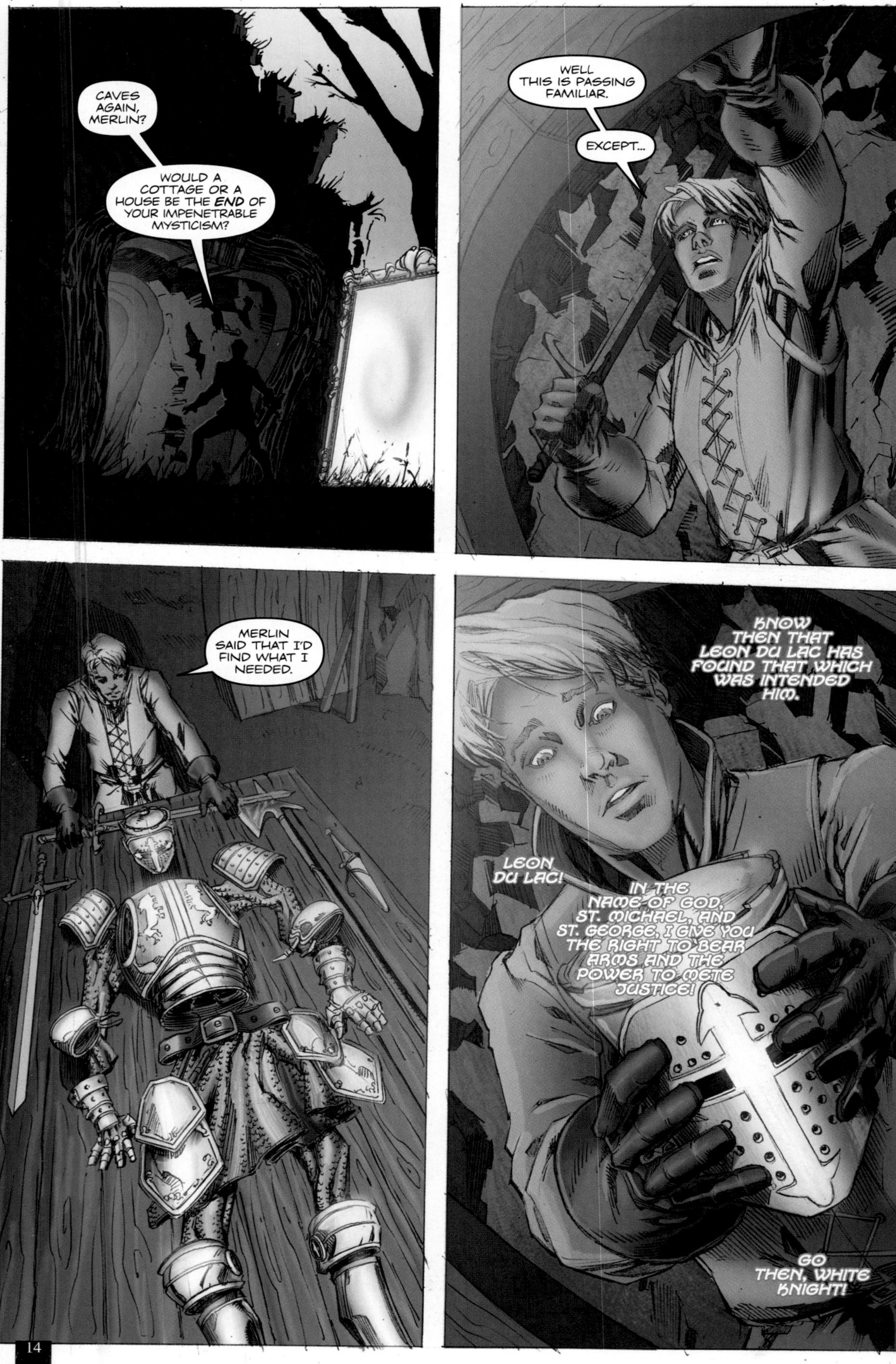
CAVES AGAIN, MERLIN?
WOULD A COTTAGE OR A HOUSE BE THE **END** OF YOUR IMPENETRABLE MYSTICISM?
WELL THIS IS PASSING FAMILIAR.
EXCEPT...
MERLIN SAID THAT I'D FIND WHAT I NEEDED.
KNOW THEN THAT LEON DU LAC HAS FOUND THAT WHICH WAS INTENDED HIM.
LEON DU LAC!
IN THE NAME OF GOD, ST. MICHAEL, AND ST. GEORGE, I GIVE YOU THE RIGHT TO BEAR ARMS AND THE POWER TO METE JUSTICE!
GO THEN, WHITE KNIGHT!

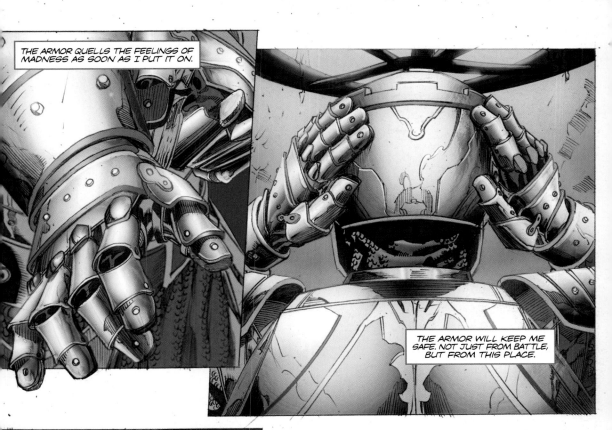

THE ARMOR QUELLS THE FEELINGS OF MADNESS AS SOON AS I PUT IT ON.

THE ARMOR WILL KEEP ME SAFE. NOT JUST FROM BATTLE, BUT FROM THIS PLACE.

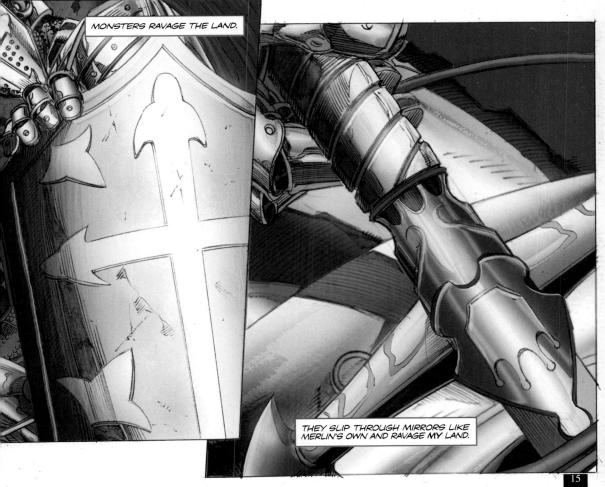

MONSTERS RAVAGE THE LAND.

THEY SLIP THROUGH MIRRORS LIKE MERLIN'S OWN AND RAVAGE MY LAND.

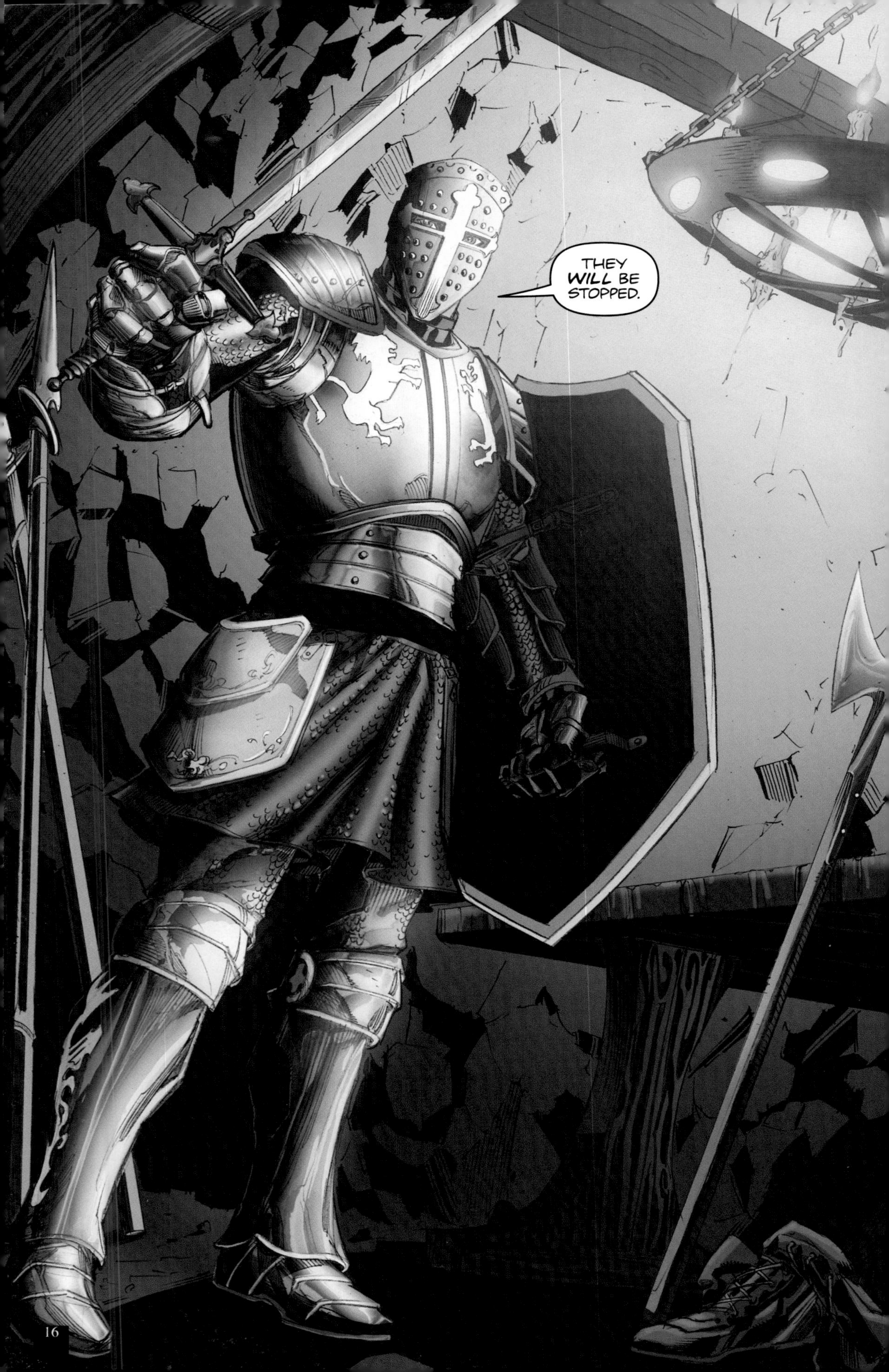
THEY WILL BE STOPPED.

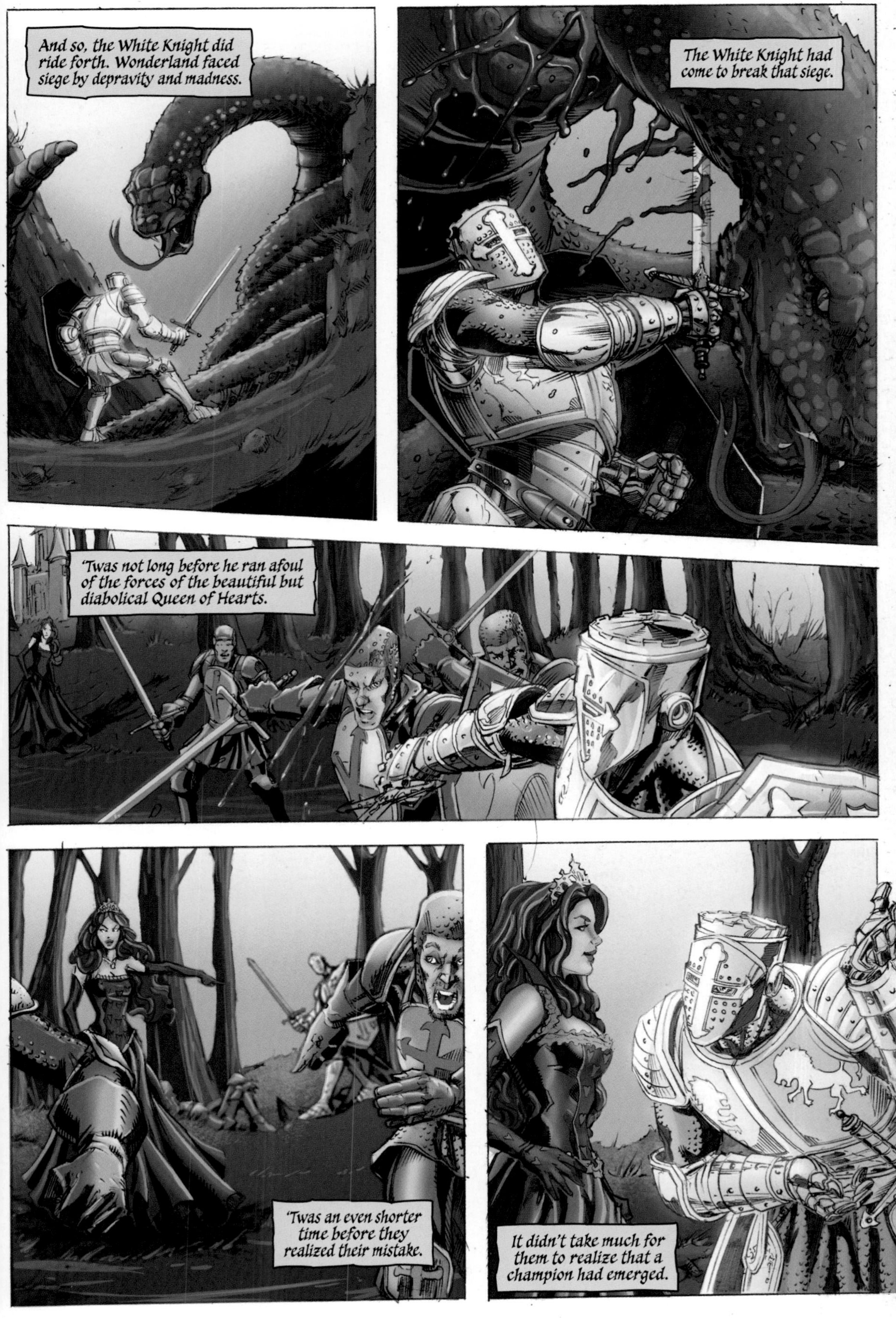
And so, the White Knight did ride forth. Wonderland faced siege by depravity and madness.
The White Knight had come to break that siege.
'Twas not long before he ran afoul of the forces of the beautiful but diabolical Queen of Hearts.
'Twas an even shorter time before they realized their mistake.
It didn't take much for them to realize that a champion had emerged.

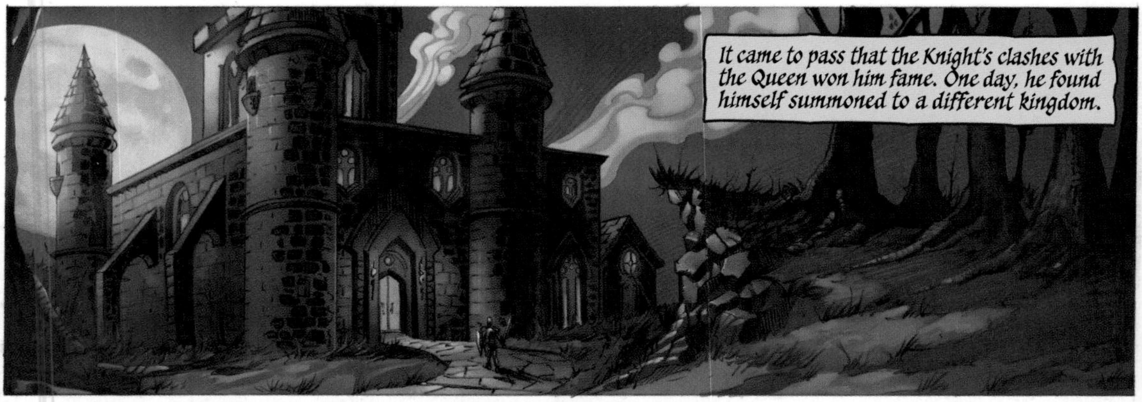
It came to pass that the Knight's clashes with the Queen won him fame. One day, he found himself summoned to a different kingdom.

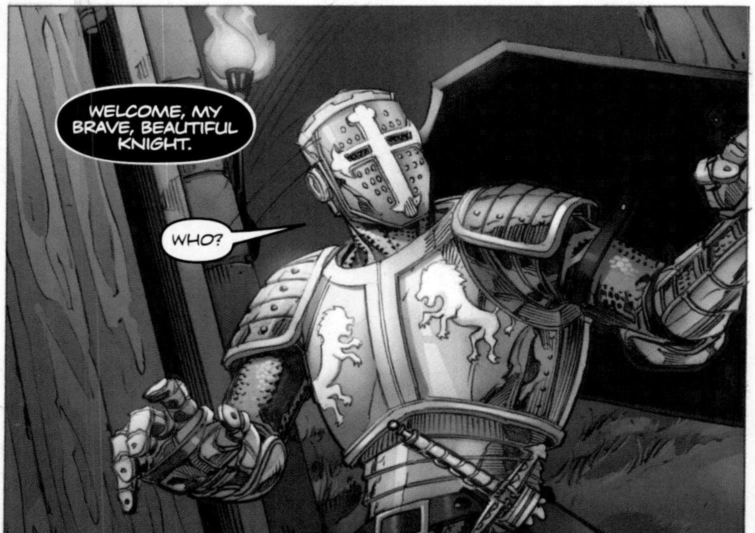
WELCOME, MY BRAVE, BEAUTIFUL KNIGHT.
WHO?

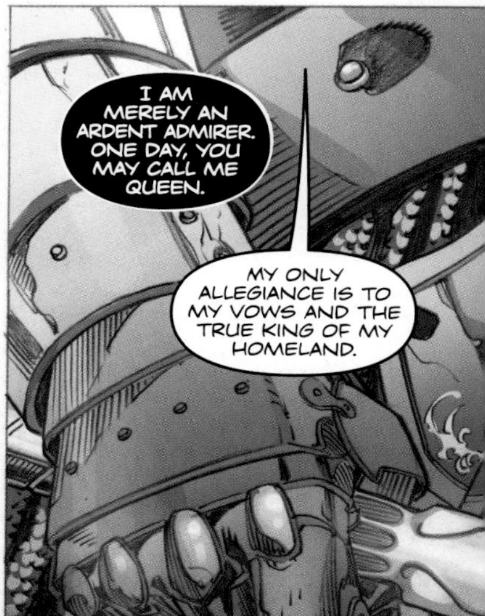
I AM MERELY AN ARDENT ADMIRER. ONE DAY, YOU MAY CALL ME QUEEN.
MY ONLY ALLEGIANCE IS TO MY VOWS AND THE TRUE KING OF MY HOMELAND.

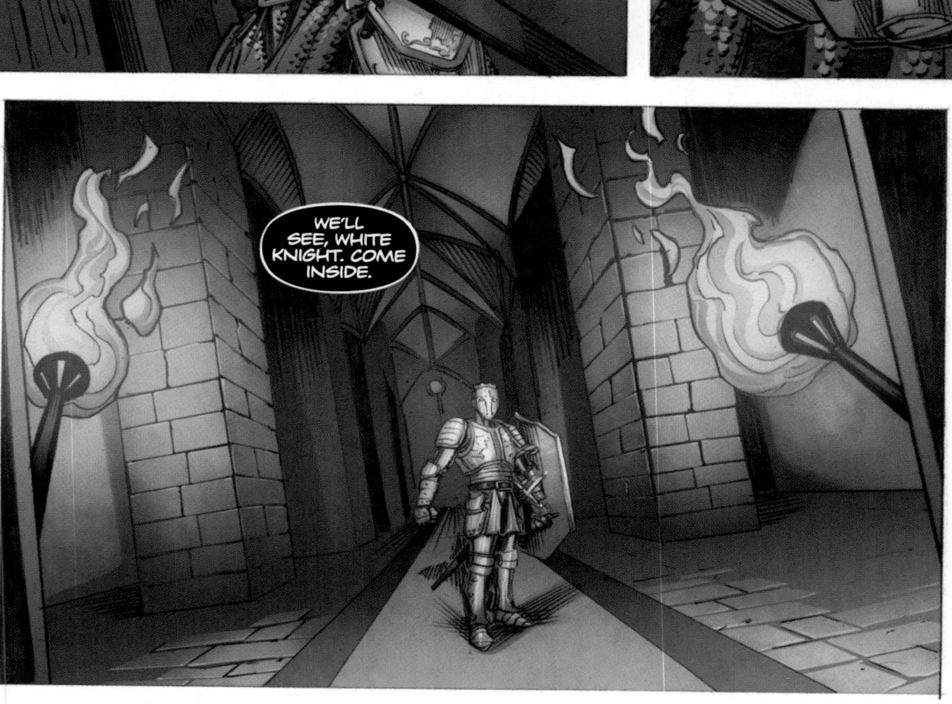
WE'LL SEE, WHITE KNIGHT. COME INSIDE.

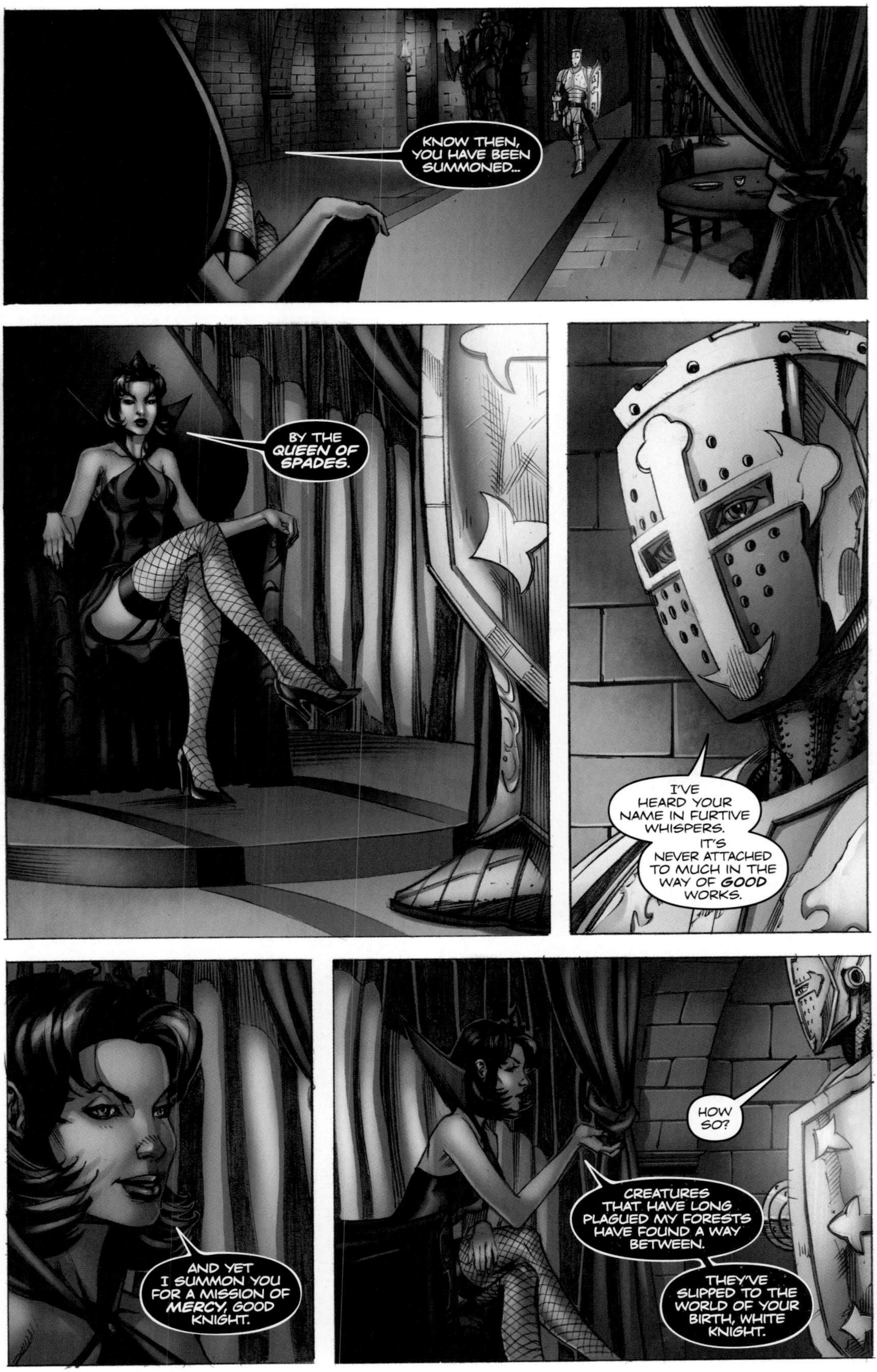
KNOW THEN, YOU HAVE BEEN SUMMONED...
BY THE QUEEN OF SPADES.
I'VE HEARD YOUR NAME IN FURTIVE WHISPERS.
IT'S NEVER ATTACHED TO MUCH IN THE WAY OF GOOD WORKS.
AND YET I SUMMON YOU FOR A MISSION OF MERCY, GOOD KNIGHT.
HOW SO?
CREATURES THAT HAVE LONG PLAGUED MY FORESTS HAVE FOUND A WAY BETWEEN.
THEY'VE SLIPPED TO THE WORLD OF YOUR BIRTH, WHITE KNIGHT.

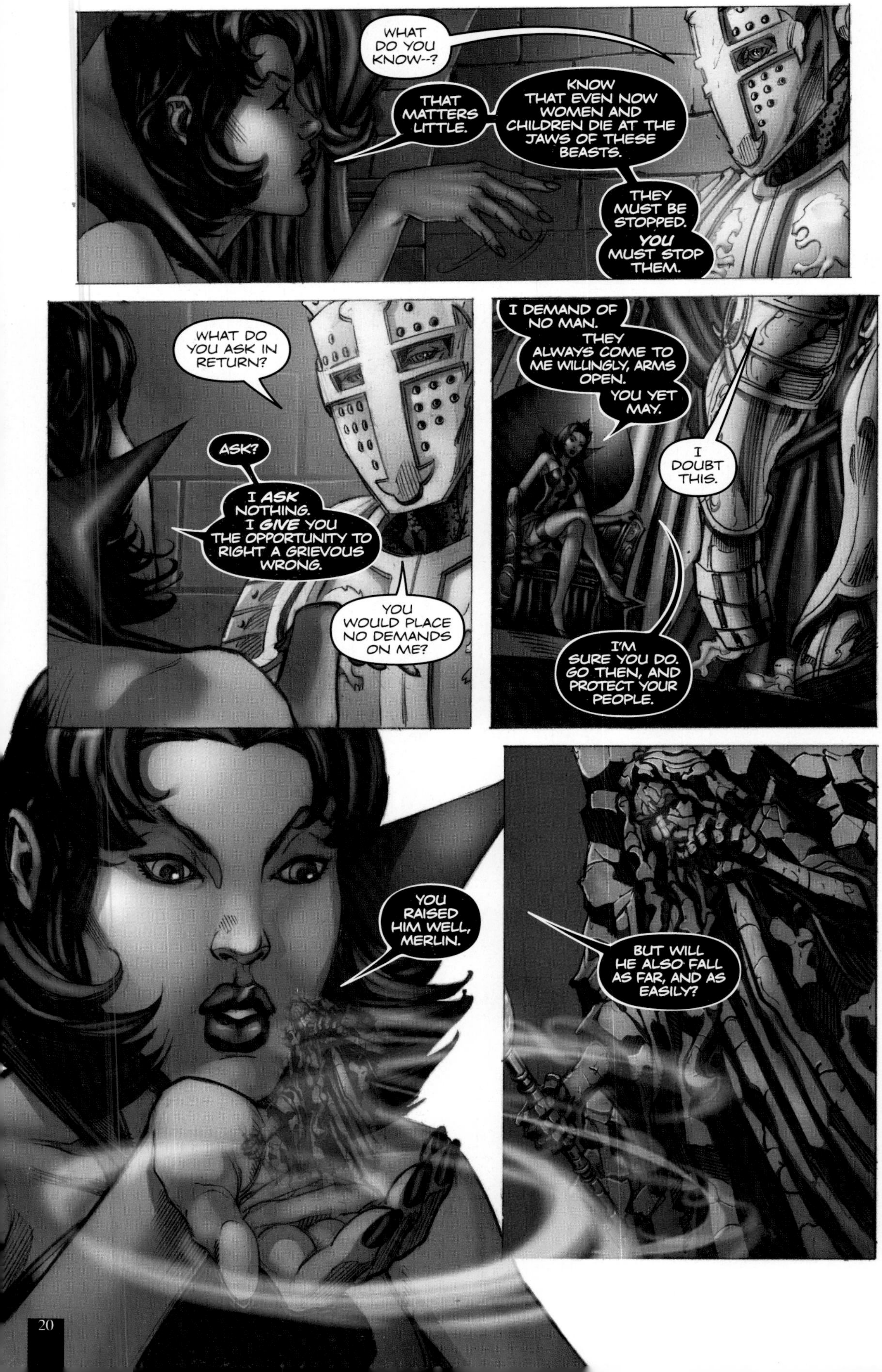
WHAT DO YOU KNOW--?
THAT MATTERS LITTLE.
KNOW THAT EVEN NOW WOMEN AND CHILDREN DIE AT THE JAWS OF THESE BEASTS.
THEY MUST BE STOPPED.
YOU MUST STOP THEM.
WHAT DO YOU ASK IN RETURN?
ASK?
I ASK NOTHING. I GIVE YOU THE OPPORTUNITY TO RIGHT A GRIEVOUS WRONG.
YOU WOULD PLACE NO DEMANDS ON ME?
I DEMAND OF NO MAN.
THEY ALWAYS COME TO ME WILLINGLY, ARMS OPEN.
YOU YET MAY.
I DOUBT THIS.
I'M SURE YOU DO. GO THEN, AND PROTECT YOUR PEOPLE.
YOU RAISED HIM WELL, MERLIN.
BUT WILL HE ALSO FALL AS FAR, AND AS EASILY?

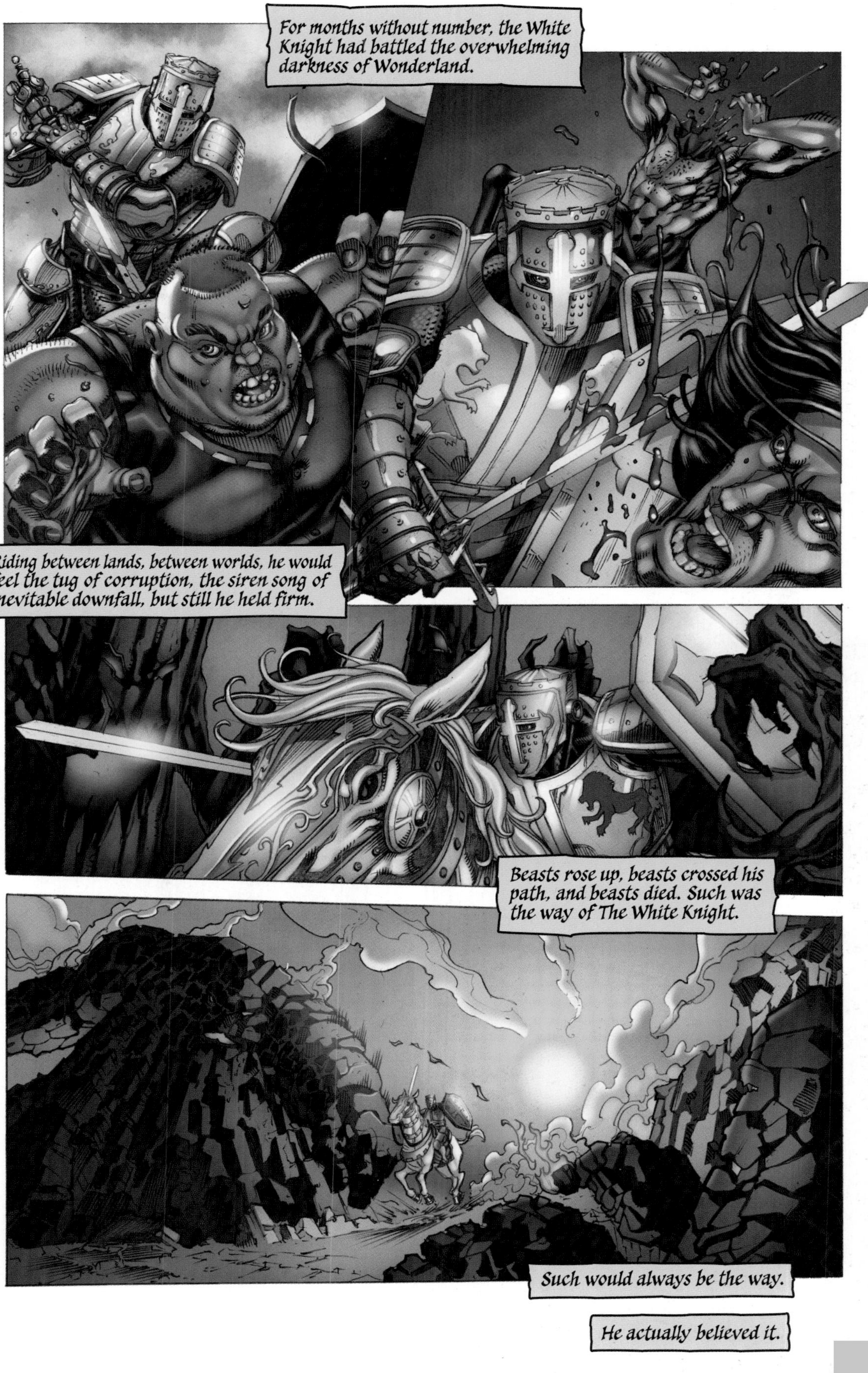
For months without number, the White Knight had battled the overwhelming darkness of Wonderland.
Riding between lands, between worlds, he would feel the tug of corruption, the siren song of inevitable downfall, but still he held firm.
Beasts rose up, beasts crossed his path, and beasts died. Such was the way of The White Knight.
Such would always be the way.
He actually believed it.

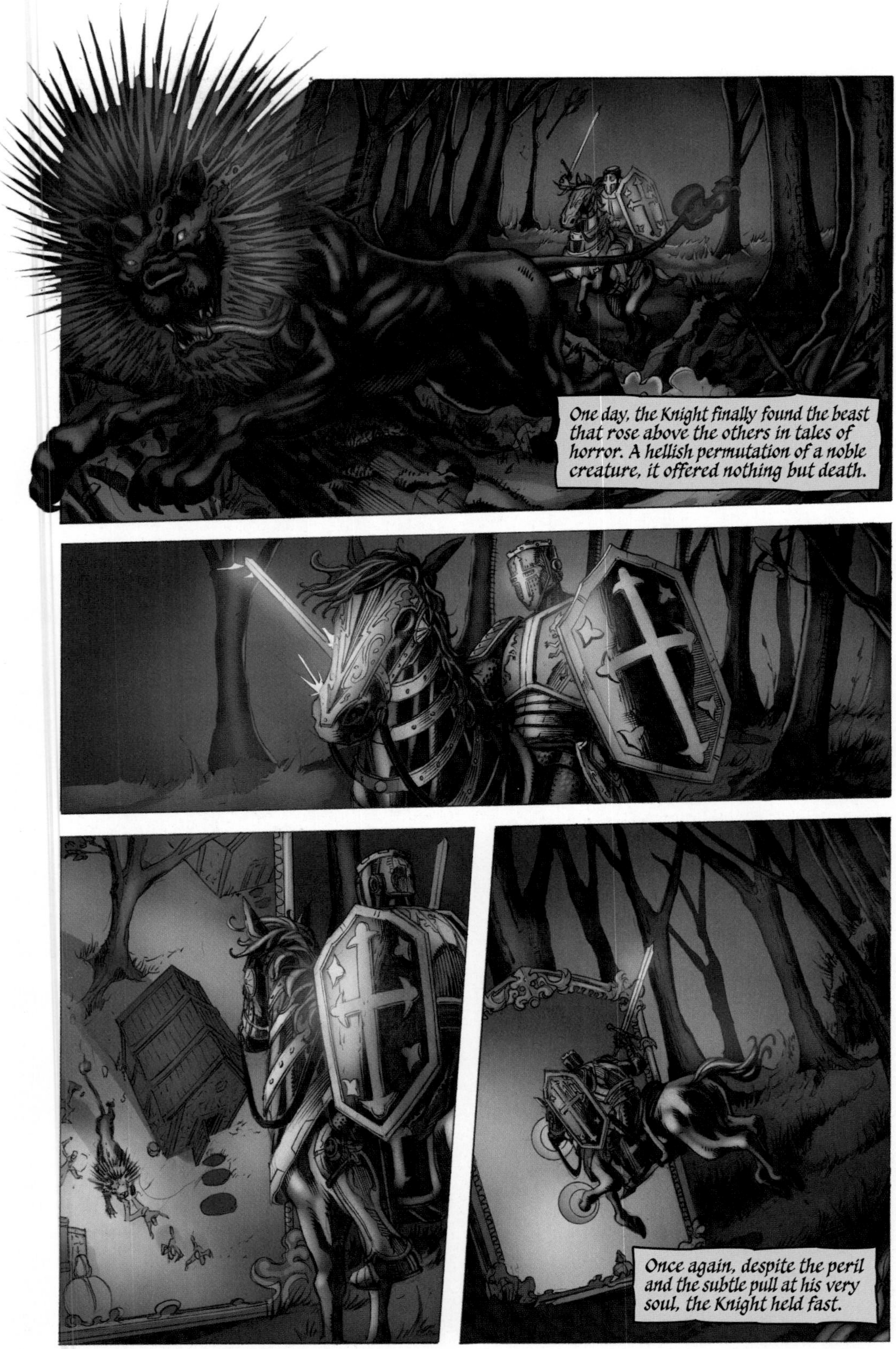
One day, the Knight finally found the beast that rose above the others in tales of horror. A hellish permutation of a noble creature, it offered nothing but death.
Once again, despite the peril and the subtle pull at his very soul, the Knight held fast.

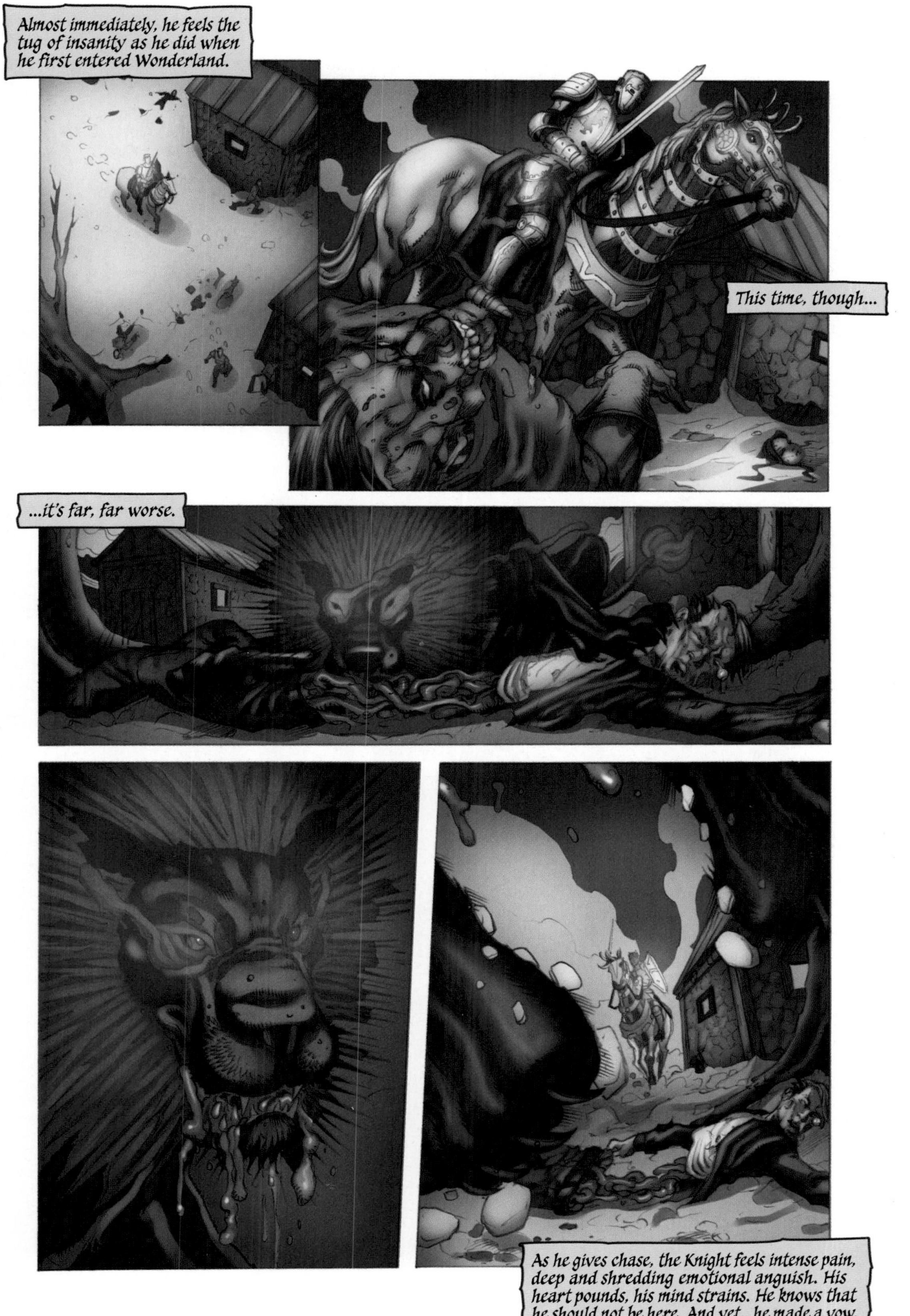
Almost immediately, he feels the tug of insanity as he did when he first entered Wonderland.
This time, though...
...it's far, far worse.
As he gives chase, the Knight feels intense pain, deep and shredding emotional anguish. His heart pounds, his mind strains. He knows that he should not be here. And yet...he made a vow.

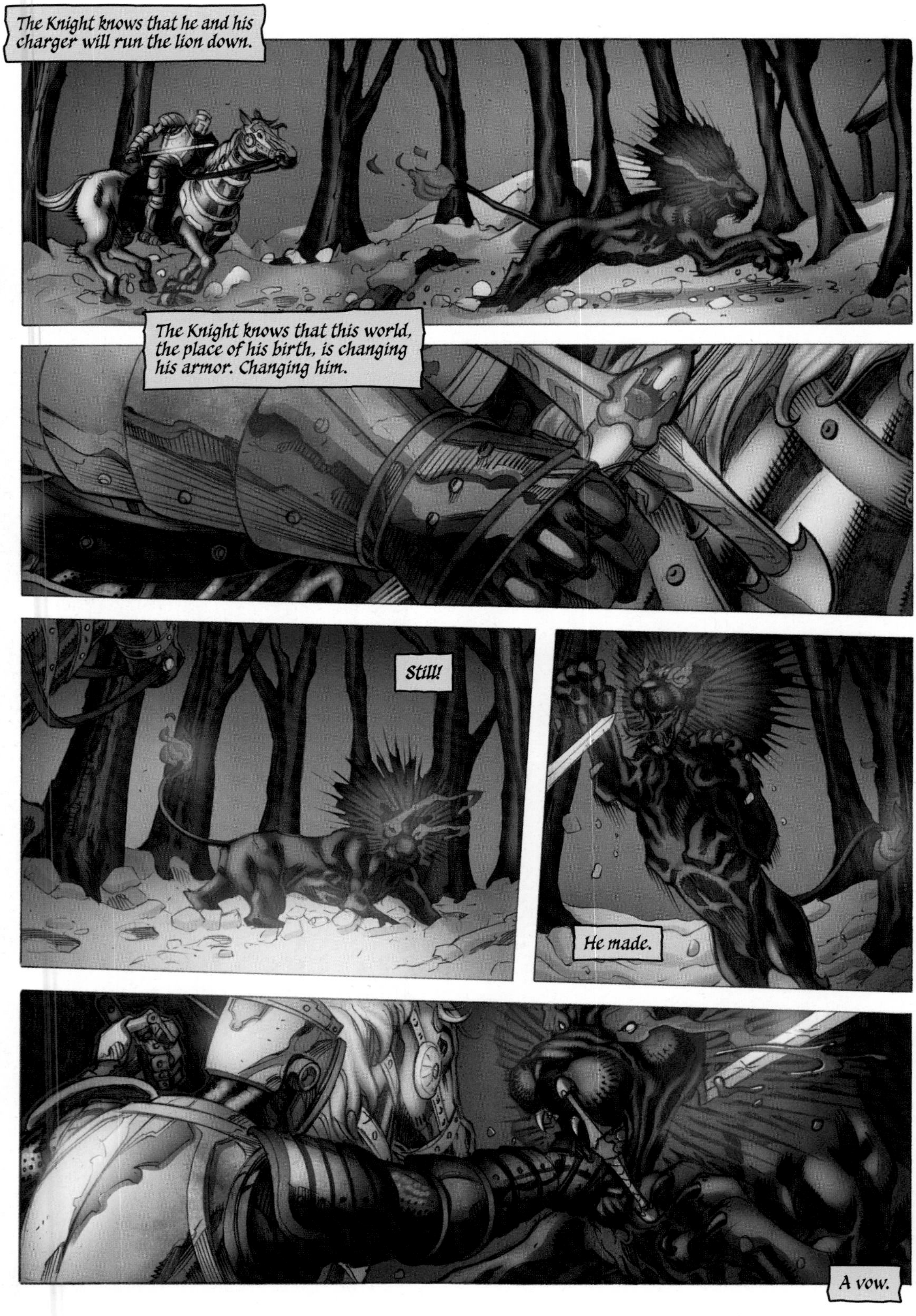
The Knight knows that he and his charger will run the lion down.
The Knight knows that this world, the place of his birth, is changing his armor. Changing him.
Still!
He made.
A vow.

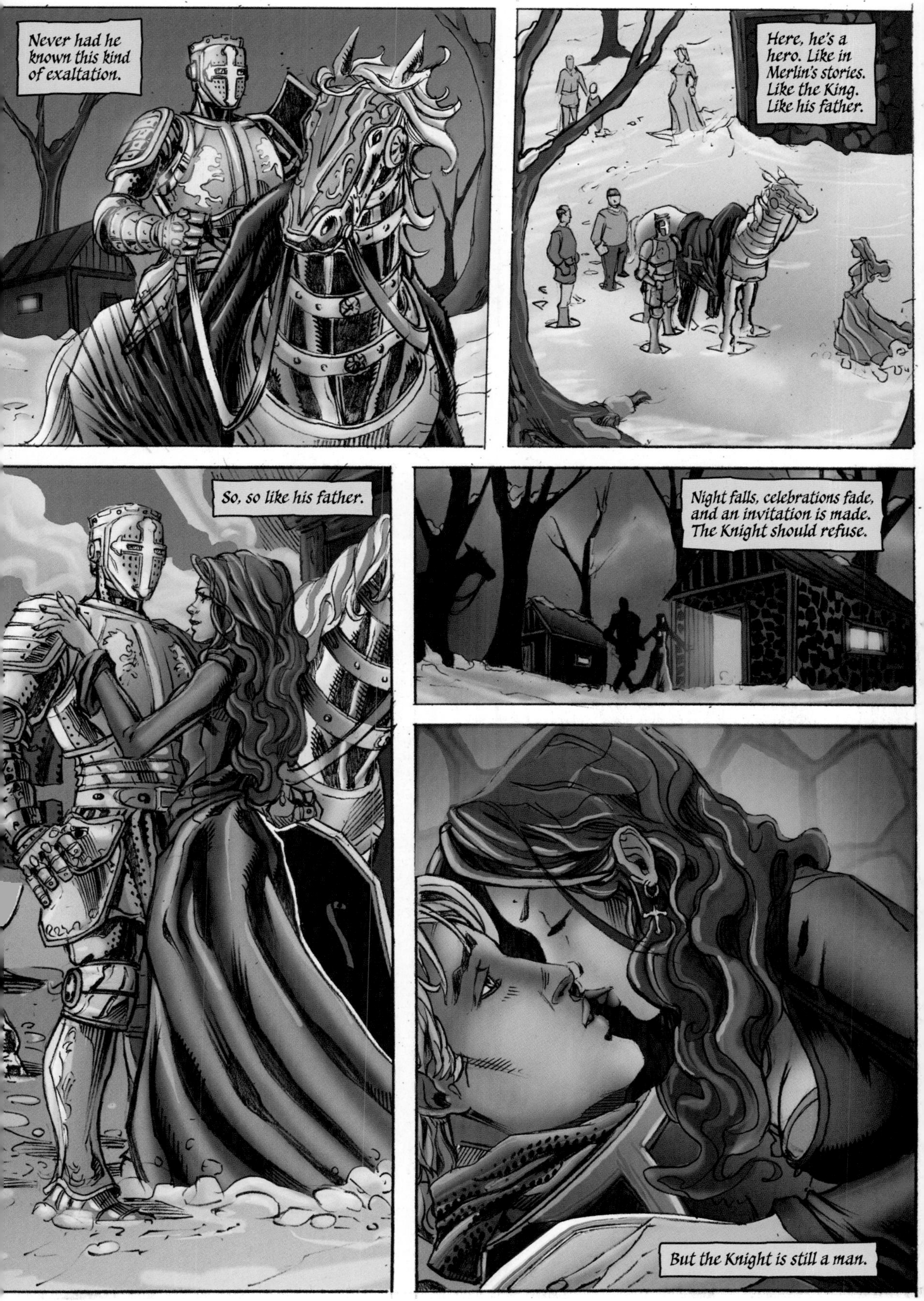
Never had he known this kind of exaltation.
Here, he's a hero. Like in Merlin's stories. Like the King. Like his father.
So, so like his father.
Night falls, celebrations fade, and an invitation is made. The Knight should refuse.
But the Knight is still a man.

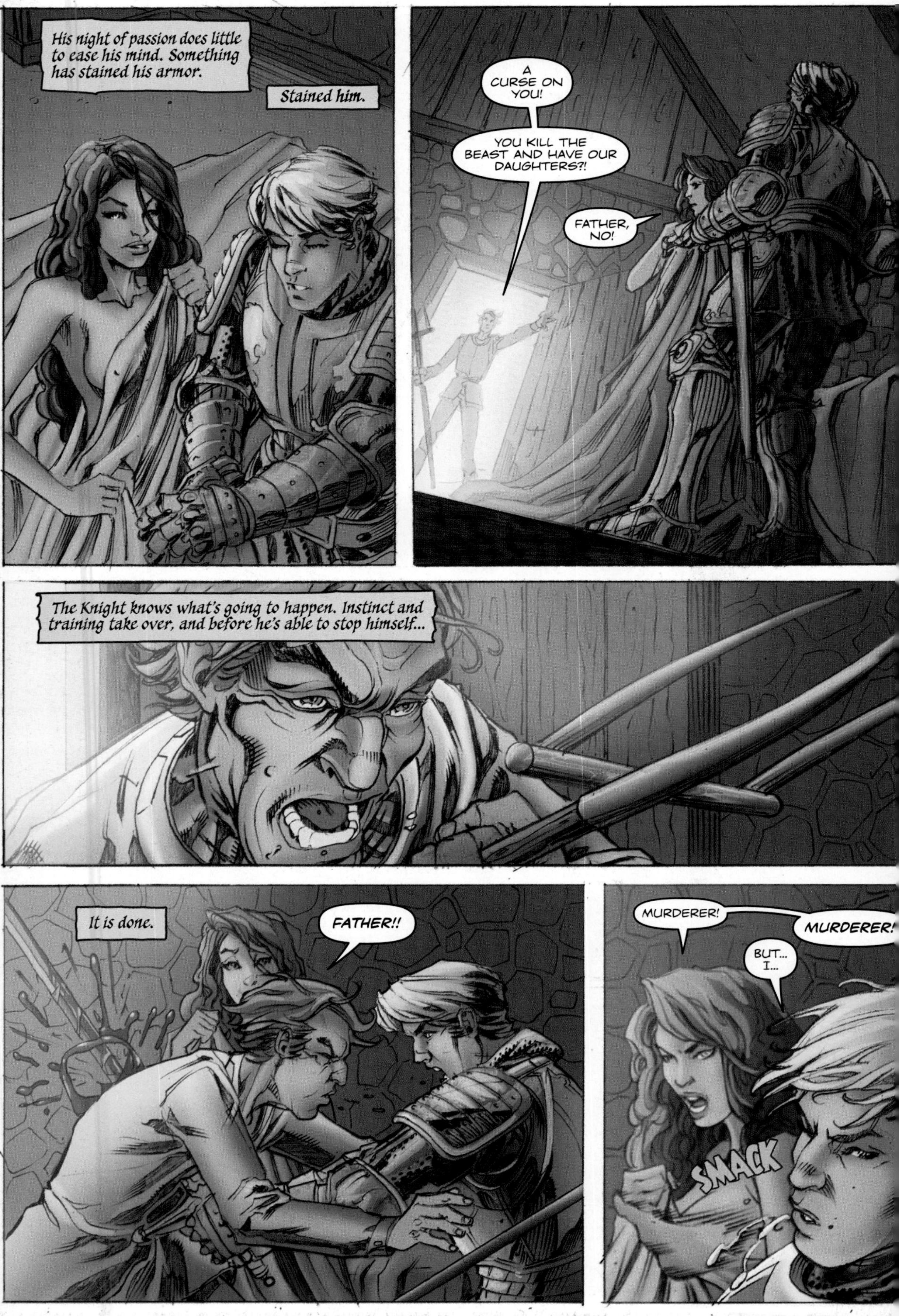

His night of passion does little to ease his mind. Something has stained his armor.
Stained him.
A CURSE ON YOU!
YOU KILL THE BEAST AND HAVE OUR DAUGHTERS?!
FATHER, NO!
The Knight knows what's going to happen. Instinct and training take over, and before he's able to stop himself...
It is done.
FATHER!!
MURDERER!
MURDERER!
BUT... I...
SMACK

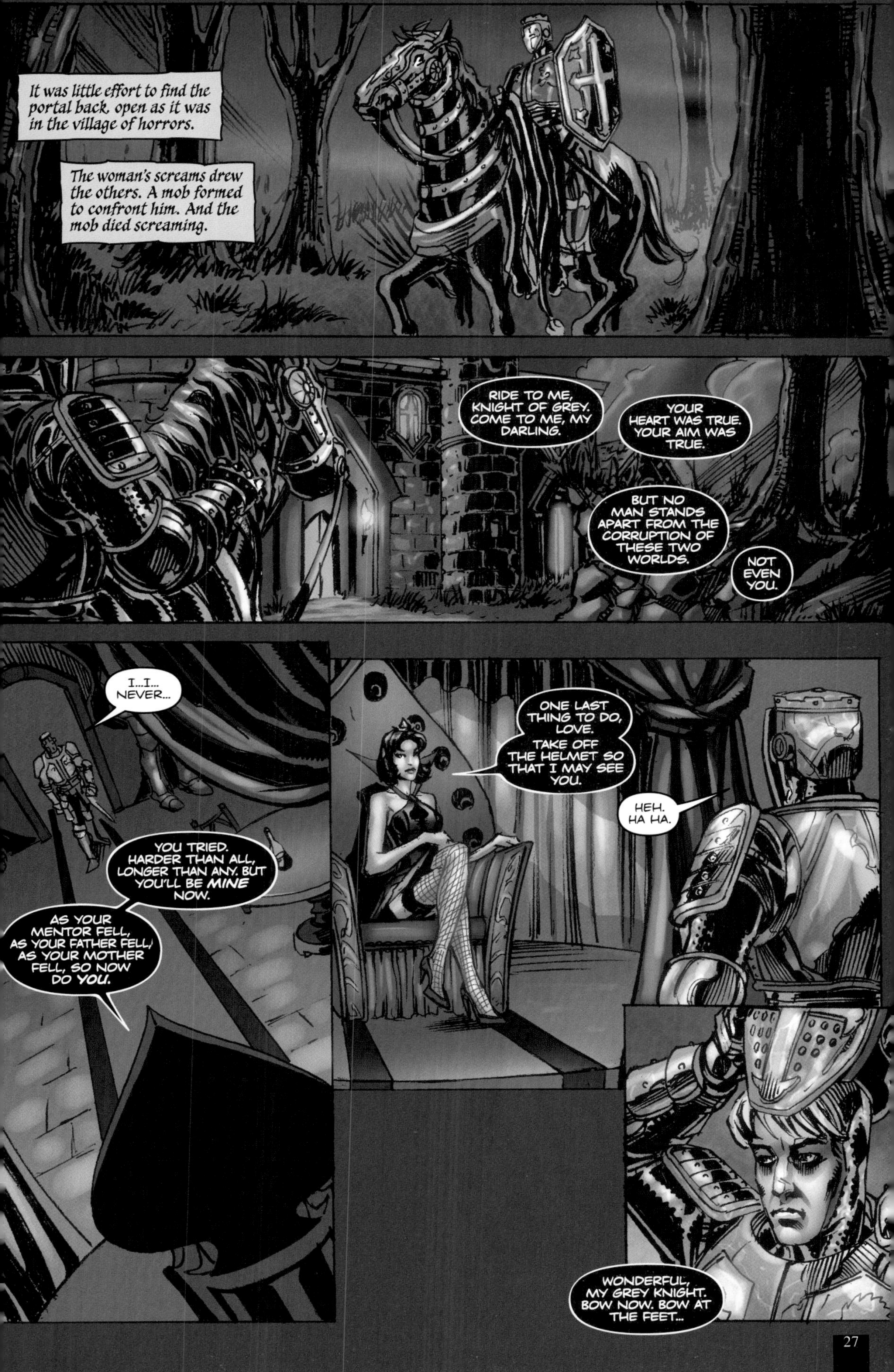
It was little effort to find the portal back, open as it was in the village of horrors.
The woman's screams drew the others. A mob formed to confront him. And the mob died screaming.
RIDE TO ME, KNIGHT OF GREY. COME TO ME, MY DARLING.
YOUR HEART WAS TRUE. YOUR AIM WAS TRUE.
BUT NO MAN STANDS APART FROM THE CORRUPTION OF THESE TWO WORLDS.
NOT EVEN YOU.
I...I... NEVER...
YOU TRIED. HARDER THAN ALL, LONGER THAN ANY. BUT YOU'LL BE MINE NOW.
AS YOUR MENTOR FELL, AS YOUR FATHER FELL, AS YOUR MOTHER FELL, SO NOW DO YOU.
ONE LAST THING TO DO, LOVE.
TAKE OFF THE HELMET SO THAT I MAY SEE YOU.
HEH. HA HA.
WONDERFUL, MY GREY KNIGHT. BOW NOW. BOW AT THE FEET...

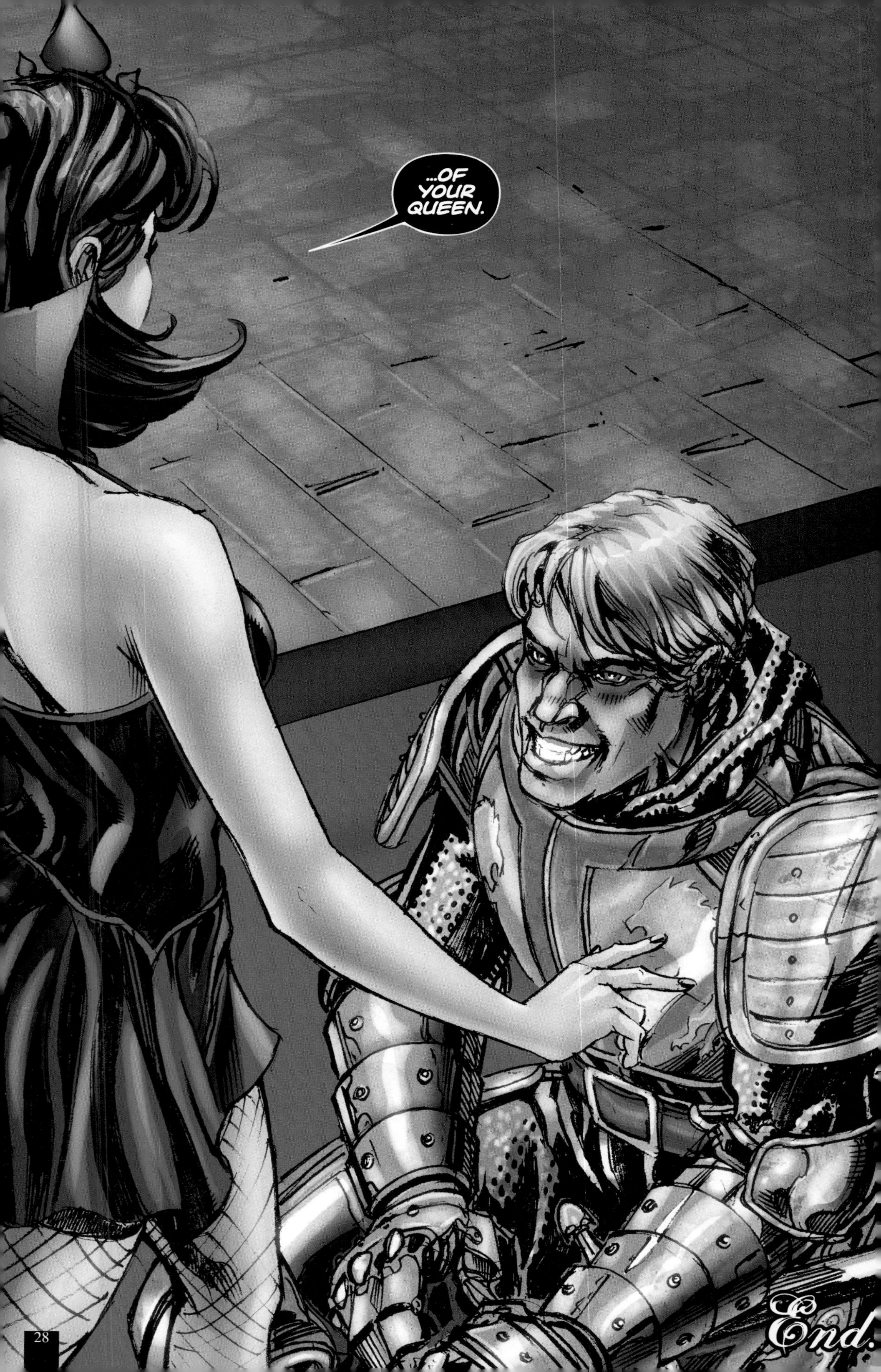
...OF YOUR QUEEN.
End.

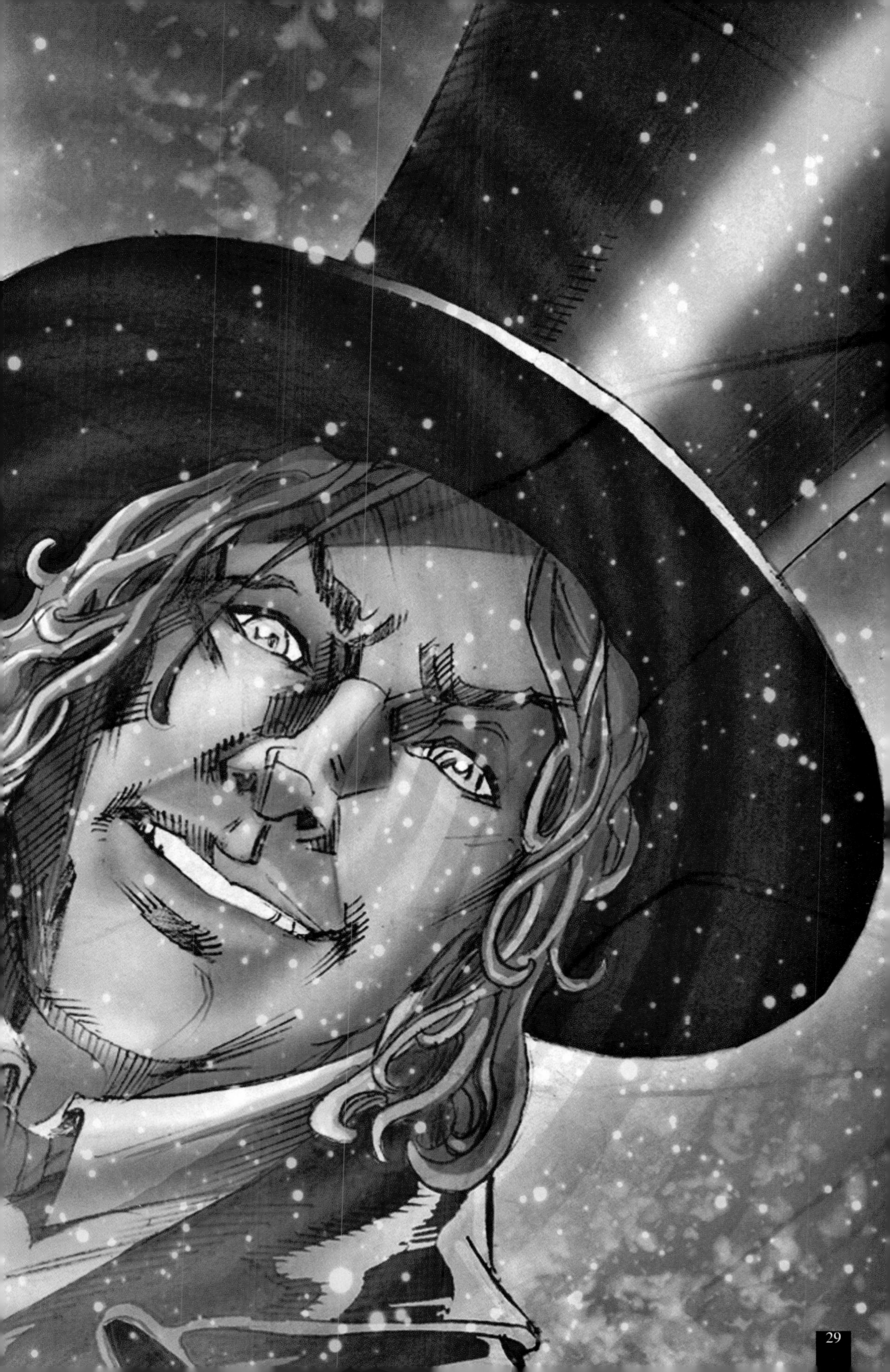

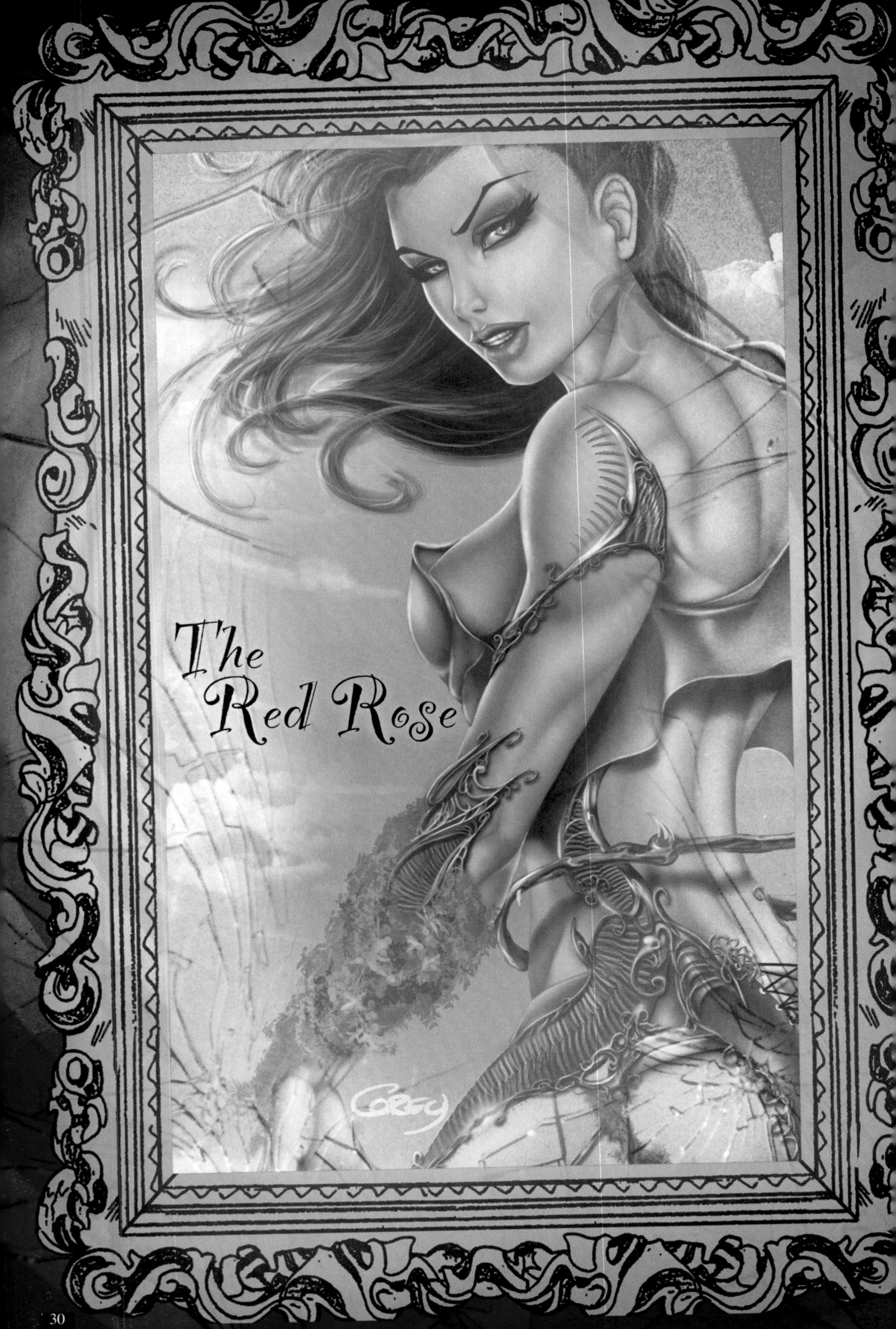
The Red Rose
Corey

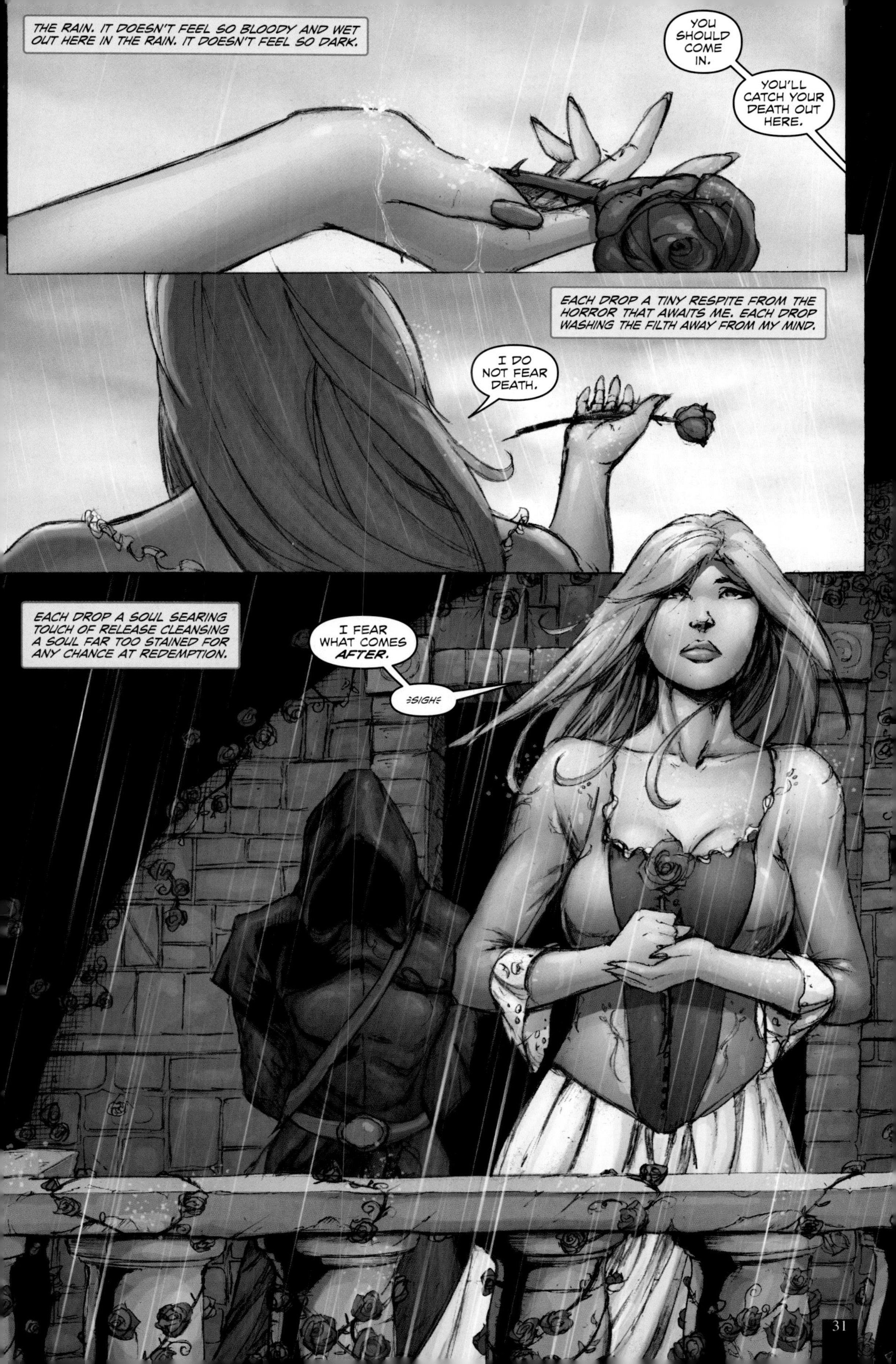
THE RAIN. IT DOESN'T FEEL SO BLOODY AND WET OUT HERE IN THE RAIN. IT DOESN'T FEEL SO DARK.
YOU SHOULD COME IN.
YOU'LL CATCH YOUR DEATH OUT HERE.
EACH DROP A TINY RESPITE FROM THE HORROR THAT AWAITS ME. EACH DROP WASHING THE FILTH AWAY FROM MY MIND.
I DO NOT FEAR DEATH.
EACH DROP A SOUL SEARING TOUCH OF RELEASE CLEANSING A SOUL FAR TOO STAINED FOR ANY CHANCE AT REDEMPTION.
I FEAR WHAT COMES AFTER.
SIGH

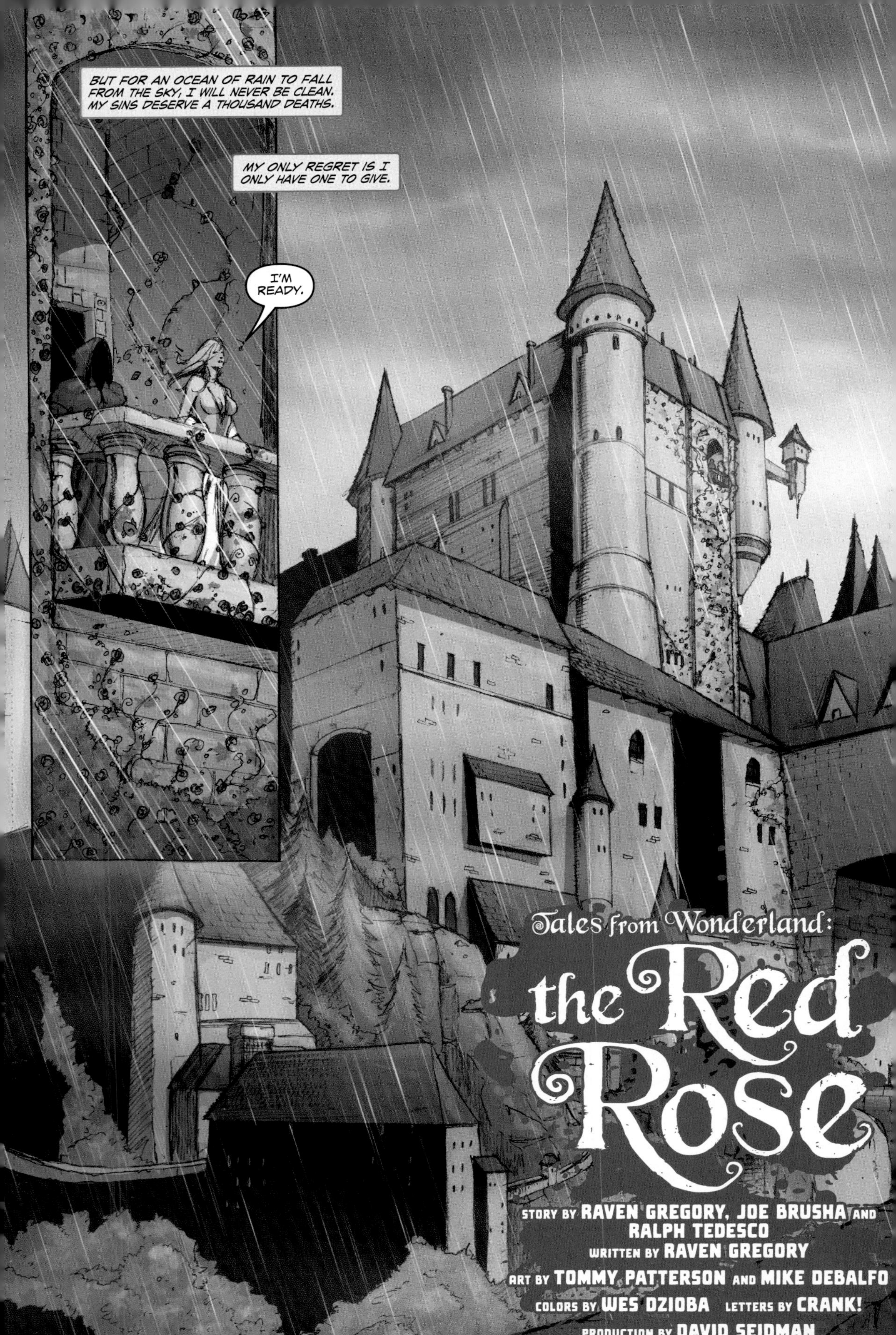

BUT FOR AN OCEAN OF RAIN TO FALL FROM THE SKY, I WILL NEVER BE CLEAN. MY SINS DESERVE A THOUSAND DEATHS.
MY ONLY REGRET IS I ONLY HAVE ONE TO GIVE.
I'M READY.
Tales from Wonderland:
the Red Rose
STORY BY RAVEN GREGORY, JOE BRUSHA AND RALPH TEDESCO
WRITTEN BY RAVEN GREGORY
ART BY TOMMY PATTERSON AND MIKE DEBALFO
COLORS BY WES DZIOBA LETTERS BY CRANK!
PRODUCTION BY DAVID SEIDMAN

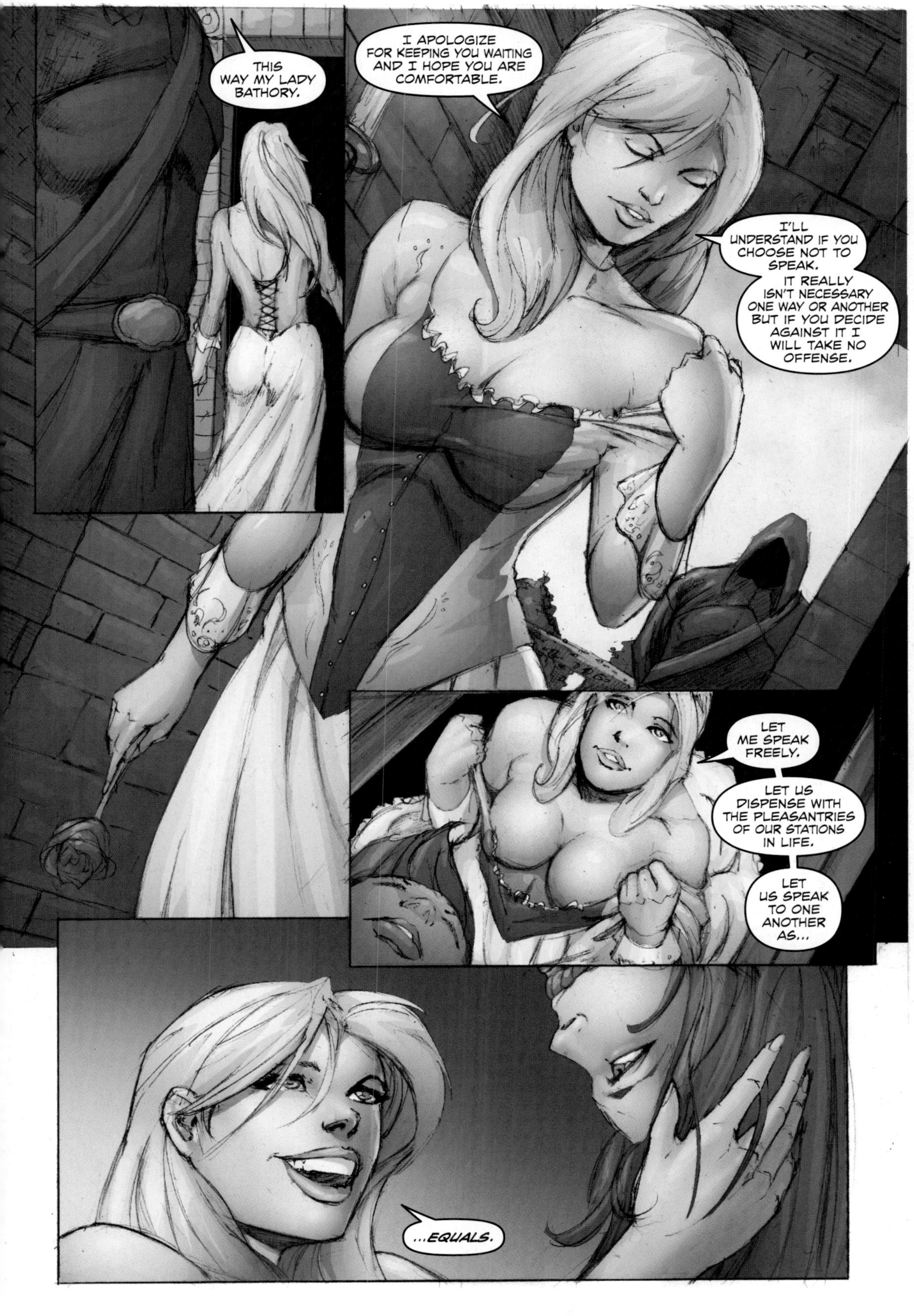
THIS WAY MY LADY BATHORY.
I APOLOGIZE FOR KEEPING YOU WAITING AND I HOPE YOU ARE COMFORTABLE.
I'LL UNDERSTAND IF YOU CHOOSE NOT TO SPEAK.
IT REALLY ISN'T NECESSARY ONE WAY OR ANOTHER BUT IF YOU DECIDE AGAINST IT I WILL TAKE NO OFFENSE.
LET ME SPEAK FREELY.
LET US DISPENSE WITH THE PLEASANTRIES OF OUR STATIONS IN LIFE.
LET US SPEAK TO ONE ANOTHER AS...
...EQUALS.

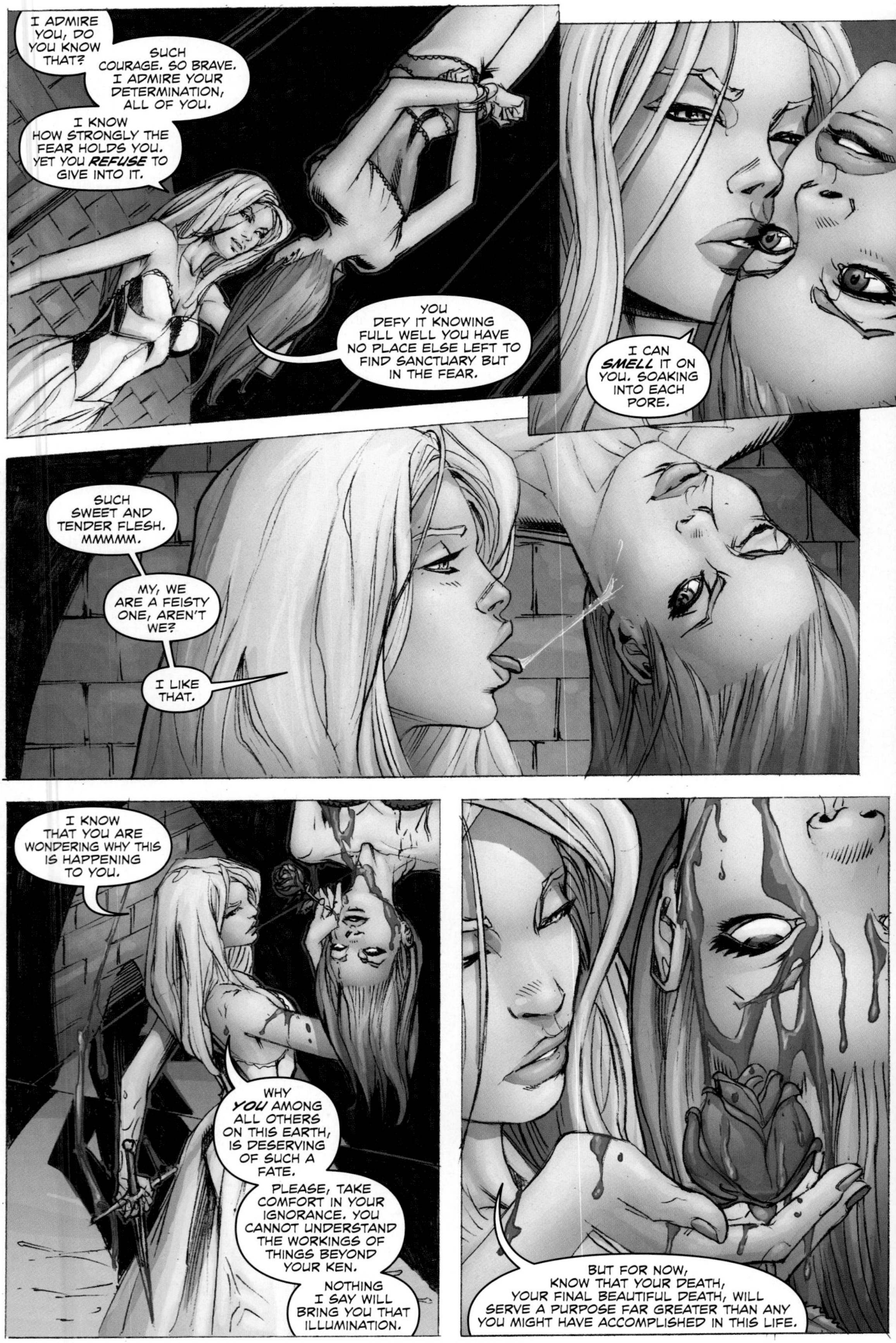
I ADMIRE YOU, DO YOU KNOW THAT?
SUCH COURAGE. SO BRAVE. I ADMIRE YOUR DETERMINATION, ALL OF YOU.
I KNOW HOW STRONGLY THE FEAR HOLDS YOU. YET YOU *REFUSE* TO GIVE INTO IT.
YOU DEFY IT KNOWING FULL WELL YOU HAVE NO PLACE ELSE LEFT TO FIND SANCTUARY BUT IN THE FEAR.
I CAN *SMELL* IT ON YOU. SOAKING INTO EACH PORE.
SUCH SWEET AND TENDER FLESH. MMMMM.
MY, WE ARE A FEISTY ONE, AREN'T WE?
I LIKE THAT.
I KNOW THAT YOU ARE WONDERING WHY THIS IS HAPPENING TO YOU.
WHY *YOU* AMONG ALL OTHERS ON THIS EARTH, IS DESERVING OF SUCH A FATE.
PLEASE, TAKE COMFORT IN YOUR IGNORANCE. YOU CANNOT UNDERSTAND THE WORKINGS OF THINGS BEYOND YOUR KEN.
NOTHING I SAY WILL BRING YOU THAT ILLUMINATION.
BUT FOR NOW, KNOW THAT YOUR DEATH, YOUR FINAL BEAUTIFUL DEATH, WILL SERVE A PURPOSE FAR GREATER THAN ANY YOU MIGHT HAVE ACCOMPLISHED IN THIS LIFE.

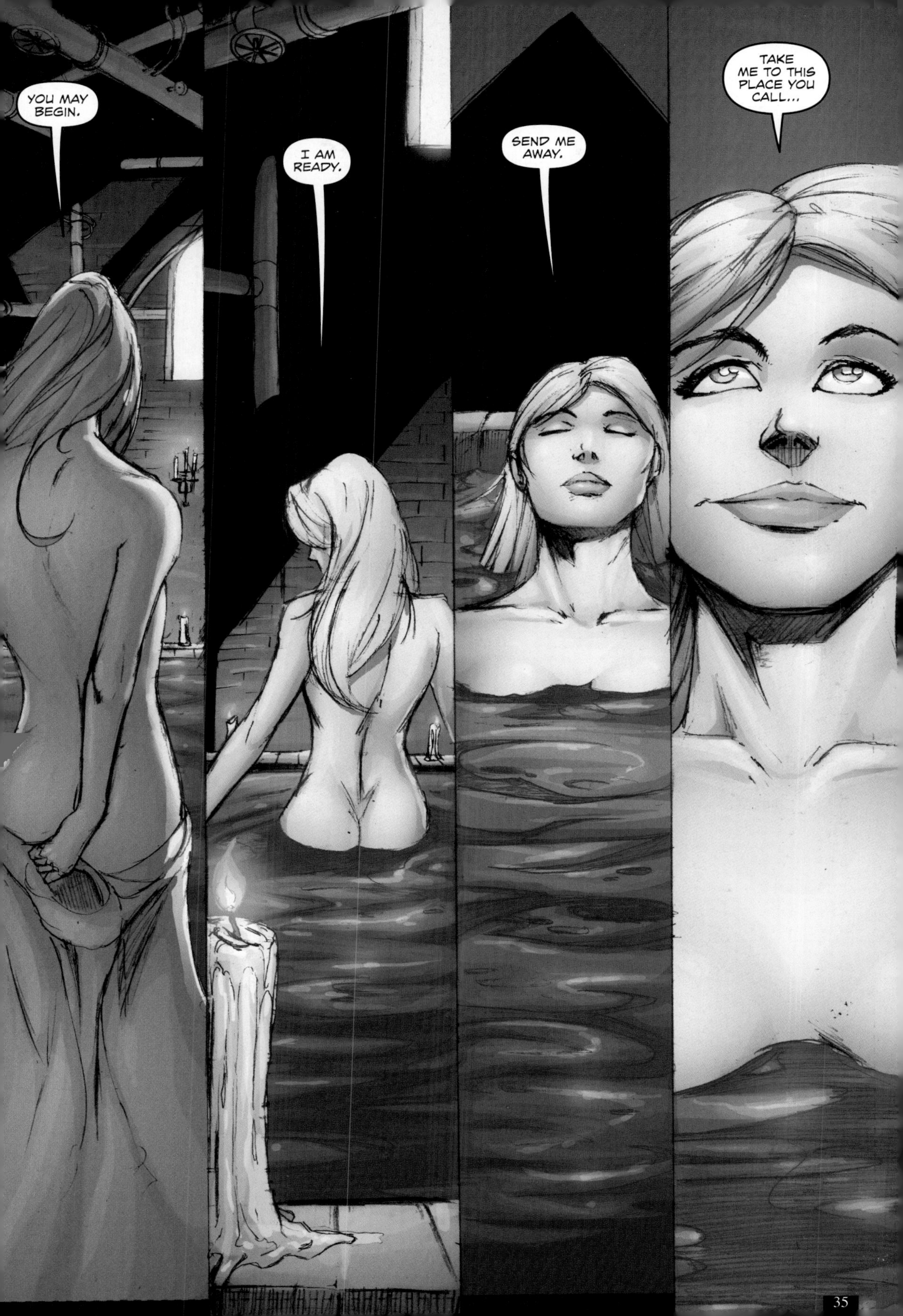
YOU MAY BEGIN.
I AM READY.
SEND ME AWAY.
TAKE ME TO THIS PLACE YOU CALL...

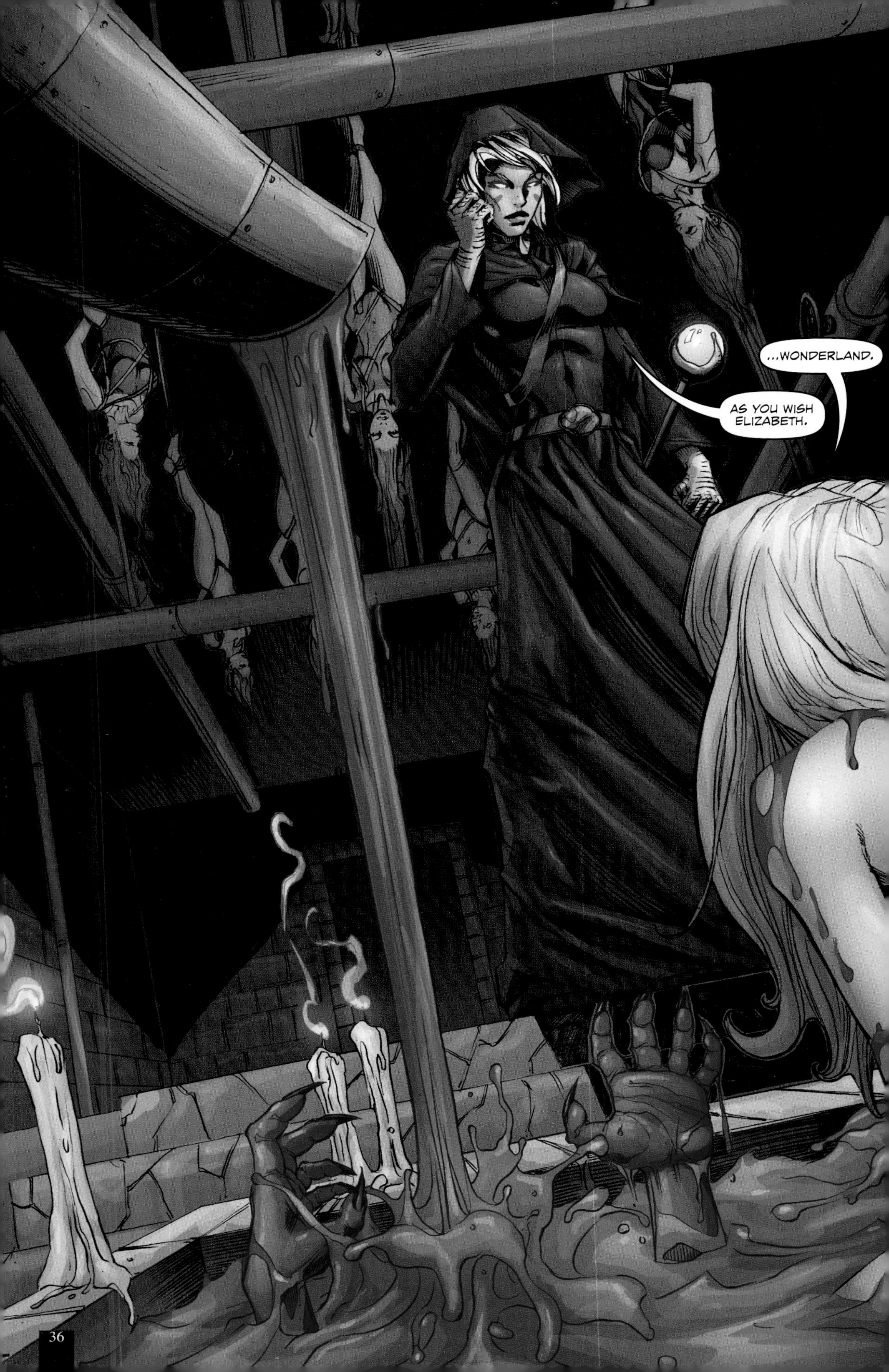
...WONDERLAND.
AS YOU WISH
ELIZABETH.

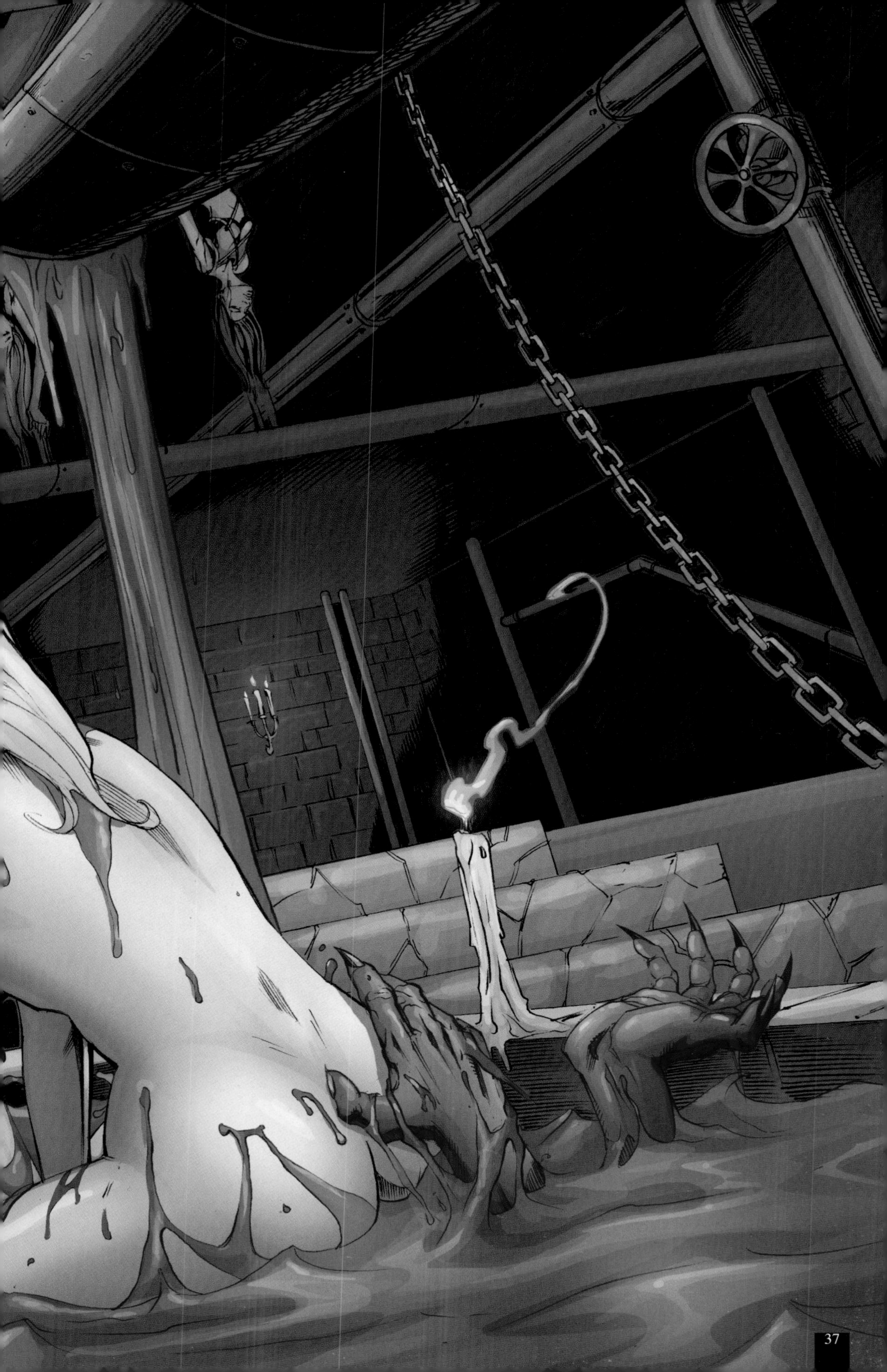

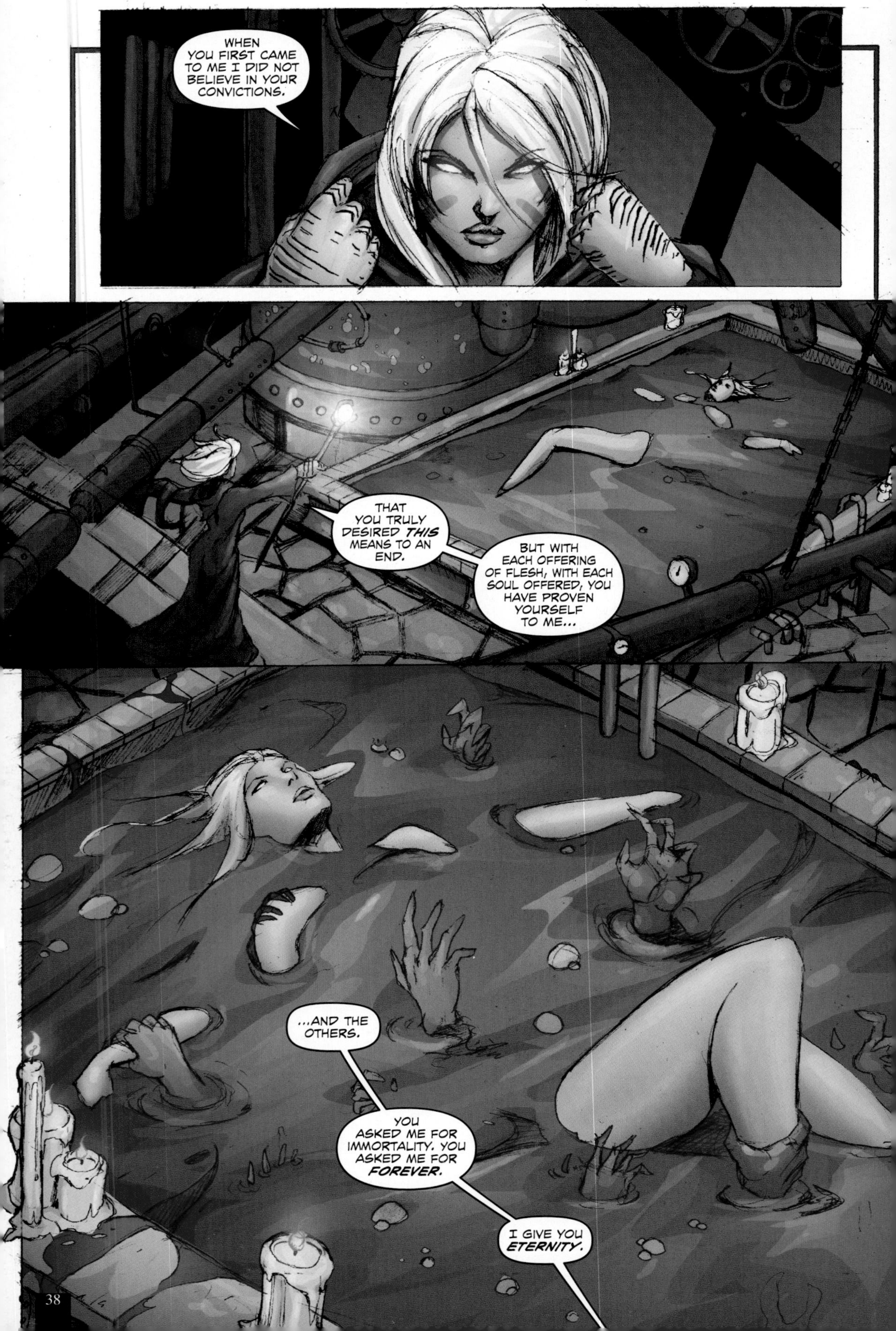
WHEN YOU FIRST CAME TO ME I DID NOT BELIEVE IN YOUR CONVICTIONS.
THAT YOU TRULY DESIRED *THIS* MEANS TO AN END.
BUT WITH EACH OFFERING OF FLESH, WITH EACH SOUL OFFERED, YOU HAVE PROVEN YOURSELF TO ME...
...AND THE OTHERS.
YOU ASKED ME FOR IMMORTALITY. YOU ASKED ME FOR *FOREVER*.
I GIVE YOU *ETERNITY*.

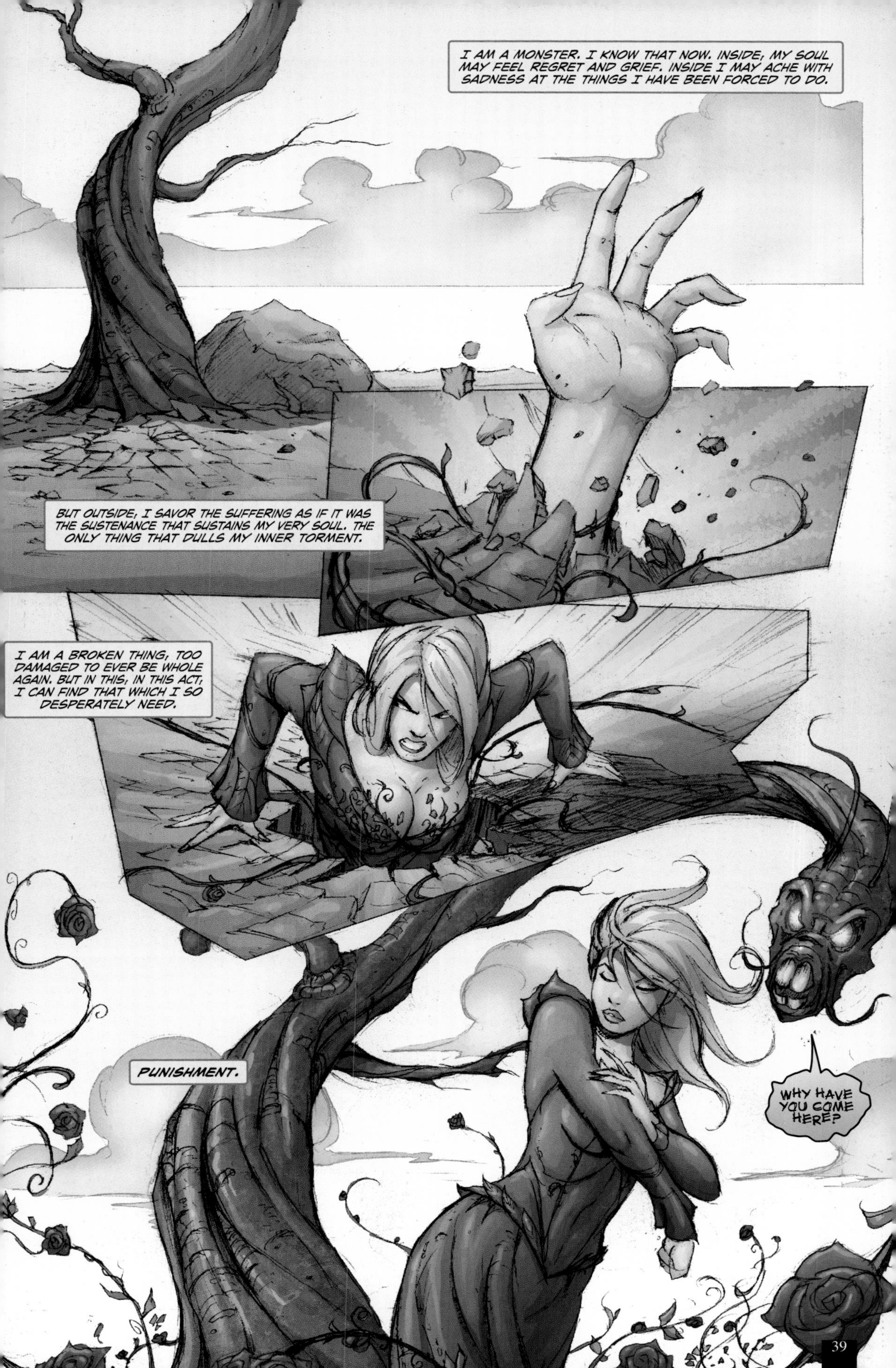
I AM A MONSTER. I KNOW THAT NOW. INSIDE, MY SOUL MAY FEEL REGRET AND GRIEF. INSIDE I MAY ACHE WITH SADNESS AT THE THINGS I HAVE BEEN FORCED TO DO.
BUT OUTSIDE, I SAVOR THE SUFFERING AS IF IT WAS THE SUSTENANCE THAT SUSTAINS MY VERY SOUL. THE ONLY THING THAT DULLS MY INNER TORMENT.
I AM A BROKEN THING, TOO DAMAGED TO EVER BE WHOLE AGAIN. BUT IN THIS, IN THIS ACT, I CAN FIND THAT WHICH I SO DESPERATELY NEED.
PUNISHMENT.
WHY HAVE YOU COME HERE?

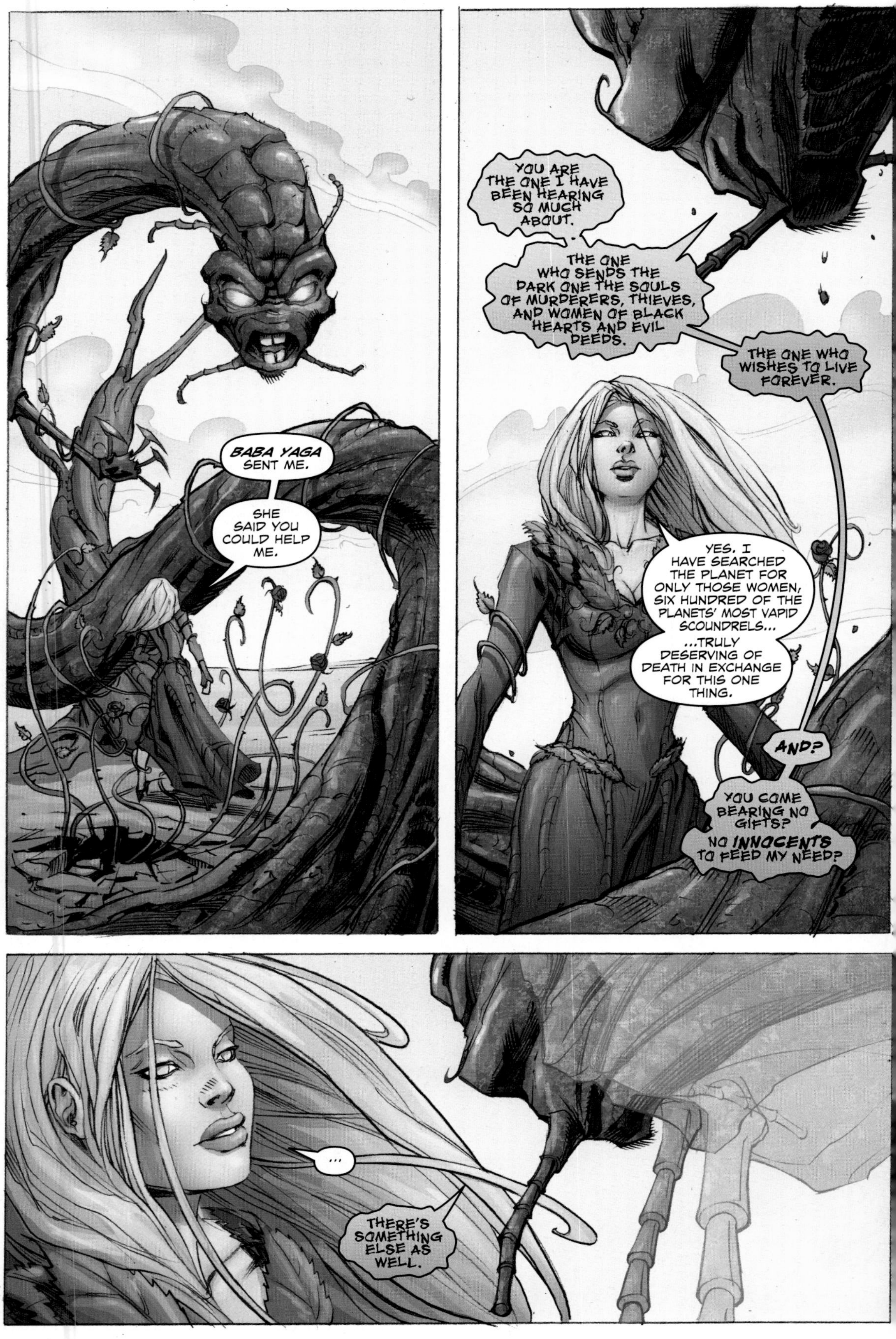
BABA YAGA SENT ME.
SHE SAID YOU COULD HELP ME.
YOU ARE THE ONE I HAVE BEEN HEARING SO MUCH ABOUT.
THE ONE WHO SENDS THE DARK ONE THE SOULS OF MURDERERS, THIEVES, AND WOMEN OF BLACK HEARTS AND EVIL DEEDS.
THE ONE WHO WISHES TO LIVE FOREVER.
YES. I HAVE SEARCHED THE PLANET FOR ONLY THOSE WOMEN, SIX HUNDRED OF THE PLANETS' MOST VAPID SCOUNDRELS...
...TRULY DESERVING OF DEATH IN EXCHANGE FOR THIS ONE THING.
AND?
YOU COME BEARING NO GIFTS?
NO INNOCENTS TO FEED MY NEED?
...
THERE'S SOMETHING ELSE AS WELL.

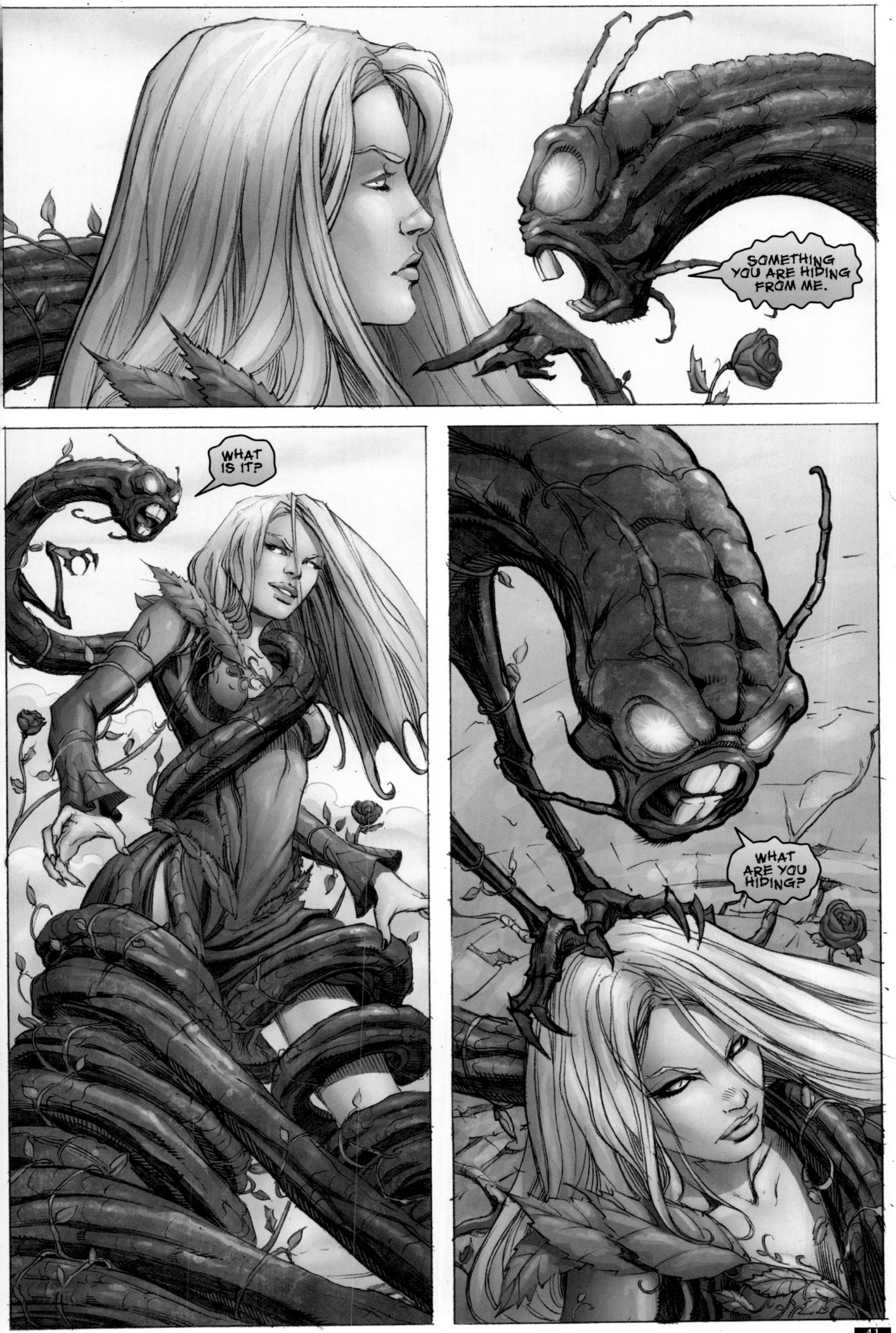
SOMETHING YOU ARE HIDING FROM ME.
WHAT IS IT?
WHAT ARE YOU HIDING?

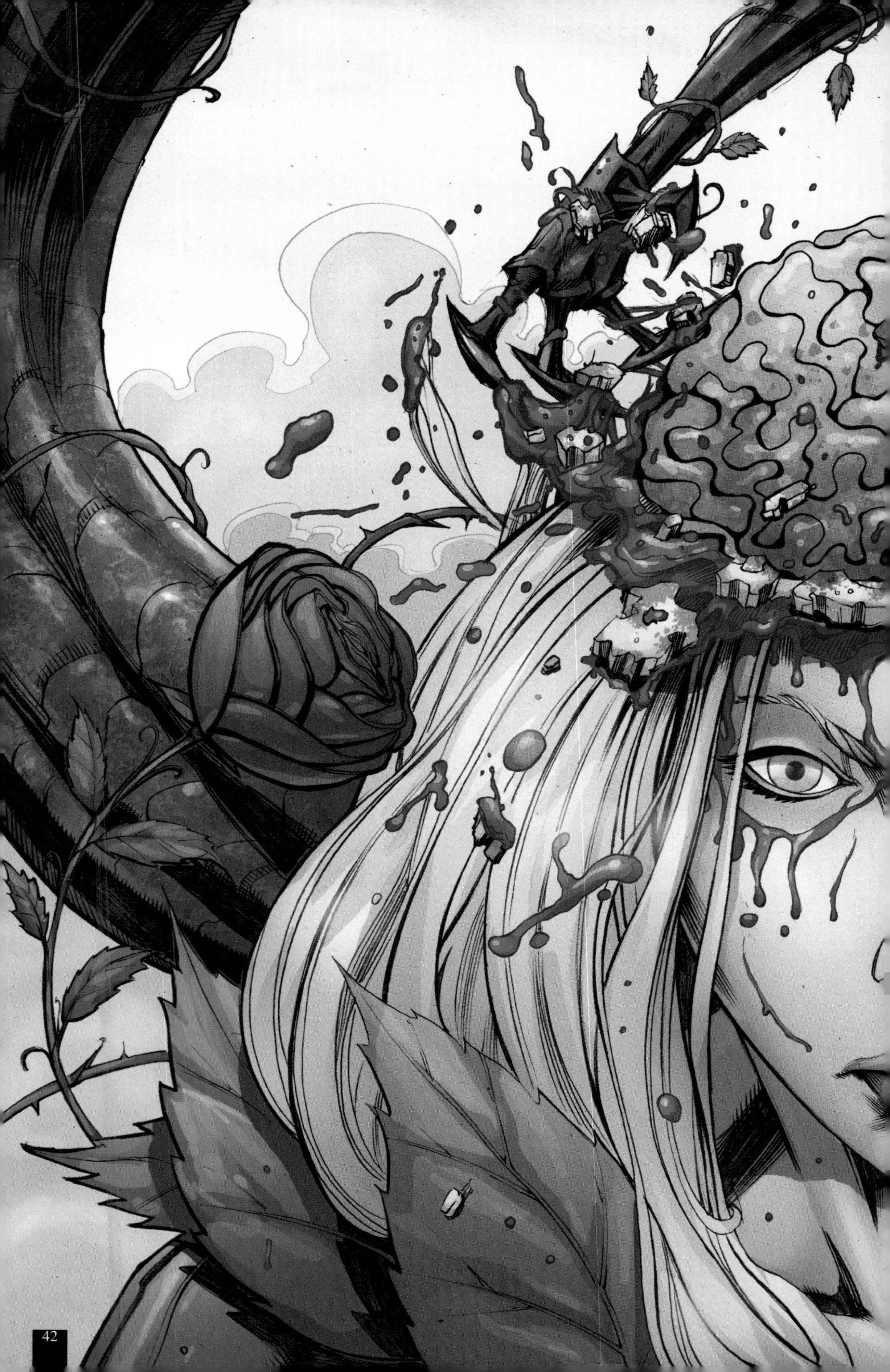

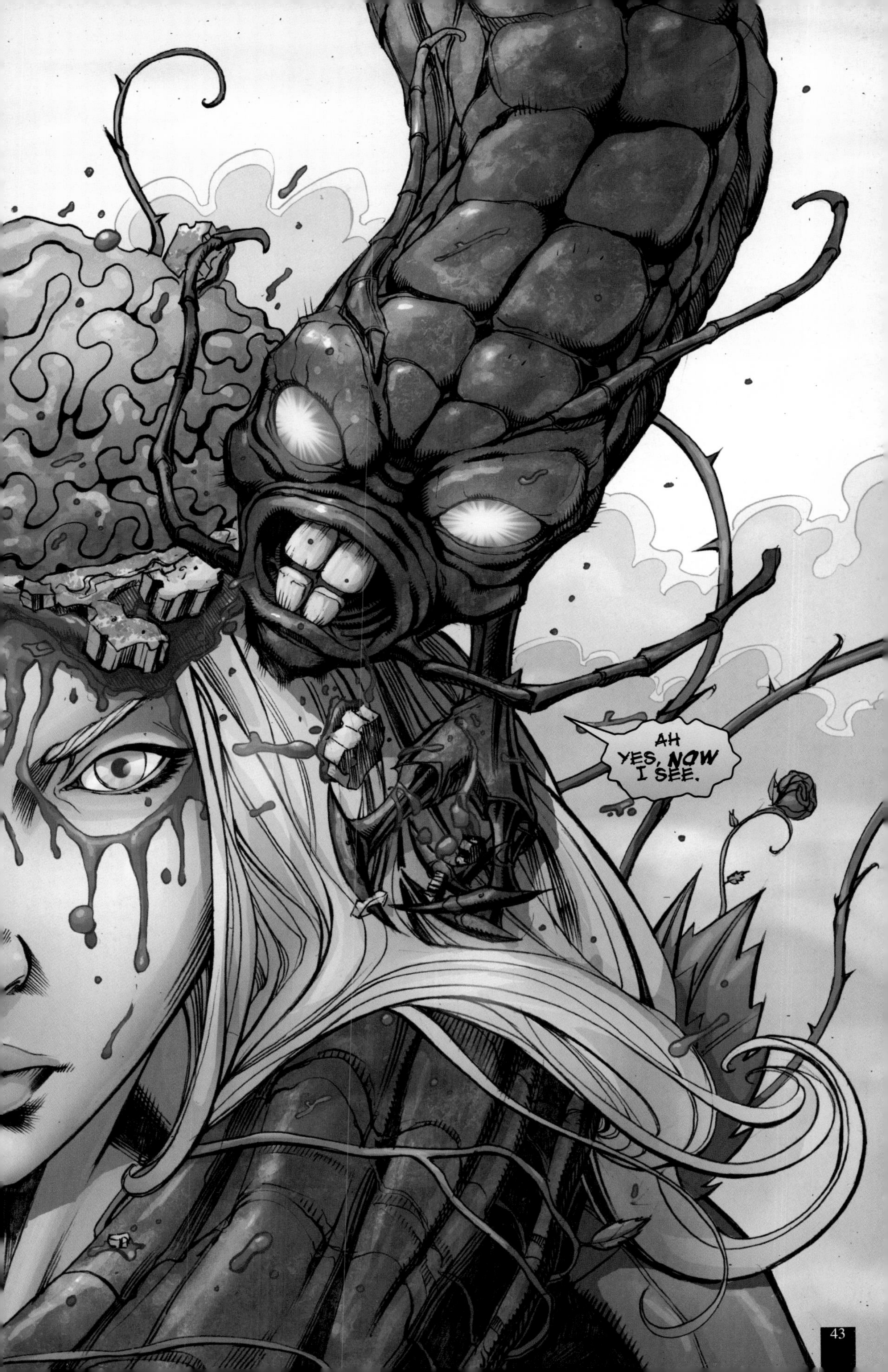
AH YES, NOW I SEE.

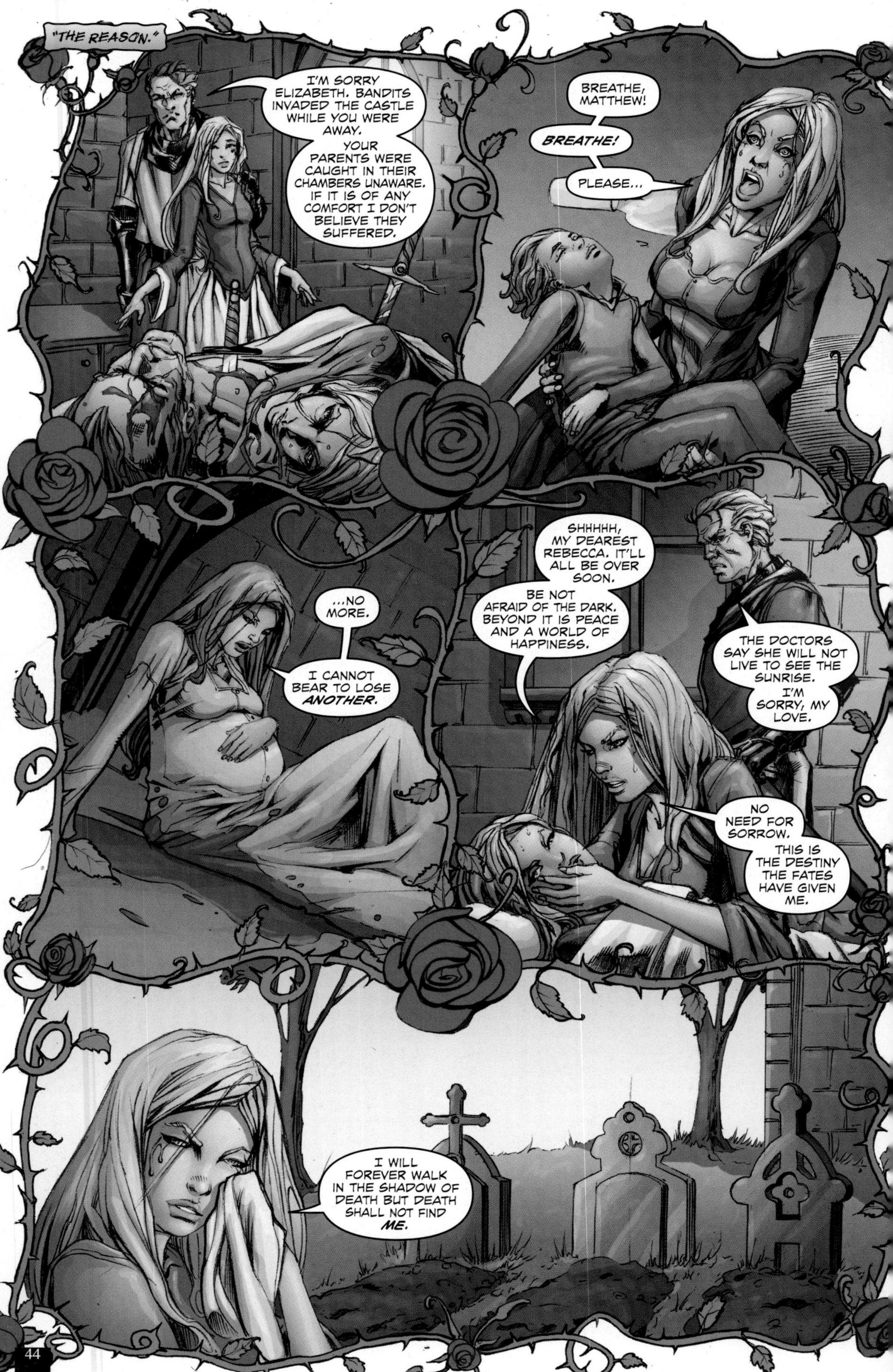
"THE REASON."
I'M SORRY ELIZABETH. BANDITS INVADED THE CASTLE WHILE YOU WERE AWAY.
YOUR PARENTS WERE CAUGHT IN THEIR CHAMBERS UNAWARE. IF IT IS OF ANY COMFORT I DON'T BELIEVE THEY SUFFERED.
BREATHE, MATTHEW!
BREATHE!
PLEASE...
...NO MORE.
I CANNOT BEAR TO LOSE ANOTHER.
SHHHHH, MY DEAREST REBECCA. IT'LL ALL BE OVER SOON.
BE NOT AFRAID OF THE DARK. BEYOND IT IS PEACE AND A WORLD OF HAPPINESS.
THE DOCTORS SAY SHE WILL NOT LIVE TO SEE THE SUNRISE.
I'M SORRY, MY LOVE.
NO NEED FOR SORROW.
THIS IS THE DESTINY THE FATES HAVE GIVEN ME.
I WILL FOREVER WALK IN THE SHADOW OF DEATH BUT DEATH SHALL NOT FIND ME.

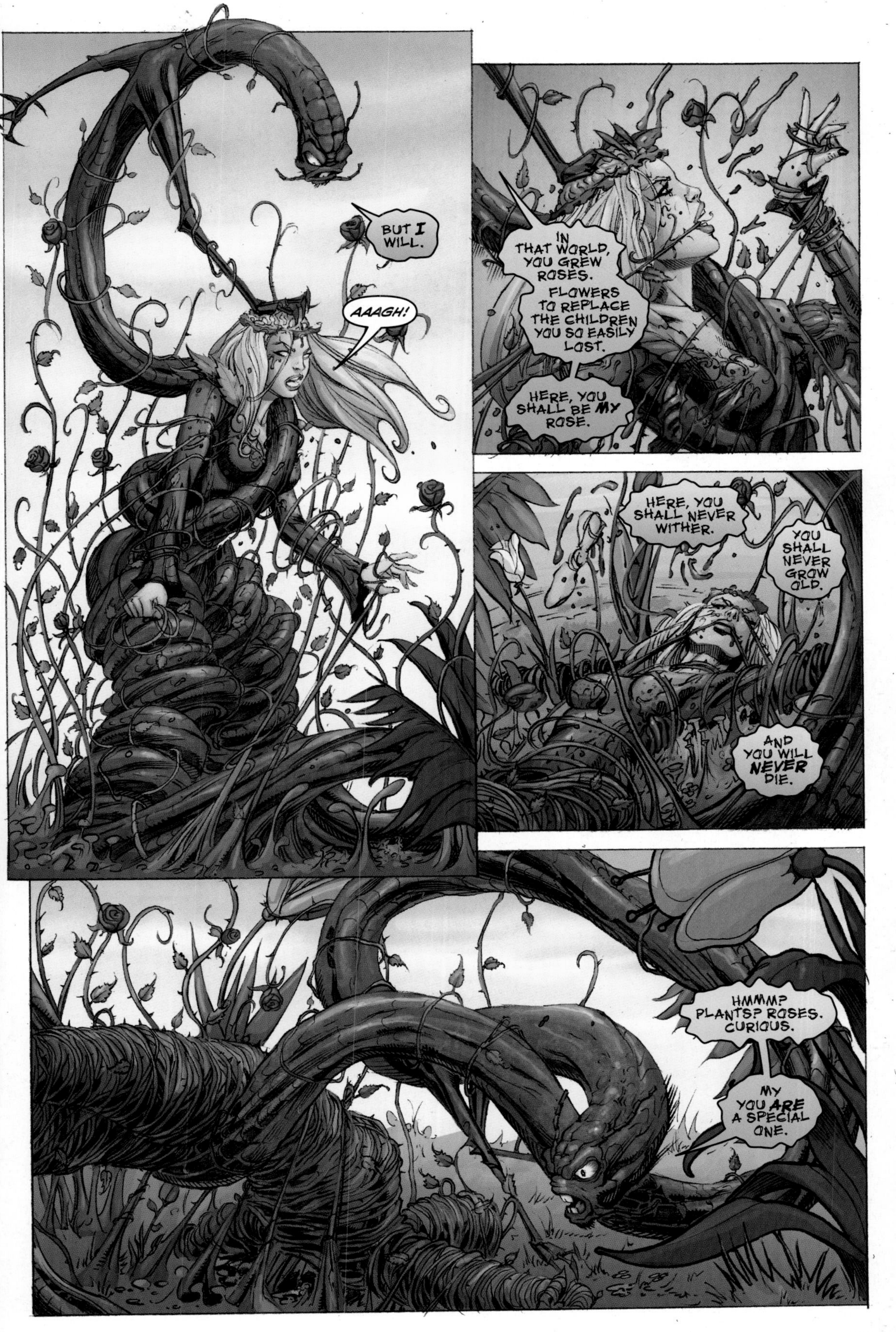
BUT I WILL.
AAAGH!
IN THAT WORLD, YOU GREW ROSES.
FLOWERS TO REPLACE THE CHILDREN YOU SO EASILY LOST.
HERE, YOU SHALL BE MY ROSE.
HERE, YOU SHALL NEVER WITHER.
YOU SHALL NEVER GROW OLD.
AND YOU WILL NEVER DIE.
HMMM? PLANTS? ROSES. CURIOUS.
MY YOU ARE A SPECIAL ONE.

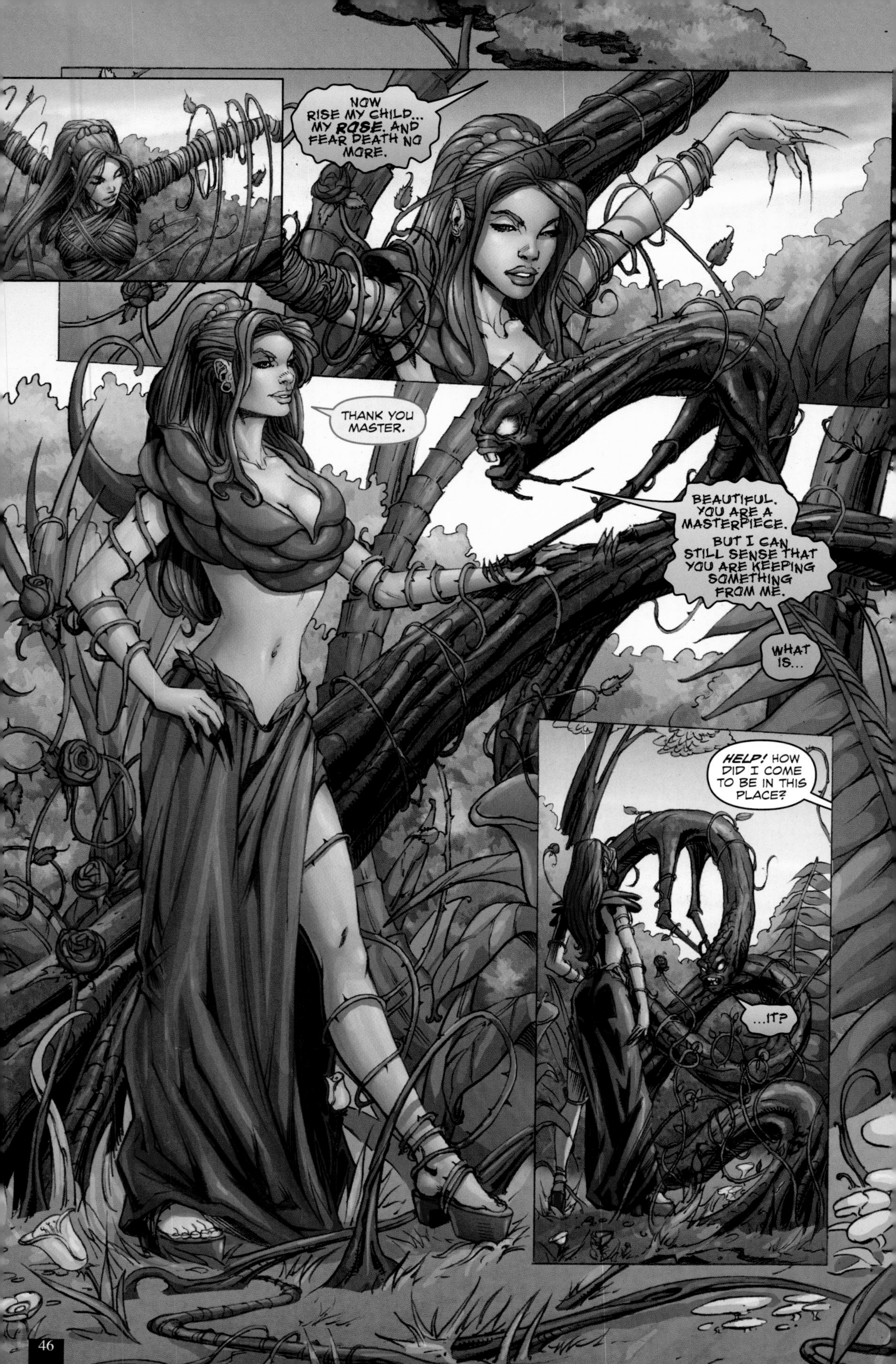
NOW RISE MY CHILD... MY ROSE. AND FEAR DEATH NO MORE.
THANK YOU MASTER.
BEAUTIFUL. YOU ARE A MASTERPIECE.
BUT I CAN STILL SENSE THAT YOU ARE KEEPING SOMETHING FROM ME.
WHAT IS...
HELP! HOW DID I COME TO BE IN THIS PLACE?
...IT?

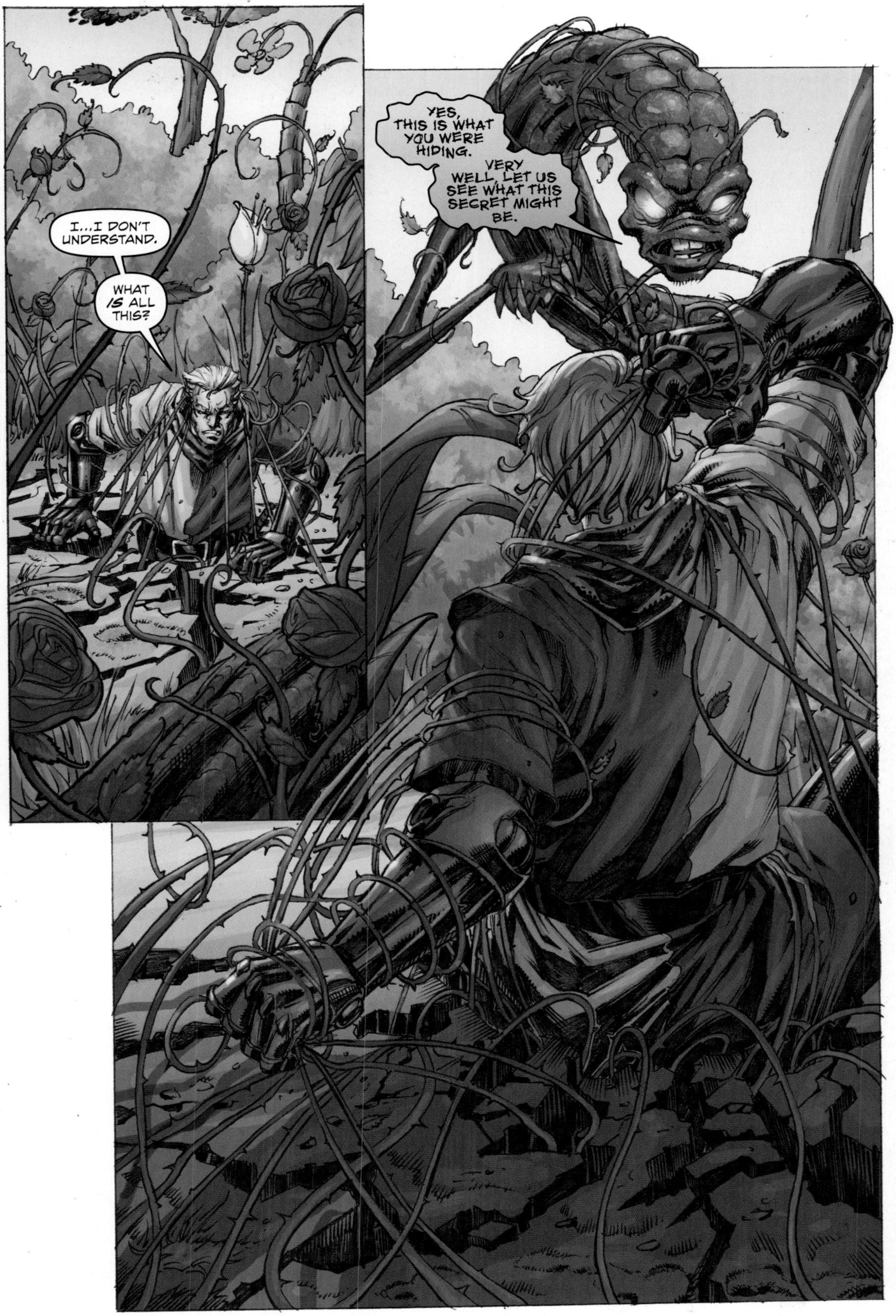
I...I DON'T UNDERSTAND.
WHAT IS ALL THIS?
YES, THIS IS WHAT YOU WERE HIDING.
VERY WELL, LET US SEE WHAT THIS SECRET MIGHT BE.

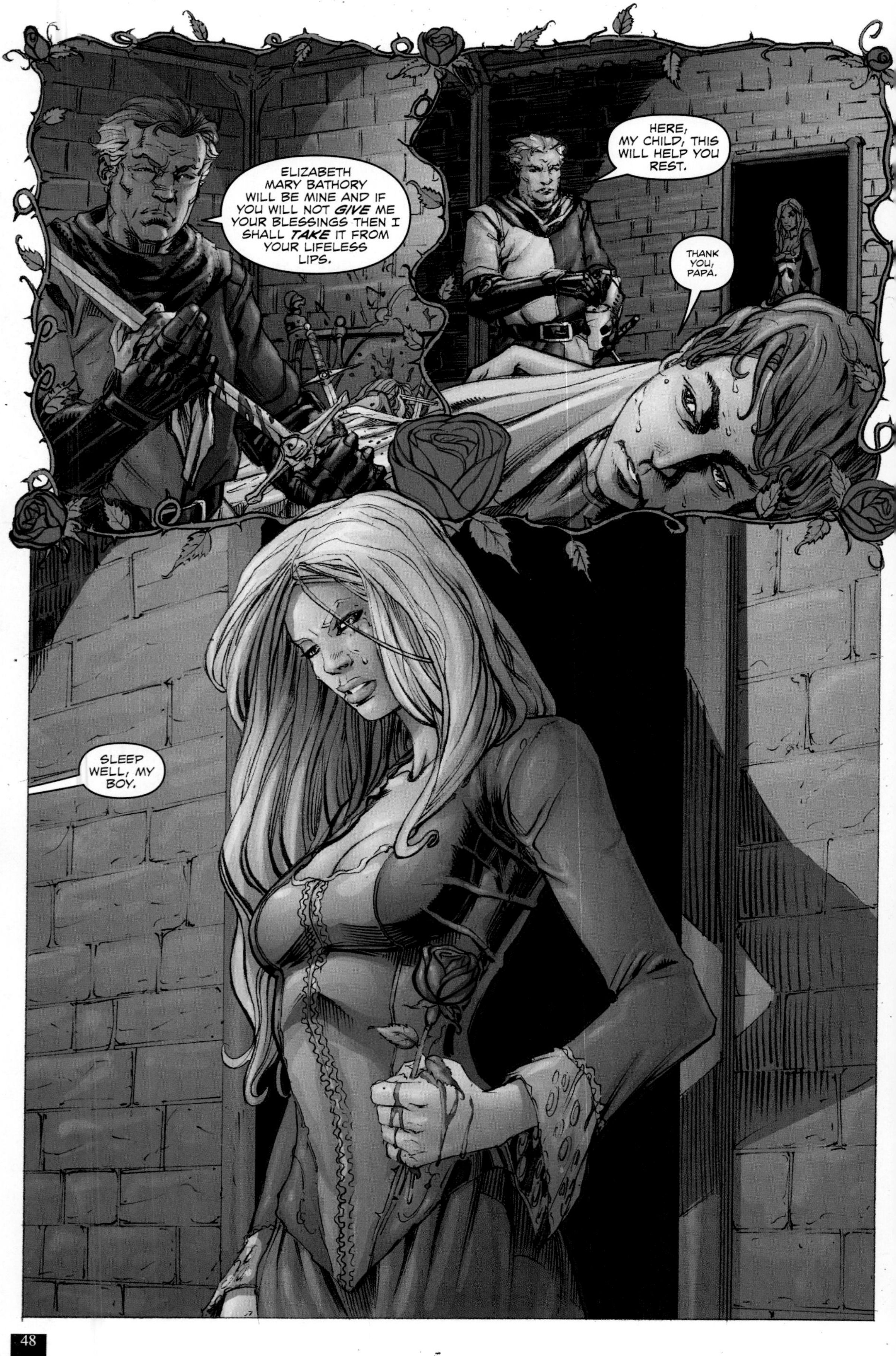
ELIZABETH MARY BATHORY WILL BE MINE AND IF YOU WILL NOT *GIVE* ME YOUR BLESSINGS THEN I SHALL *TAKE* IT FROM YOUR LIFELESS LIPS.
HERE, MY CHILD, THIS WILL HELP YOU REST.
THANK YOU, PAPA.
SLEEP WELL, MY BOY.

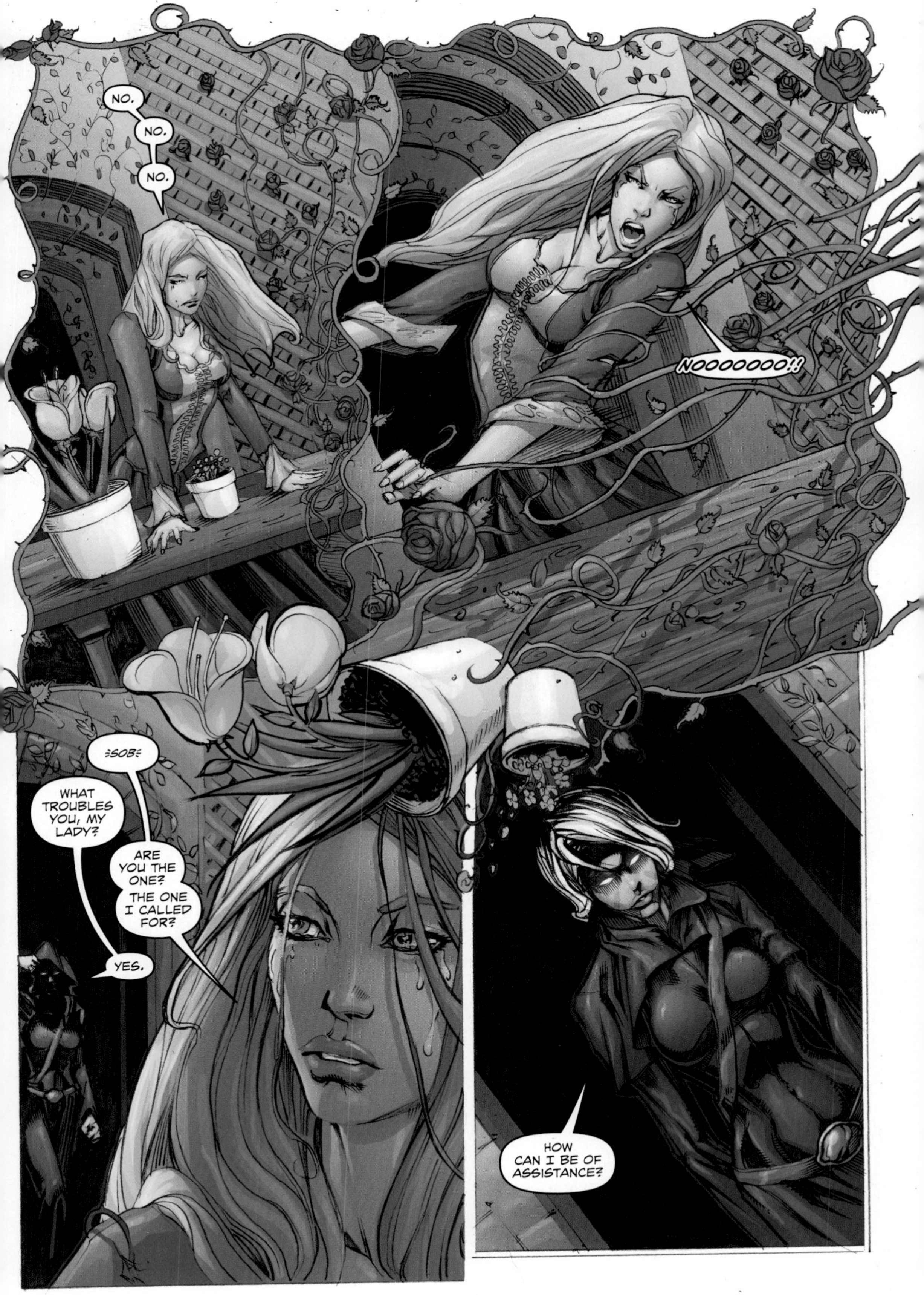
NO.
NO.
NO.
NOOOOOOO!!
≈SOB≈
WHAT TROUBLES YOU, MY LADY?
ARE YOU THE ONE? THE ONE I CALLED FOR?
YES.
HOW CAN I BE OF ASSISTANCE?

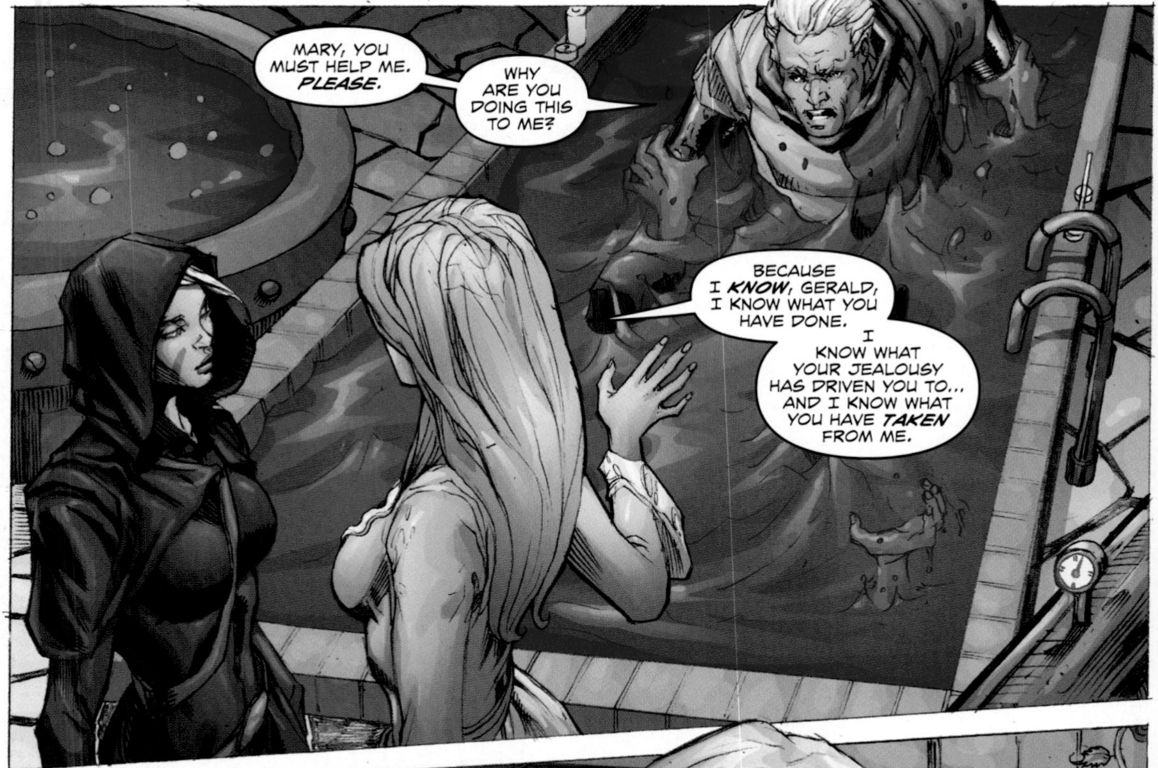
MARY, YOU MUST HELP ME. PLEASE.
WHY ARE YOU DOING THIS TO ME?
BECAUSE I KNOW, GERALD, I KNOW WHAT YOU HAVE DONE.
I KNOW WHAT YOUR JEALOUSY HAS DRIVEN YOU TO... AND I KNOW WHAT YOU HAVE TAKEN FROM ME.

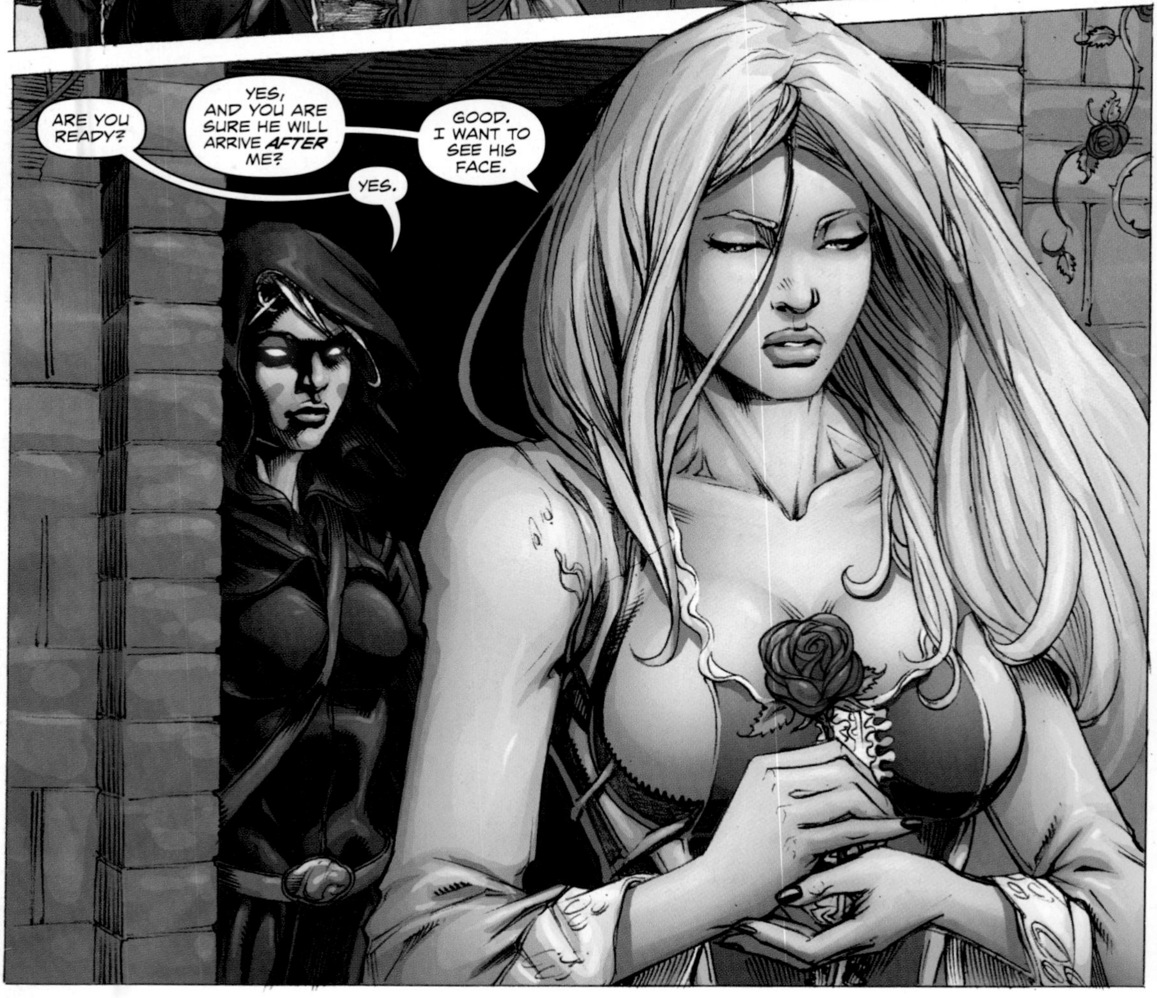
ARE YOU READY?
YES, AND YOU ARE SURE HE WILL ARRIVE AFTER ME?
YES.
GOOD. I WANT TO SEE HIS FACE.

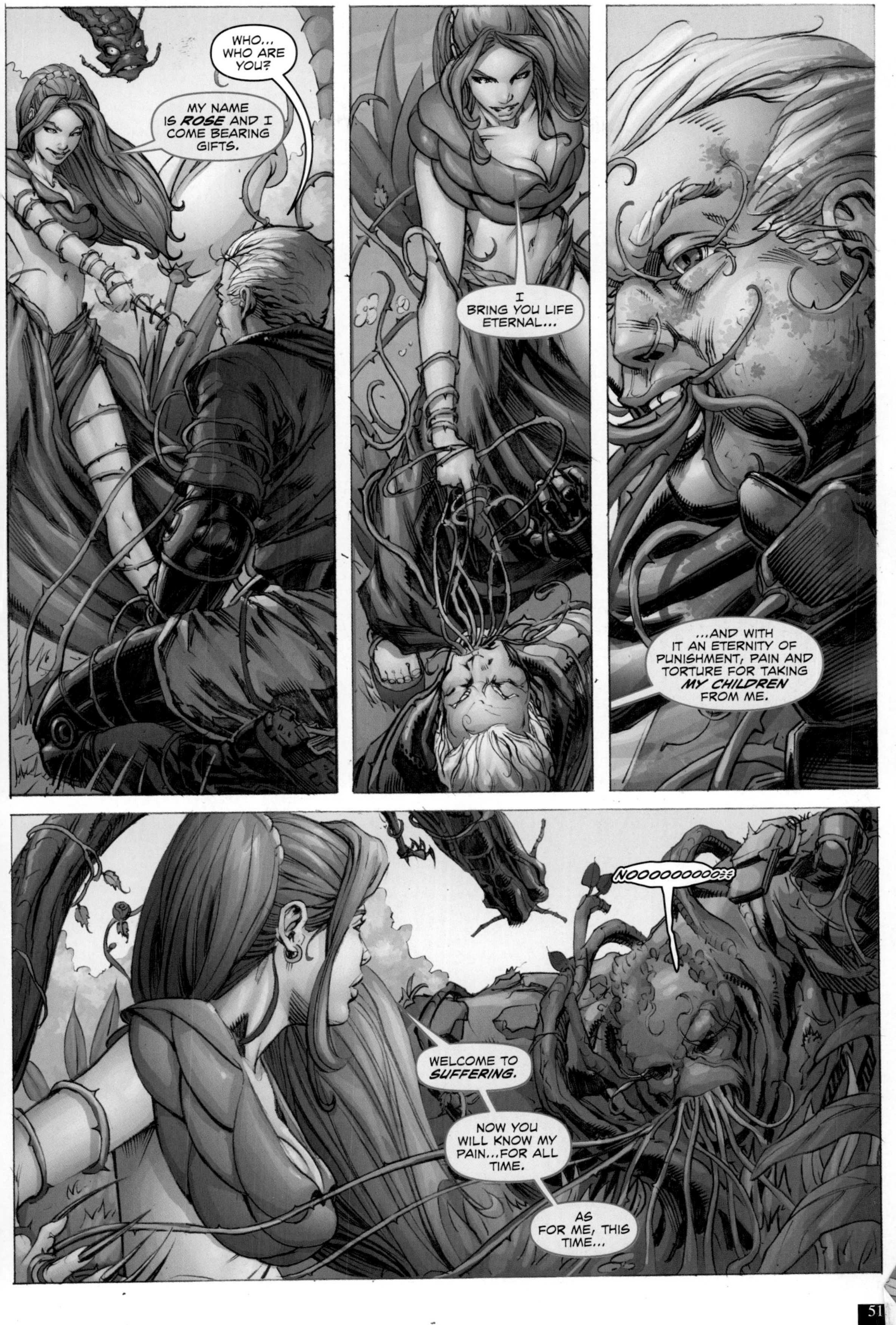
WHO... WHO ARE YOU?
MY NAME IS ROSE AND I COME BEARING GIFTS.
I BRING YOU LIFE ETERNAL...
...AND WITH IT AN ETERNITY OF PUNISHMENT, PAIN AND TORTURE FOR TAKING MY CHILDREN FROM ME.
NOOOOOOOOO!!
WELCOME TO SUFFERING.
NOW YOU WILL KNOW MY PAIN...FOR ALL TIME.
AS FOR ME, THIS TIME...

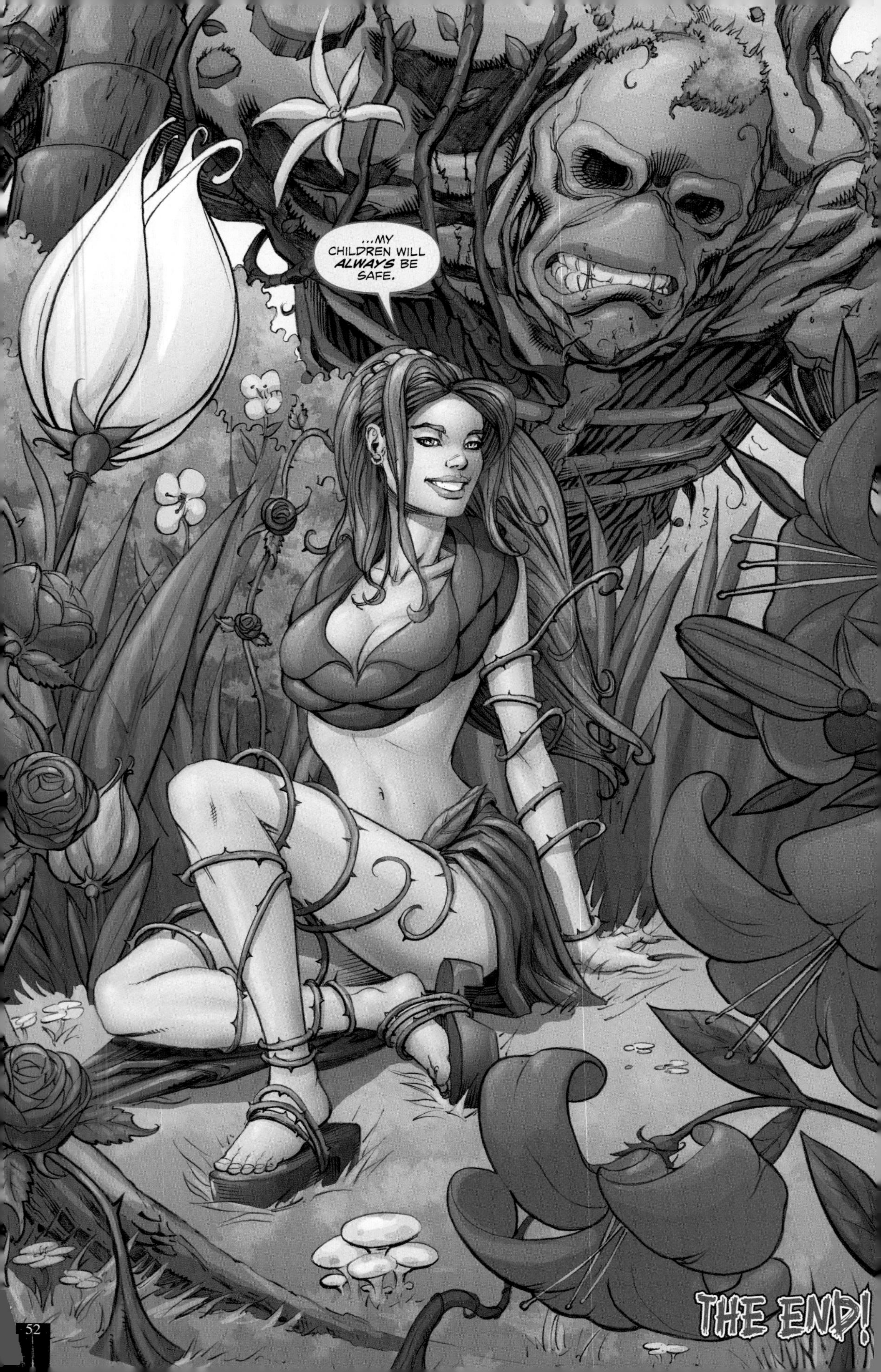
...MY CHILDREN WILL ALWAYS BE SAFE.
THE END!

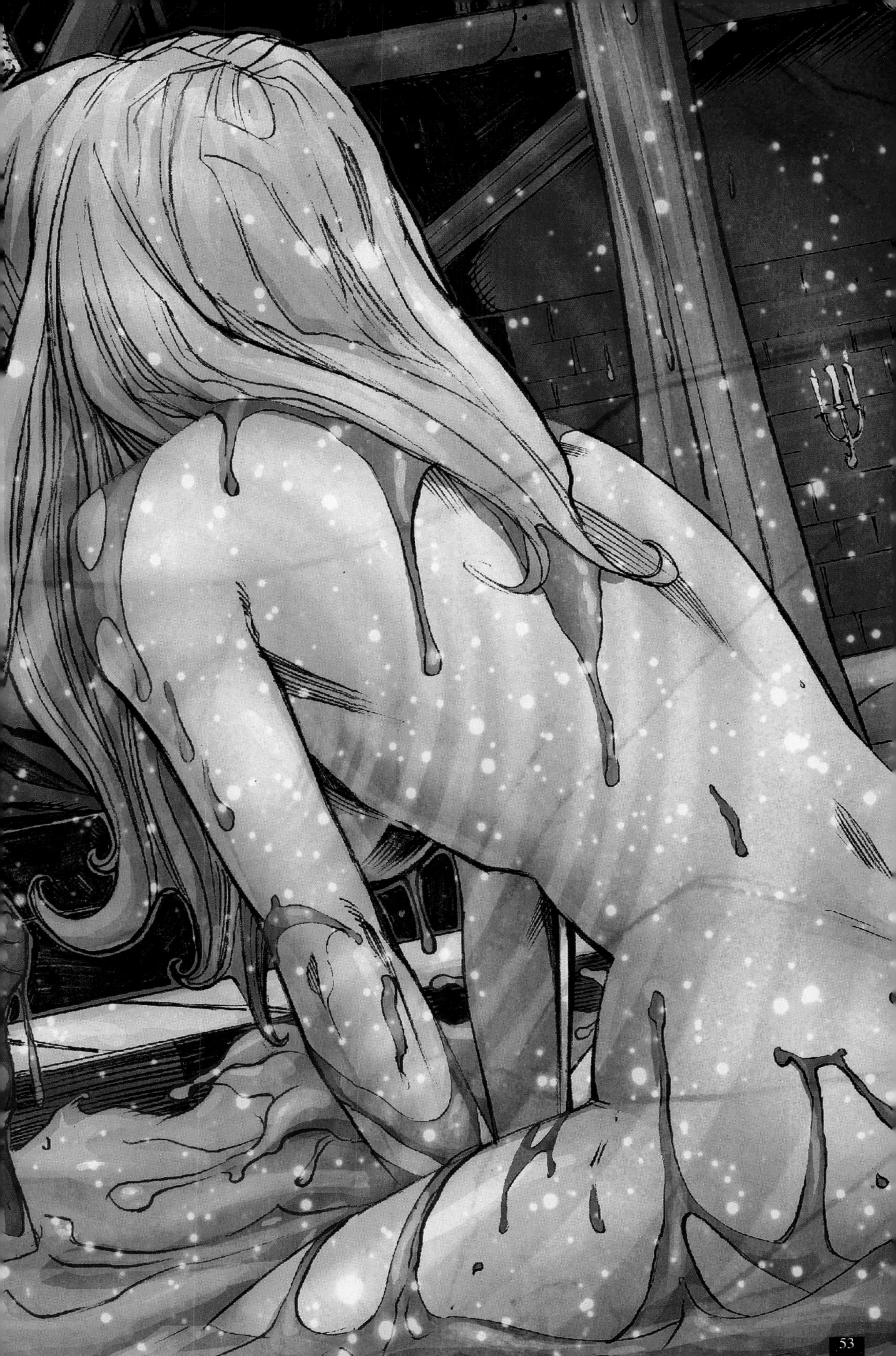

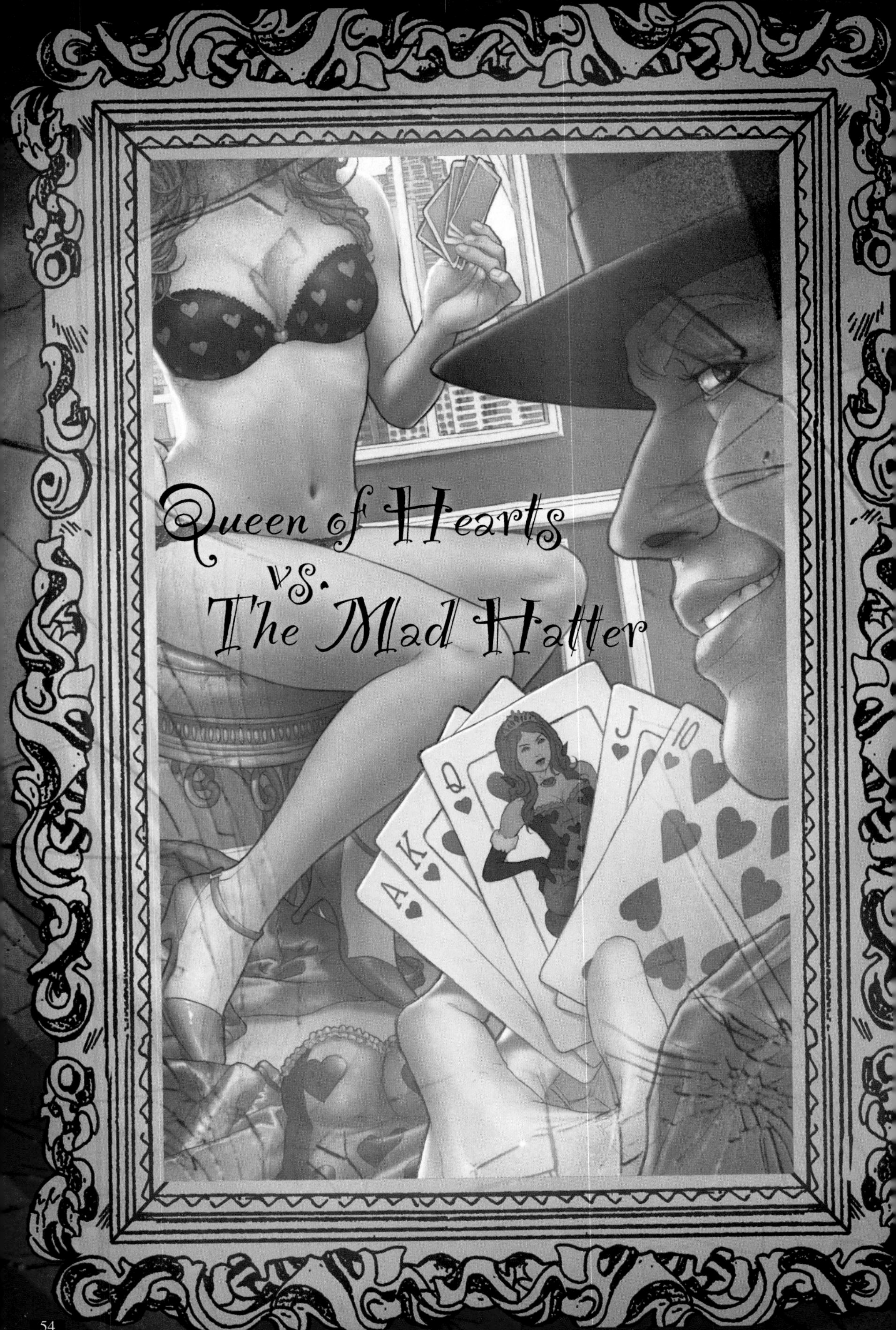
Queen of Hearts
vs.
The Mad Hatter

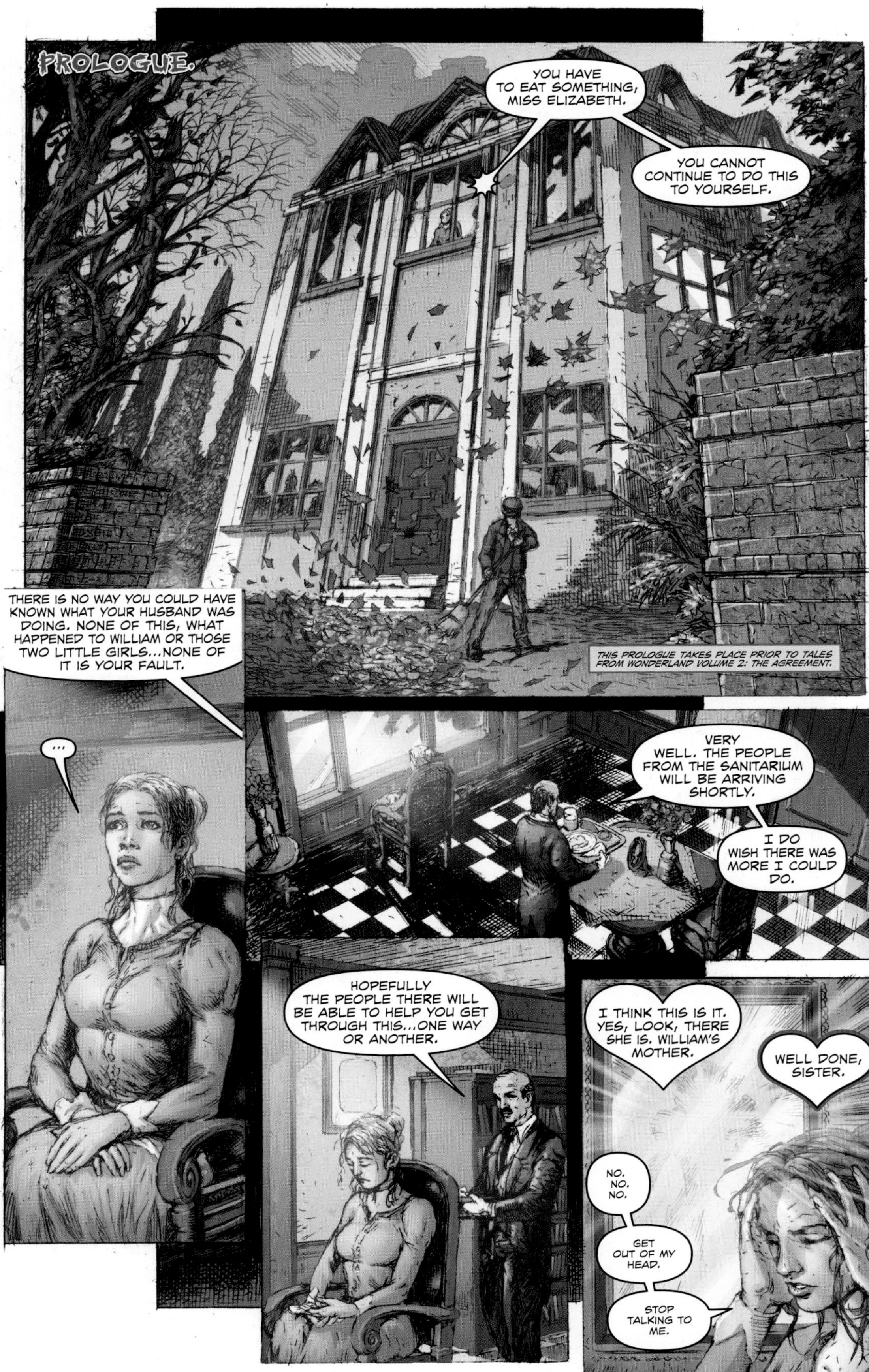
PROLOGUE.
YOU HAVE TO EAT SOMETHING, MISS ELIZABETH.
YOU CANNOT CONTINUE TO DO THIS TO YOURSELF.
THIS PROLOGUE TAKES PLACE PRIOR TO TALES FROM WONDERLAND VOLUME 2: THE AGREEMENT.
THERE IS NO WAY YOU COULD HAVE KNOWN WHAT YOUR HUSBAND WAS DOING. NONE OF THIS, WHAT HAPPENED TO WILLIAM OR THOSE TWO LITTLE GIRLS...NONE OF IT IS YOUR FAULT.
...
VERY WELL. THE PEOPLE FROM THE SANITARIUM WILL BE ARRIVING SHORTLY.
I DO WISH THERE WAS MORE I COULD DO.
HOPEFULLY THE PEOPLE THERE WILL BE ABLE TO HELP YOU GET THROUGH THIS...ONE WAY OR ANOTHER.
I THINK THIS IS IT. YES, LOOK, THERE SHE IS. WILLIAM'S MOTHER.
WELL DONE, SISTER.
NO. NO. NO.
GET OUT OF MY HEAD.
STOP TALKING TO ME.

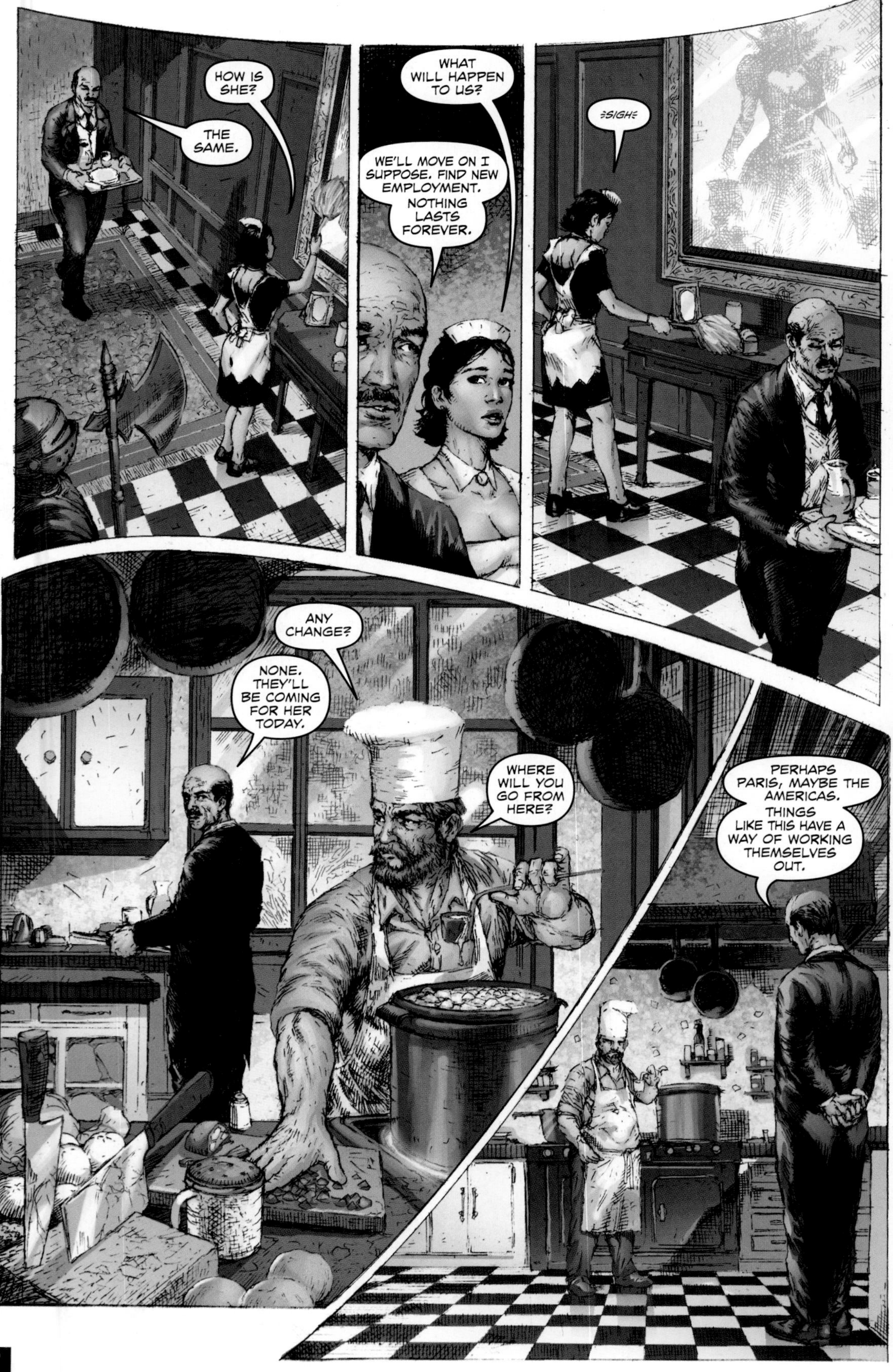
HOW IS SHE?
THE SAME.
WHAT WILL HAPPEN TO US?
WE'LL MOVE ON I SUPPOSE. FIND NEW EMPLOYMENT.
NOTHING LASTS FOREVER.
=SIGH=
ANY CHANGE?
NONE. THEY'LL BE COMING FOR HER TODAY.
WHERE WILL YOU GO FROM HERE?
PERHAPS PARIS, MAYBE THE AMERICAS.
THINGS LIKE THIS HAVE A WAY OF WORKING THEMSELVES OUT.

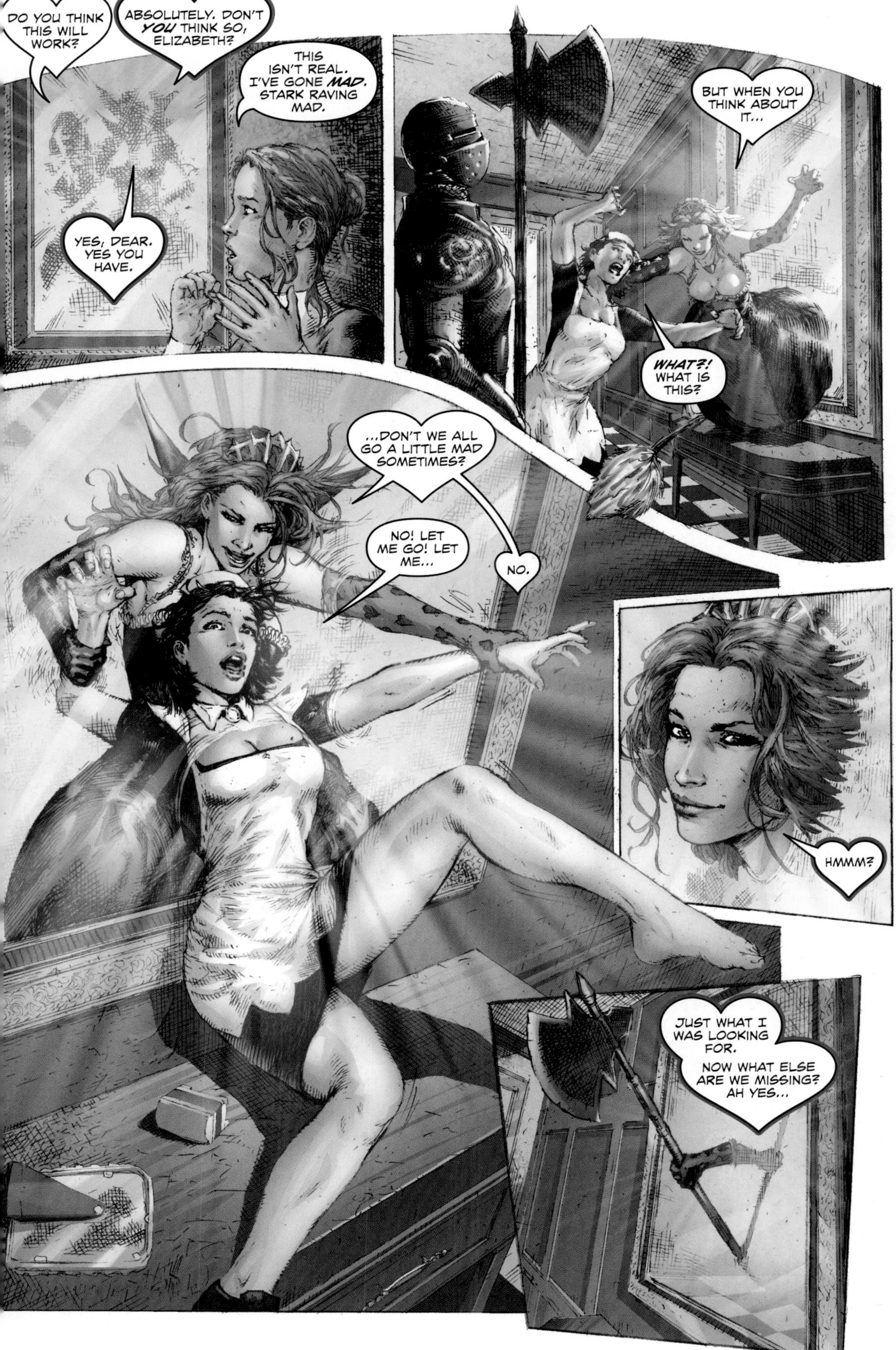
DO YOU THINK THIS WILL WORK?
ABSOLUTELY. DON'T YOU THINK SO, ELIZABETH?
THIS ISN'T REAL. I'VE GONE MAD. STARK RAVING MAD.
YES, DEAR. YES YOU HAVE.
BUT WHEN YOU THINK ABOUT IT...
WHAT?! WHAT IS THIS?
...DON'T WE ALL GO A LITTLE MAD SOMETIMES?
NO! LET ME GO! LET ME...
NO.
HMMM?
JUST WHAT I WAS LOOKING FOR.
NOW WHAT ELSE ARE WE MISSING? AH YES...

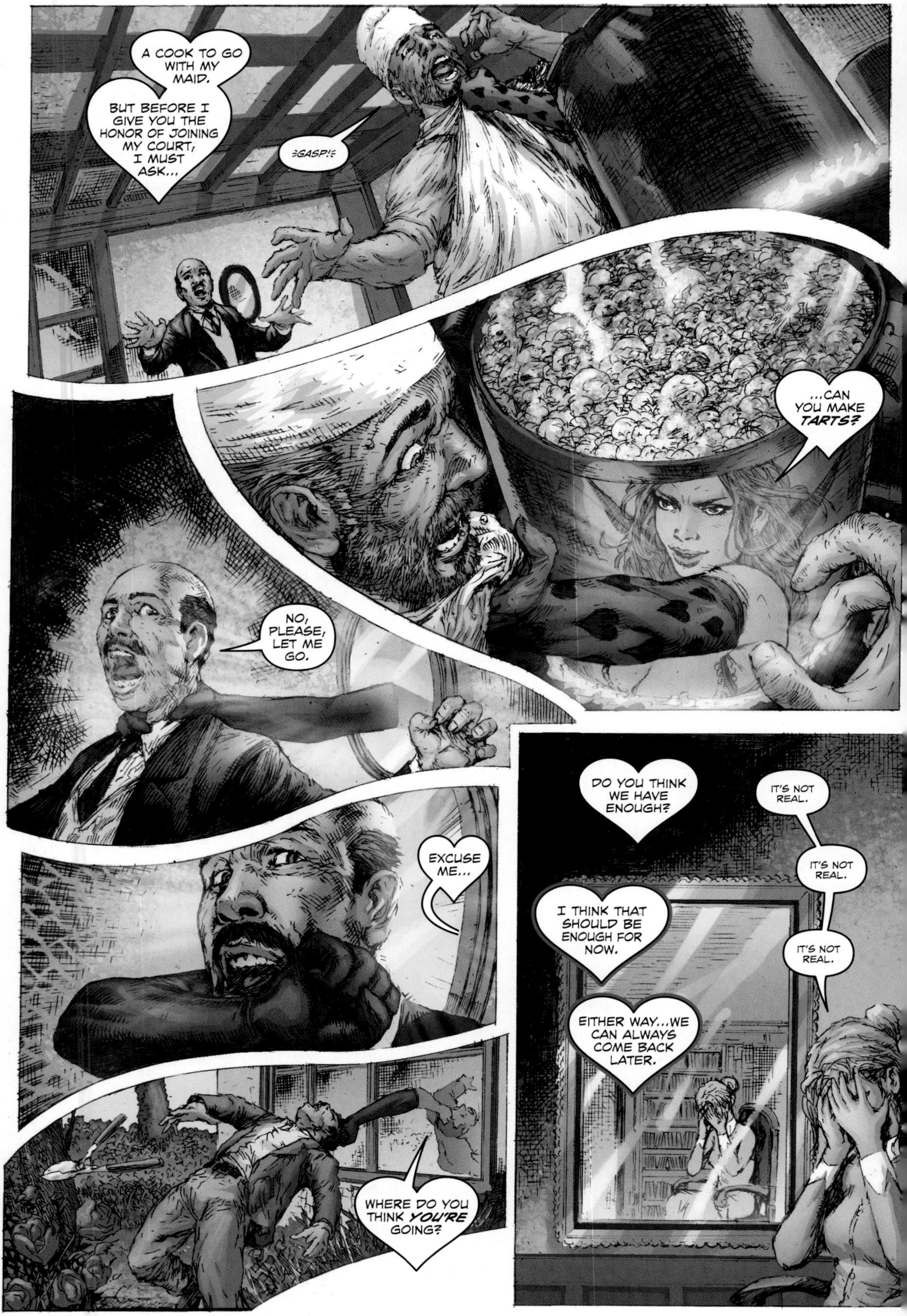
A COOK TO GO WITH MY MAID.
BUT BEFORE I GIVE YOU THE HONOR OF JOINING MY COURT, I MUST ASK...
GASP!
...CAN YOU MAKE TARTS?
NO, PLEASE, LET ME GO.
EXCUSE ME...
WHERE DO YOU THINK YOU'RE GOING?
DO YOU THINK WE HAVE ENOUGH?
IT'S NOT REAL.
IT'S NOT REAL.
I THINK THAT SHOULD BE ENOUGH FOR NOW.
IT'S NOT REAL.
EITHER WAY...WE CAN ALWAYS COME BACK LATER.

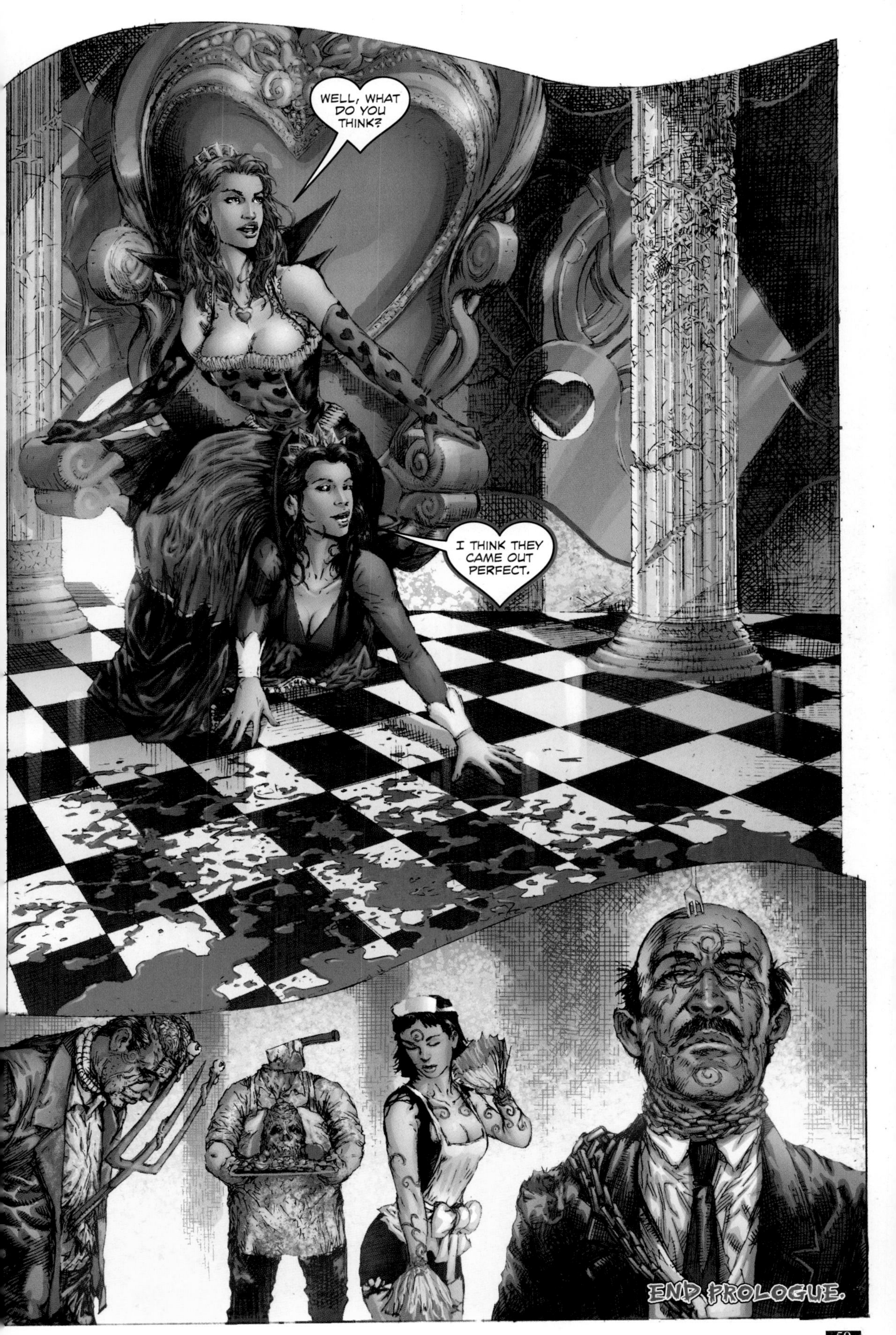
WELL, WHAT DO YOU THINK?
I THINK THEY CAME OUT PERFECT.
END PROLOGUE.

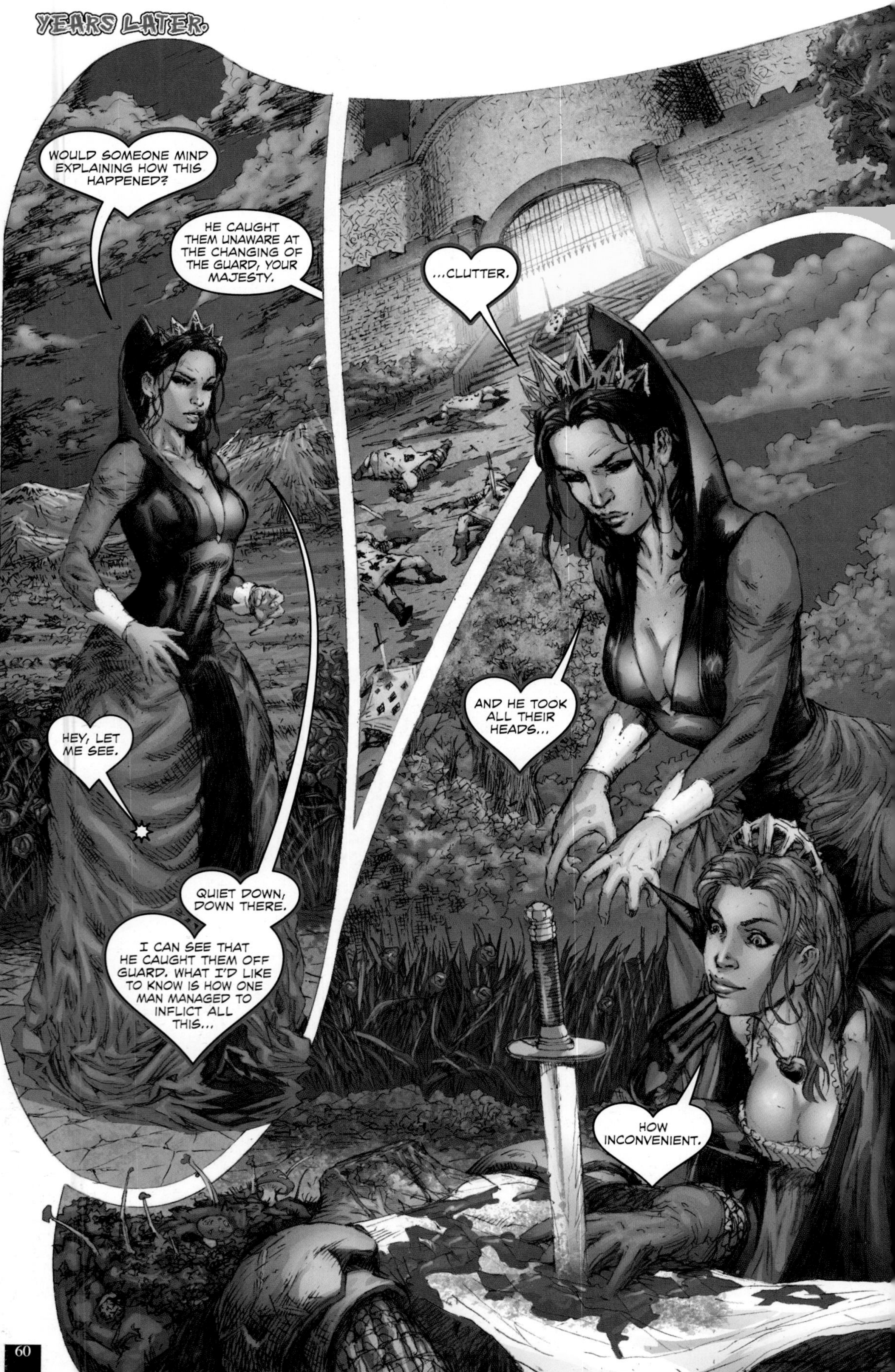
YEARS LATER.
WOULD SOMEONE MIND EXPLAINING HOW THIS HAPPENED?
HE CAUGHT THEM UNAWARE AT THE CHANGING OF THE GUARD, YOUR MAJESTY.
HEY, LET ME SEE.
QUIET DOWN, DOWN THERE.
I CAN SEE THAT HE CAUGHT THEM OFF GUARD. WHAT I'D LIKE TO KNOW IS HOW ONE MAN MANAGED TO INFLICT ALL THIS...
...CLUTTER.
AND HE TOOK ALL THEIR HEADS...
HOW INCONVENIENT.

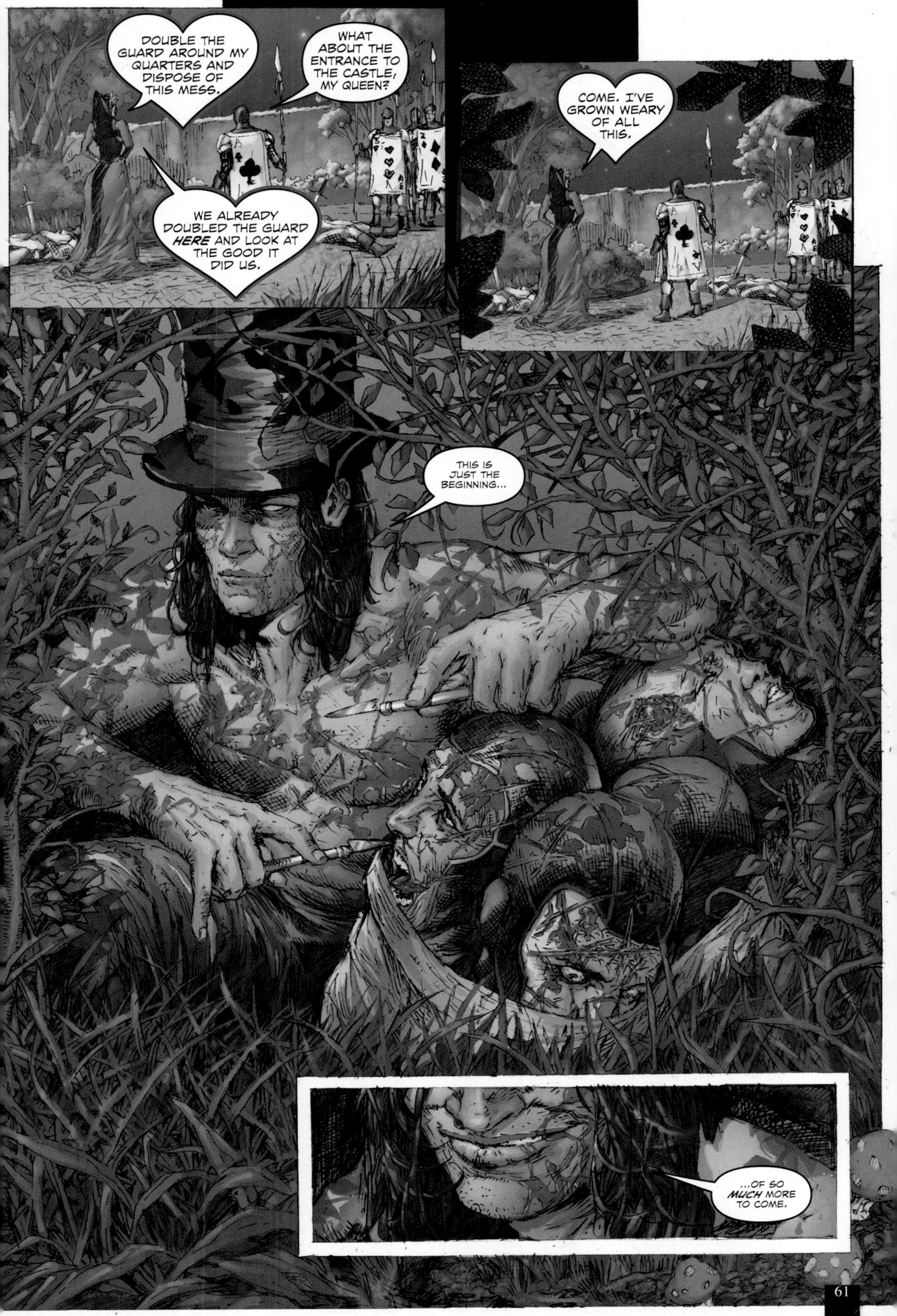
DOUBLE THE GUARD AROUND MY QUARTERS AND DISPOSE OF THIS MESS.
WHAT ABOUT THE ENTRANCE TO THE CASTLE, MY QUEEN?
WE ALREADY DOUBLED THE GUARD *HERE* AND LOOK AT THE GOOD IT DID US.
COME. I'VE GROWN WEARY OF ALL THIS.
THIS IS JUST THE BEGINNING...
...OF SO *MUCH* MORE TO COME.

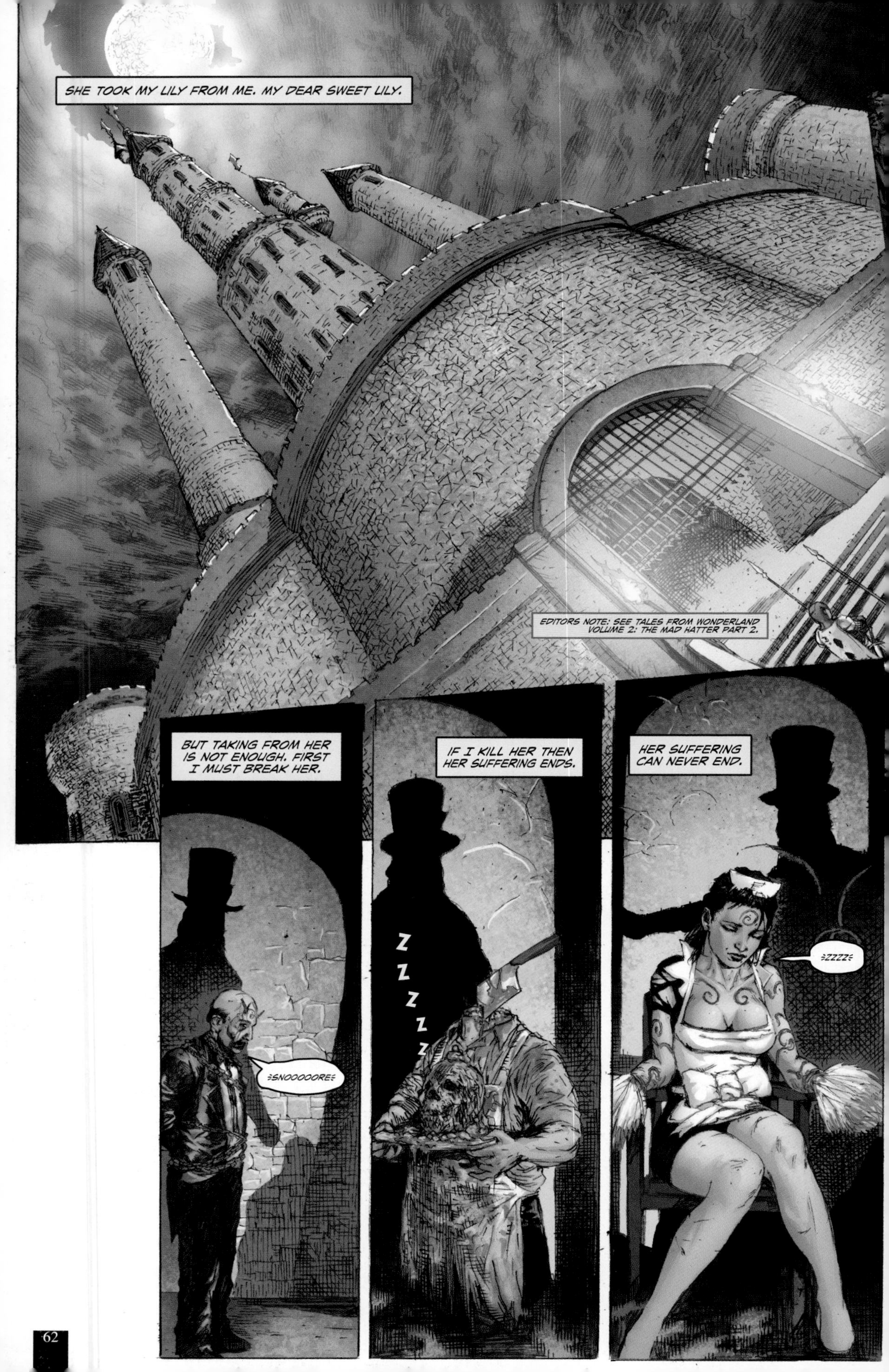
SHE TOOK MY LILY FROM ME. MY DEAR SWEET LILY.
EDITORS NOTE: SEE TALES FROM WONDERLAND VOLUME 2: THE MAD HATTER PART 2.
BUT TAKING FROM HER IS NOT ENOUGH. FIRST I MUST BREAK HER.
SNOOOOORE
IF I KILL HER THEN HER SUFFERING ENDS.
Z Z Z Z Z
HER SUFFERING CAN NEVER END.
ZZZZ

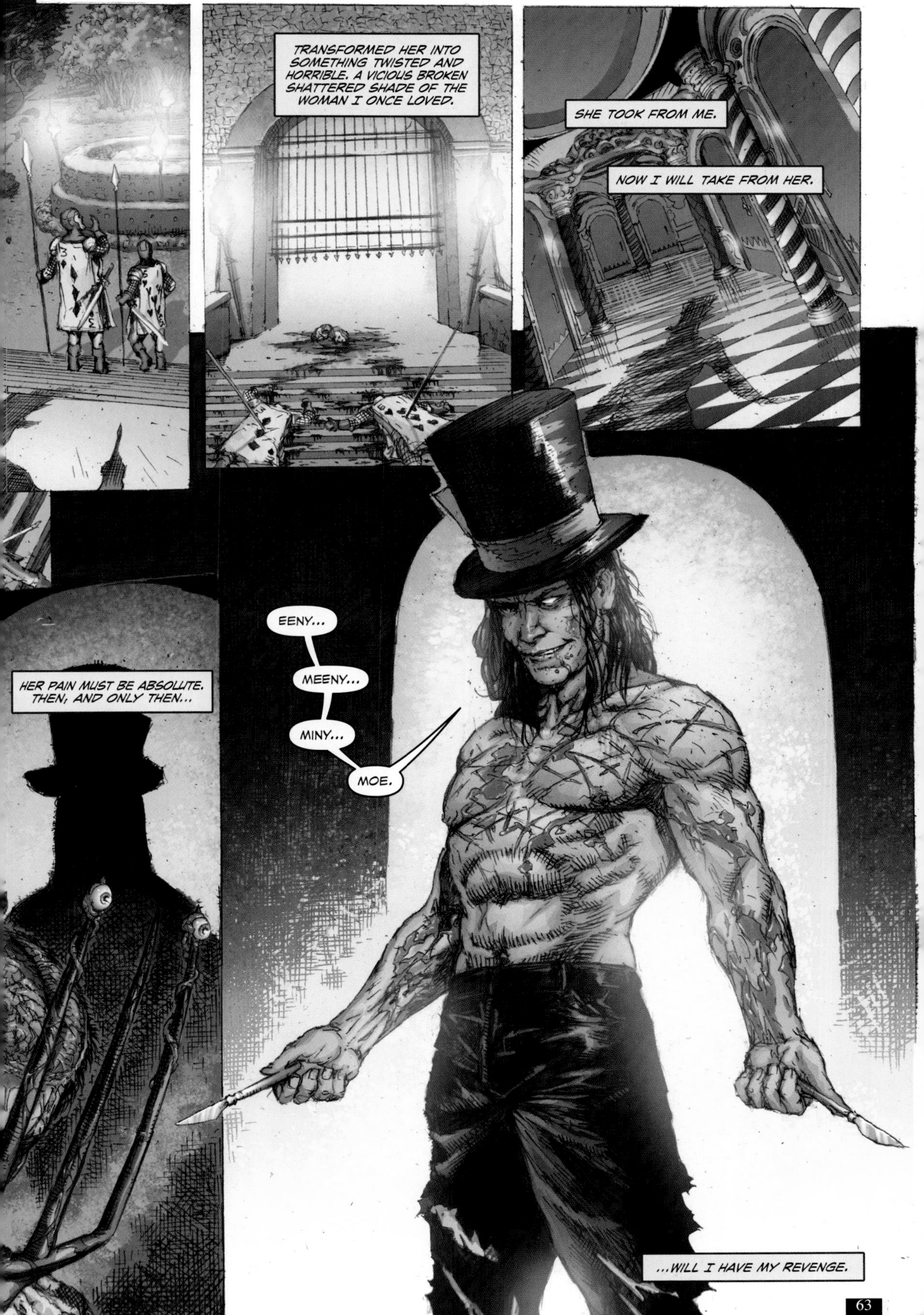
TRANSFORMED HER INTO SOMETHING TWISTED AND HORRIBLE. A VICIOUS BROKEN SHATTERED SHADE OF THE WOMAN I ONCE LOVED.
SHE TOOK FROM ME.
NOW I WILL TAKE FROM HER.
HER PAIN MUST BE ABSOLUTE. THEN, AND ONLY THEN...
EENY...
MEENY...
MINY...
MOE.
...WILL I HAVE MY REVENGE.

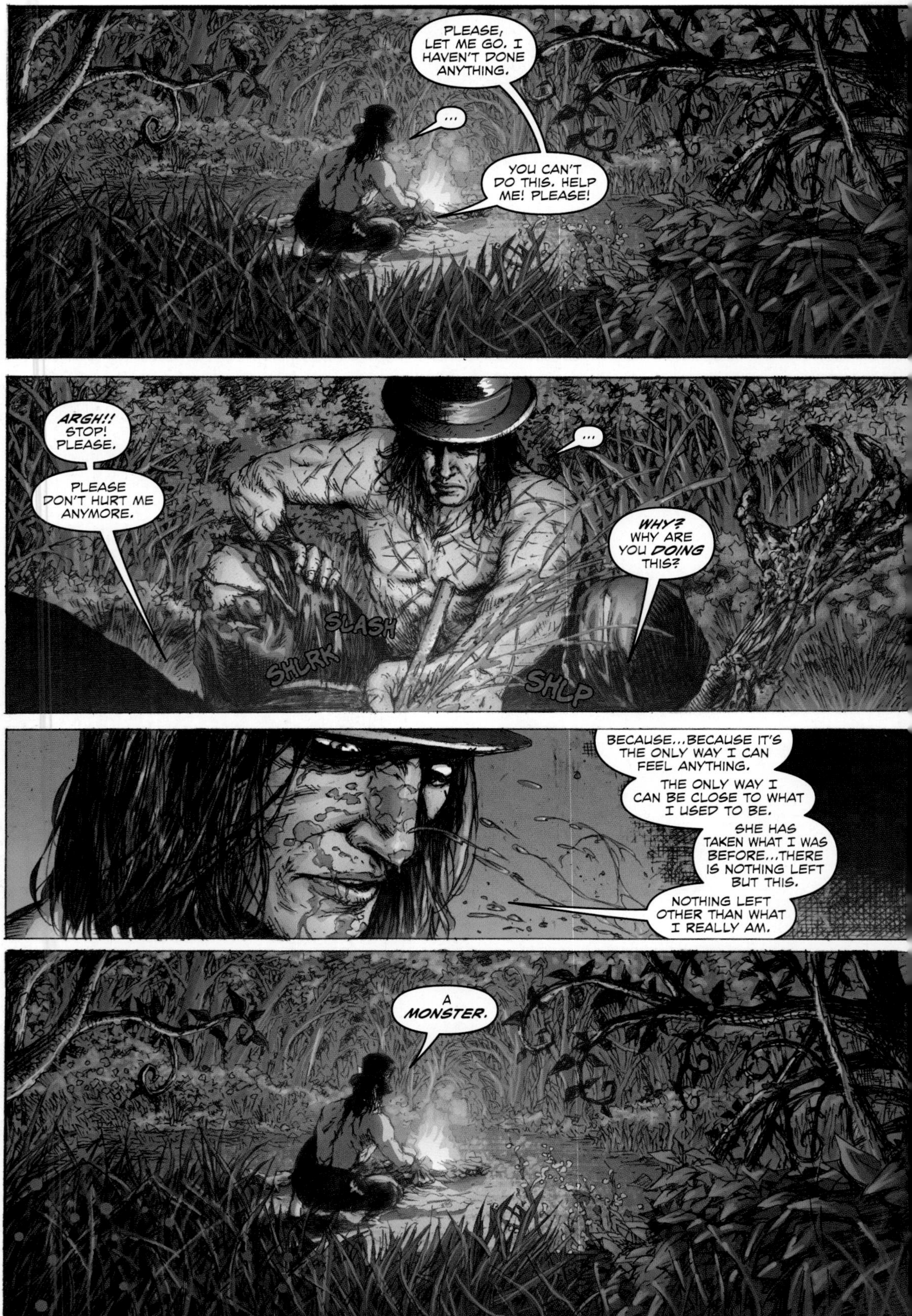
PLEASE, LET ME GO. I HAVEN'T DONE ANYTHING.
...
YOU CAN'T DO THIS. HELP ME! PLEASE!
ARGH!! STOP! PLEASE.
PLEASE DON'T HURT ME ANYMORE.
...
WHY? WHY ARE YOU DOING THIS?
SLASH
SHLRK
SHLP
BECAUSE...BECAUSE IT'S THE ONLY WAY I CAN FEEL ANYTHING.
THE ONLY WAY I CAN BE CLOSE TO WHAT I USED TO BE.
SHE HAS TAKEN WHAT I WAS BEFORE...THERE IS NOTHING LEFT BUT THIS.
NOTHING LEFT OTHER THAN WHAT I REALLY AM.
A MONSTER.

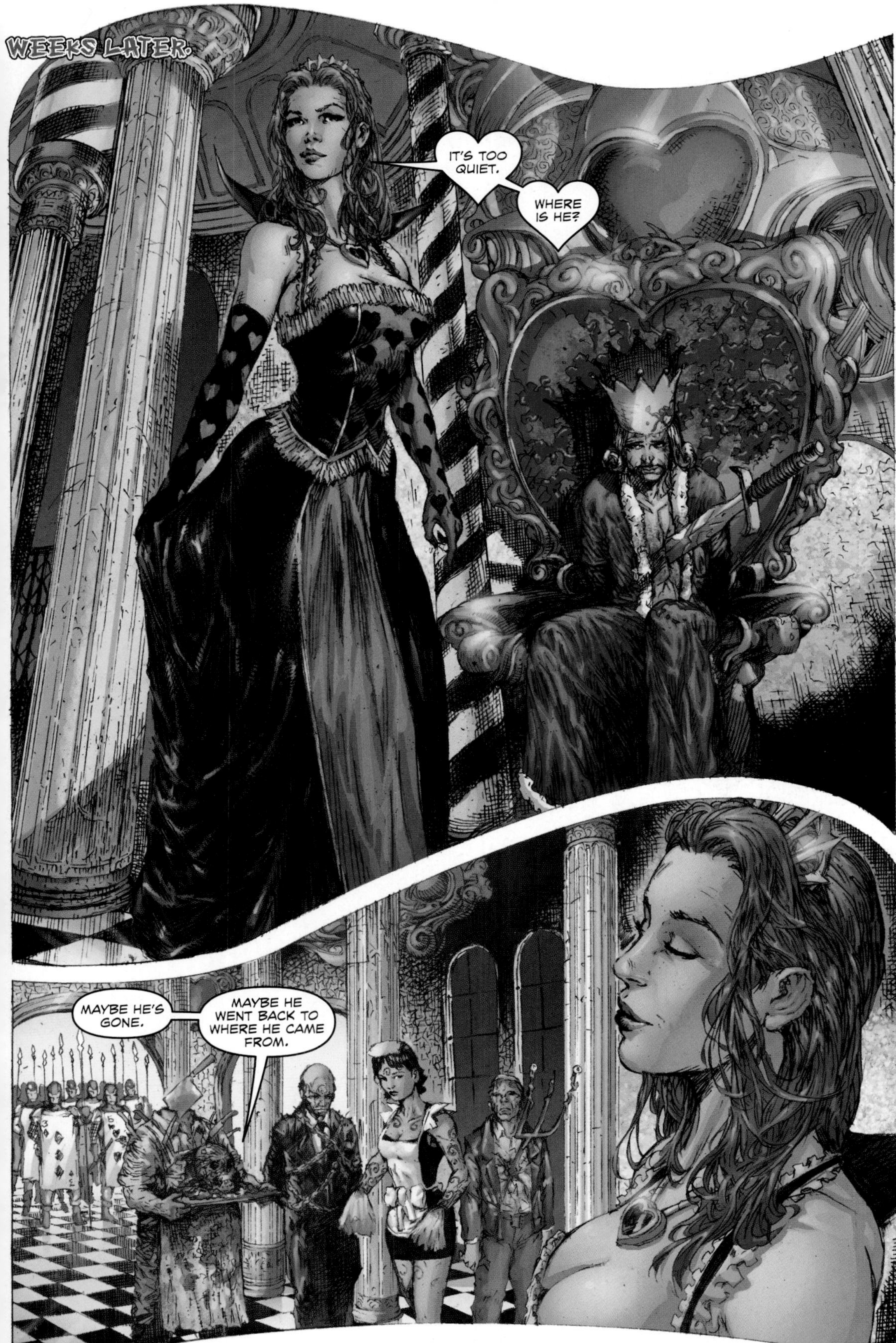
WEEKS LATER.
IT'S TOO QUIET.
WHERE IS HE?
MAYBE HE'S GONE.
MAYBE HE WENT BACK TO WHERE HE CAME FROM.

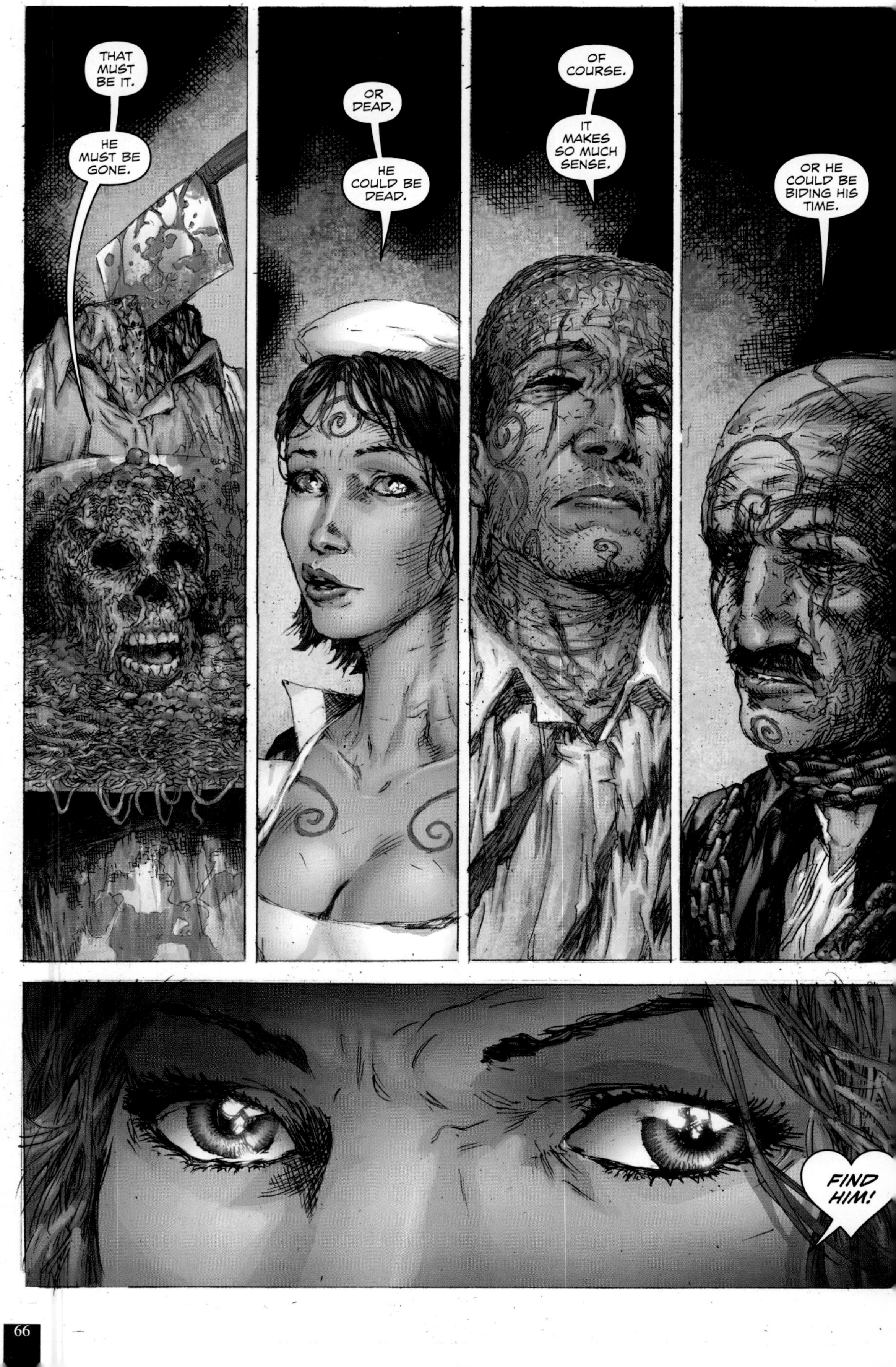
THAT MUST BE IT.
HE MUST BE GONE.
OR DEAD.
HE COULD BE DEAD.
OF COURSE.
IT MAKES SO MUCH SENSE.
OR HE COULD BE BIDING HIS TIME.
FIND HIM!

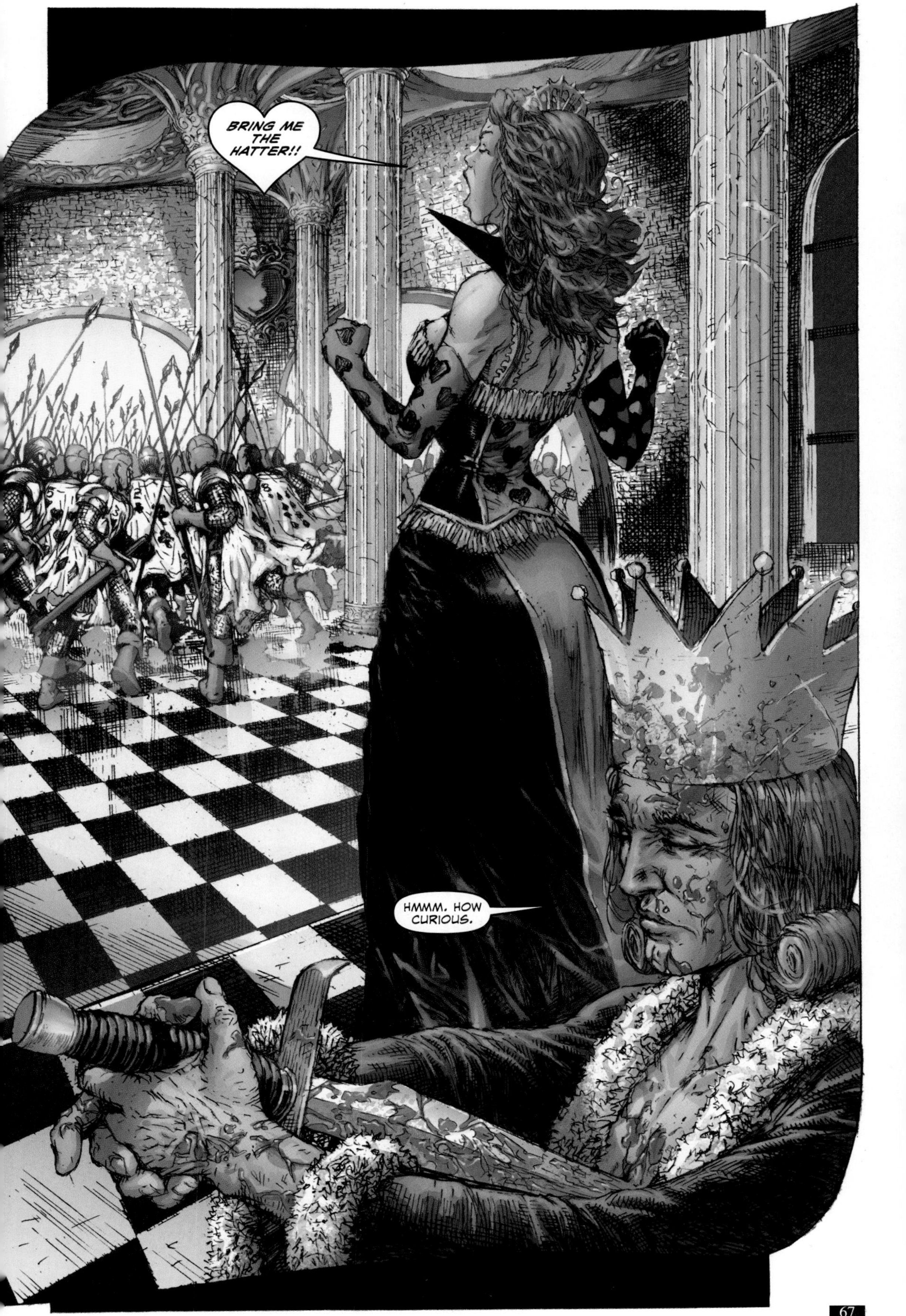
BRING ME THE HATTER!!
HMMM. HOW CURIOUS.

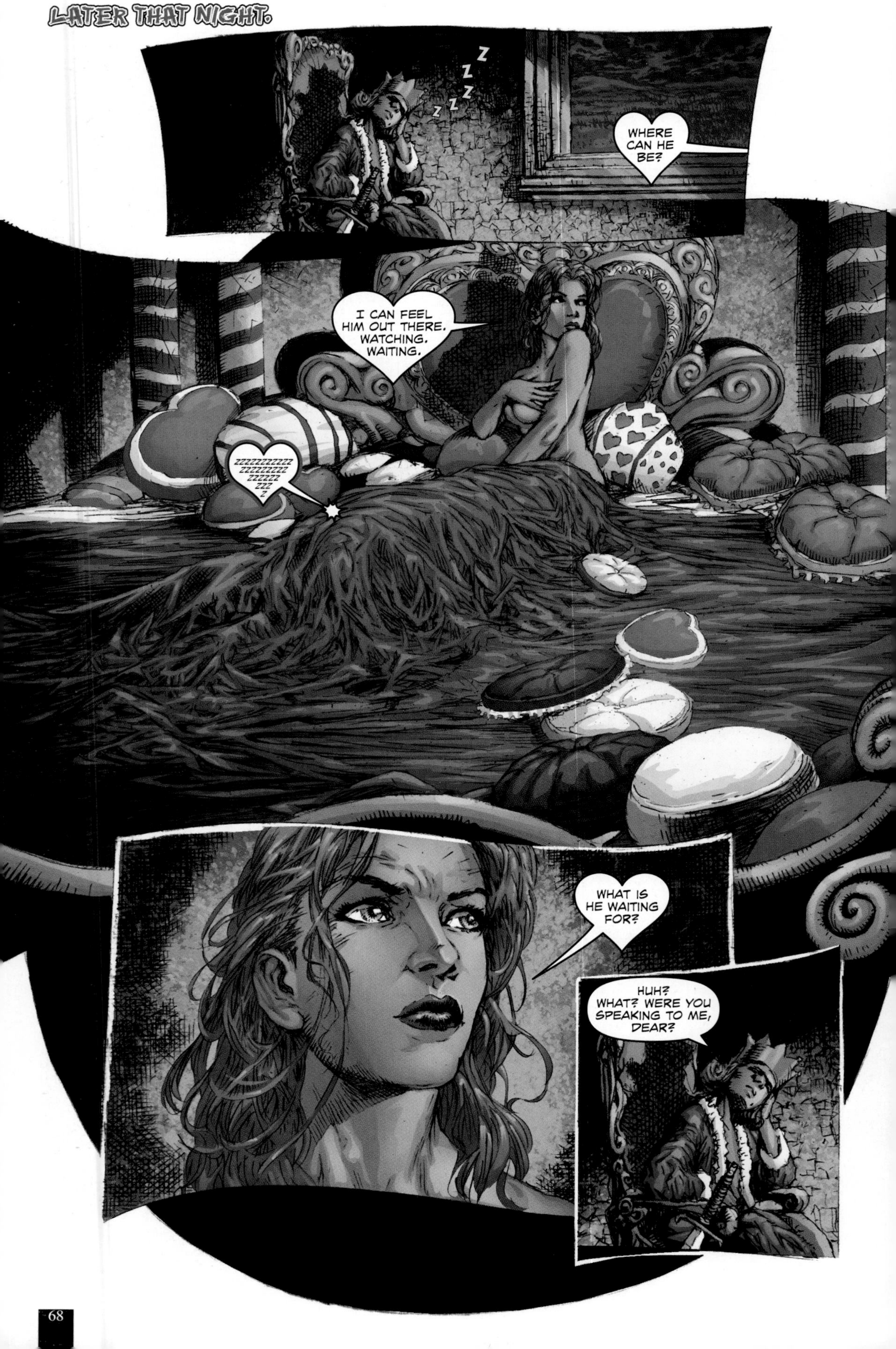
LATER THAT NIGHT.
Z Z Z Z Z Z
WHERE CAN HE BE?
I CAN FEEL HIM OUT THERE. WATCHING. WAITING.
ZZZZZZZZZZ ZZZZZZZZ ZZZZZ ZZZ Z
WHAT IS HE WAITING FOR?
HUH? WHAT? WERE YOU SPEAKING TO ME, DEAR?

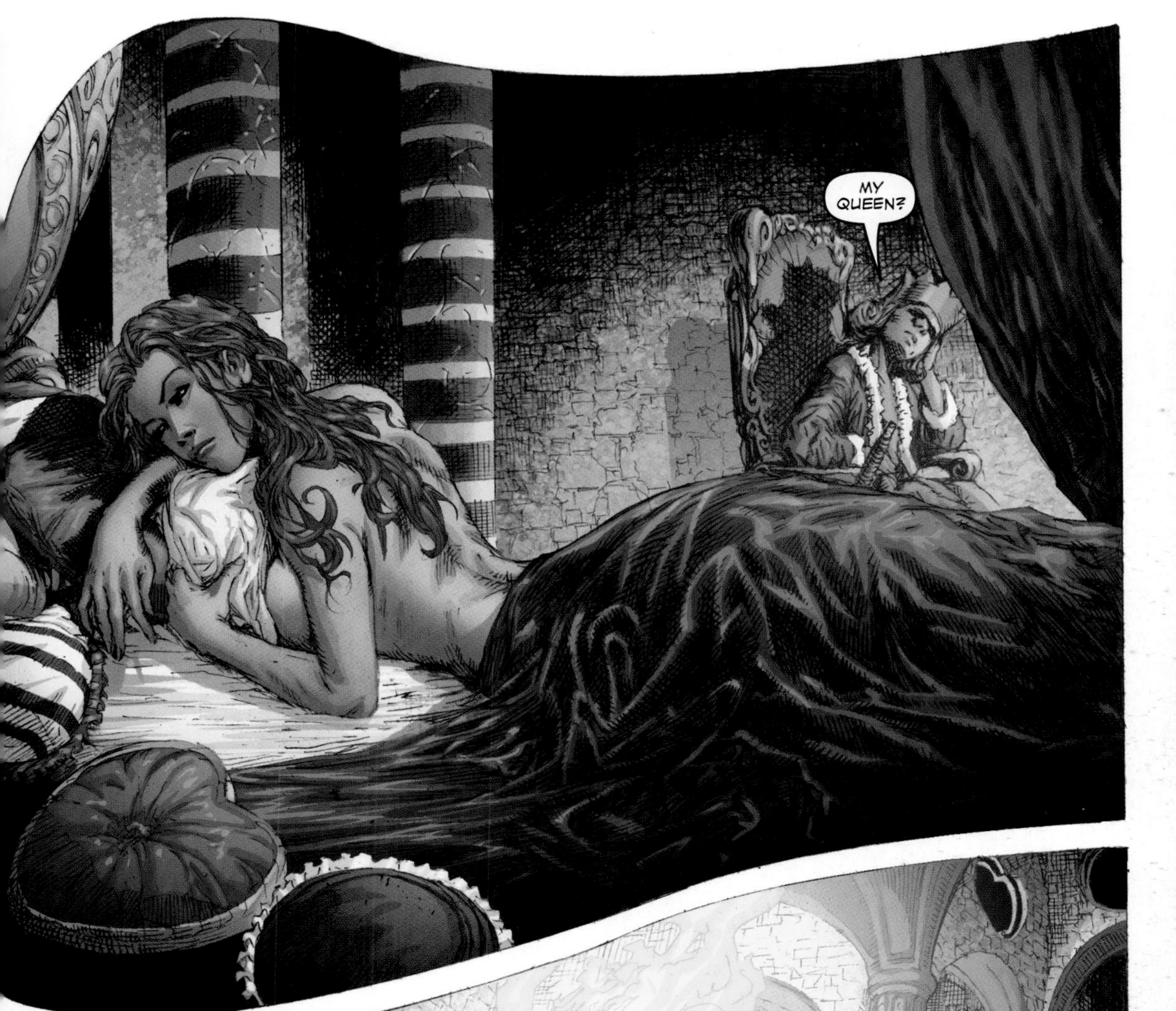
MY
QUEEN?

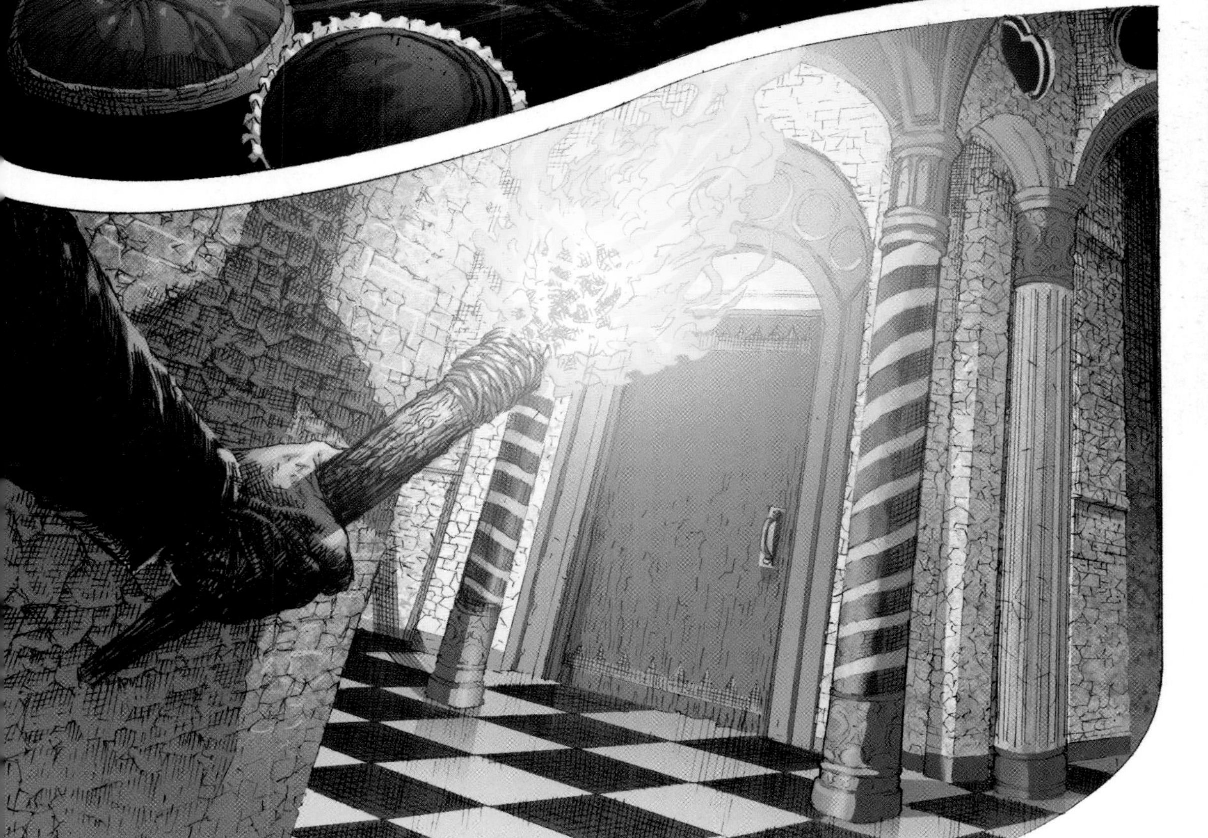

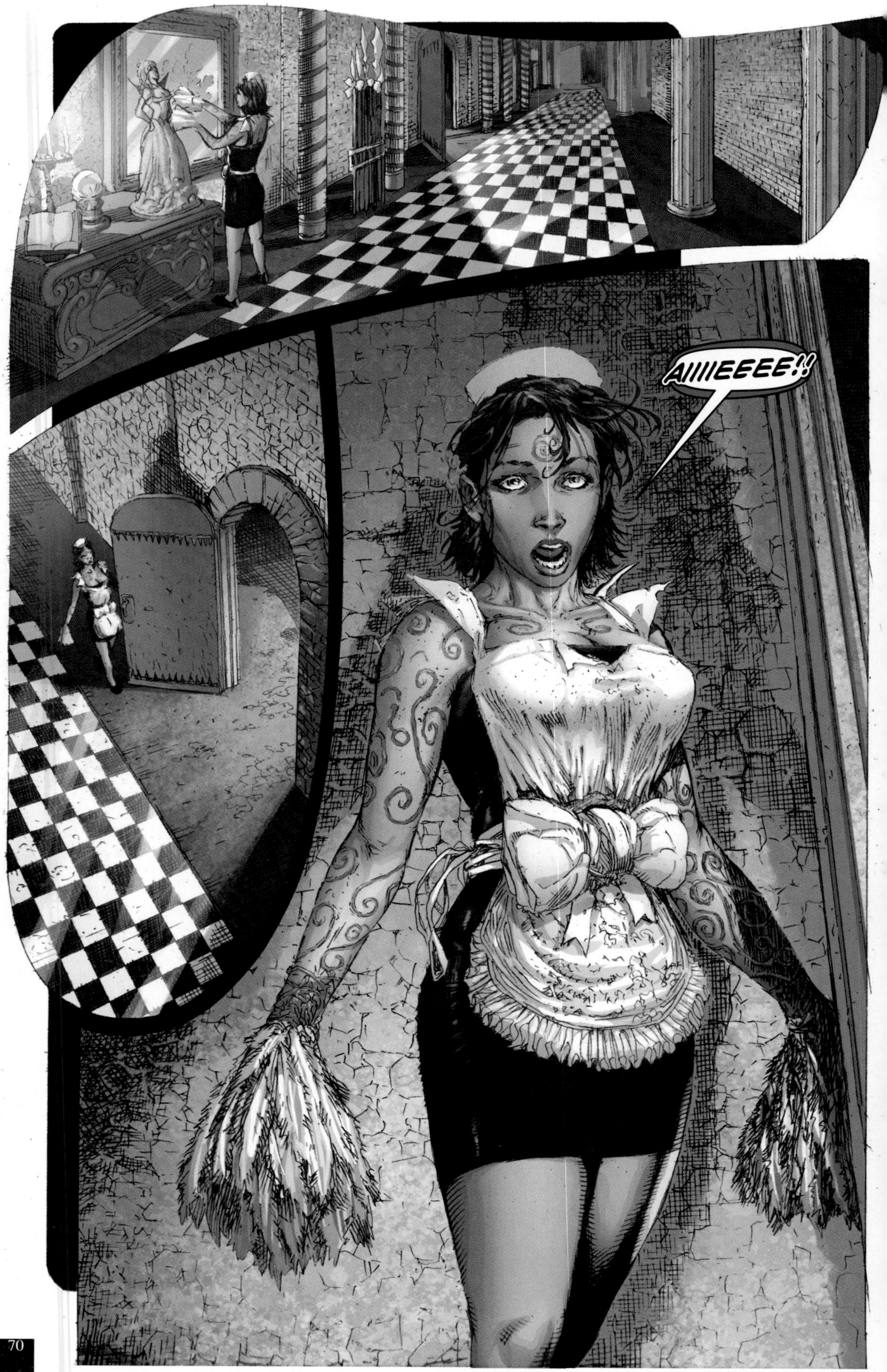
AIIIIEEEEE!!

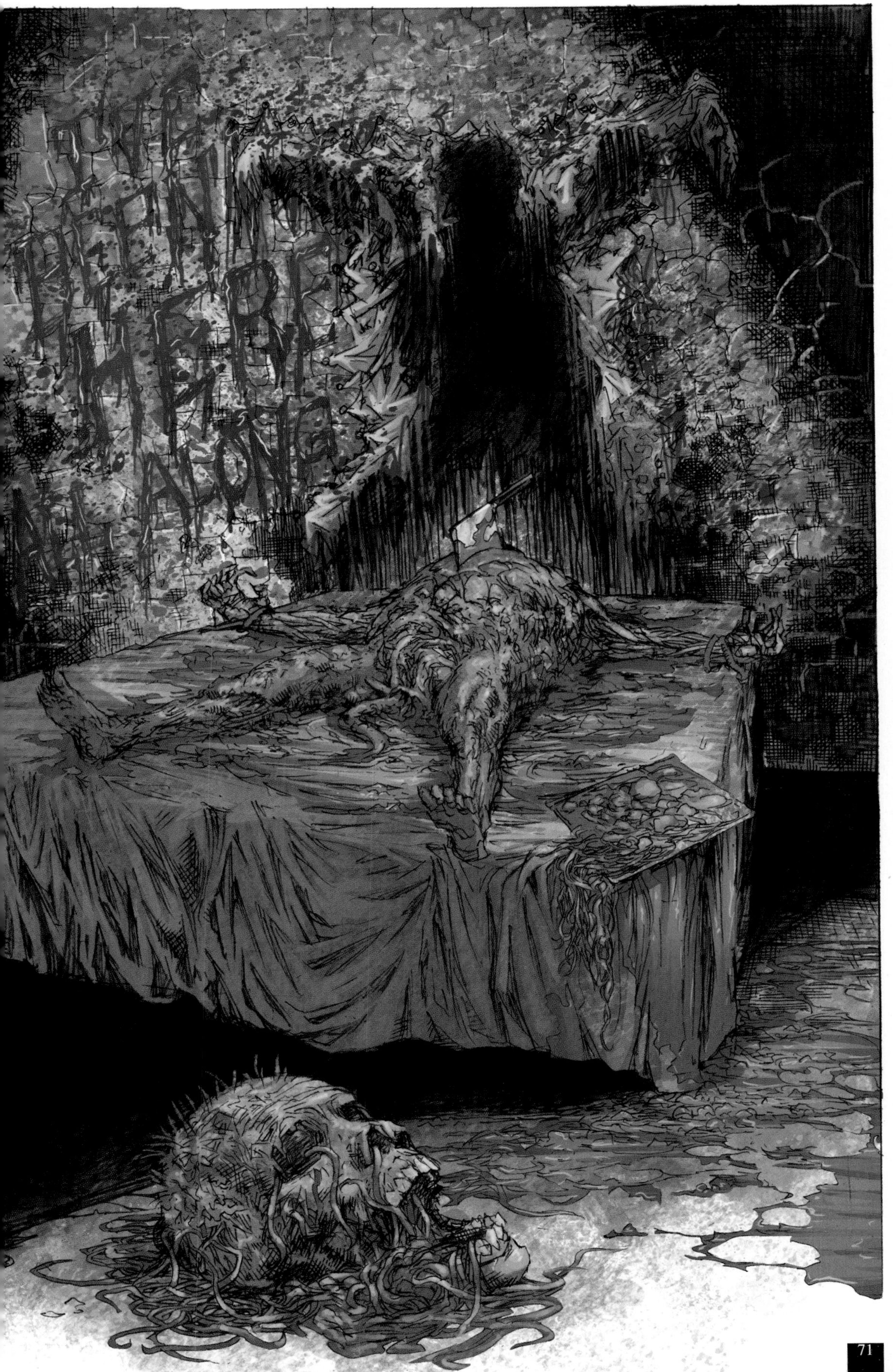

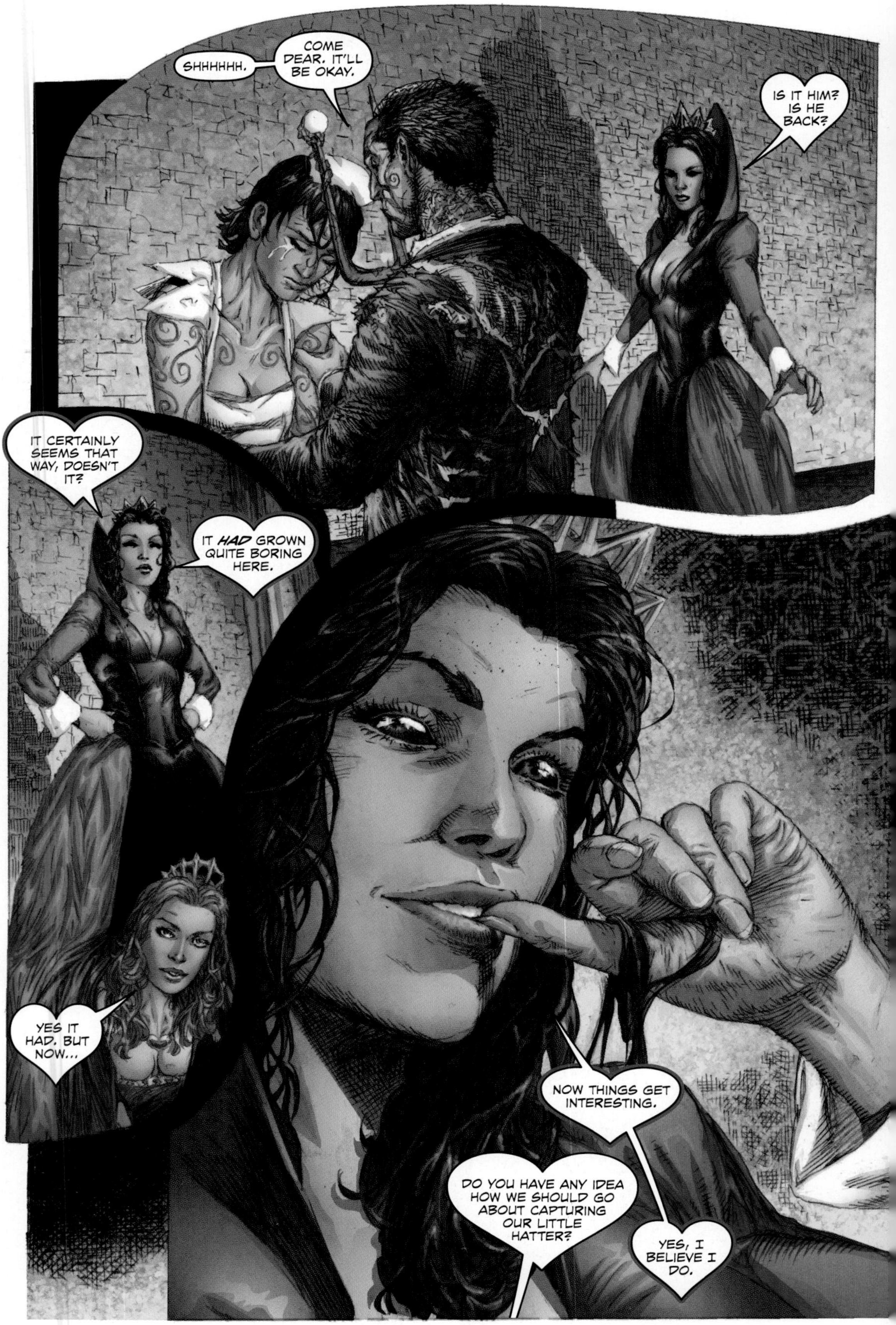
SHHHHHH.
COME DEAR. IT'LL BE OKAY.
IS IT HIM? IS HE BACK?
IT CERTAINLY SEEMS THAT WAY, DOESN'T IT?
IT *HAD* GROWN QUITE BORING HERE.
YES IT HAD. BUT NOW...
NOW THINGS GET INTERESTING.
DO YOU HAVE ANY IDEA HOW WE SHOULD GO ABOUT CAPTURING OUR LITTLE HATTER?
YES, I BELIEVE I DO.

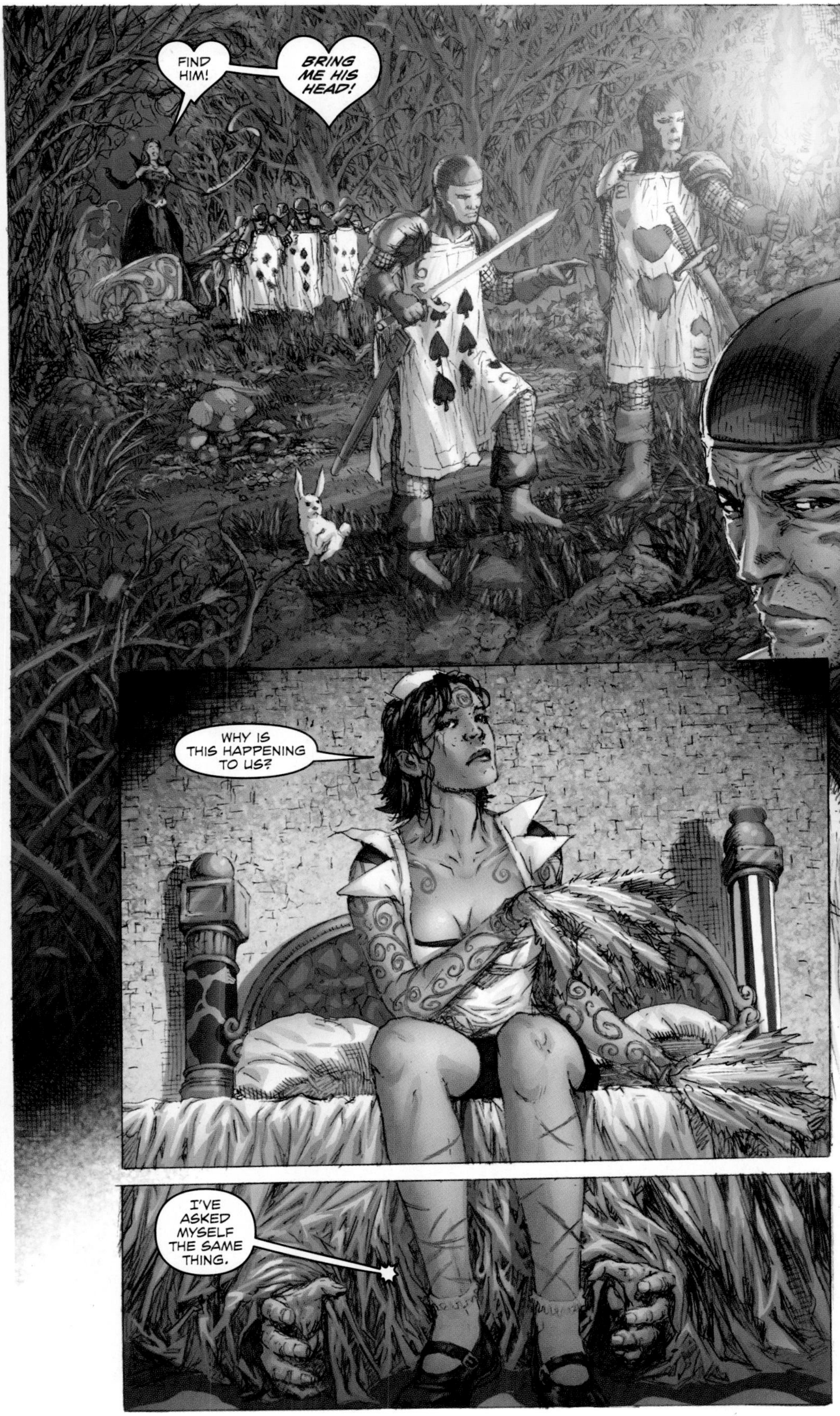
FIND HIM!
BRING ME HIS HEAD!
WHY IS THIS HAPPENING TO US?
I'VE ASKED MYSELF THE SAME THING.

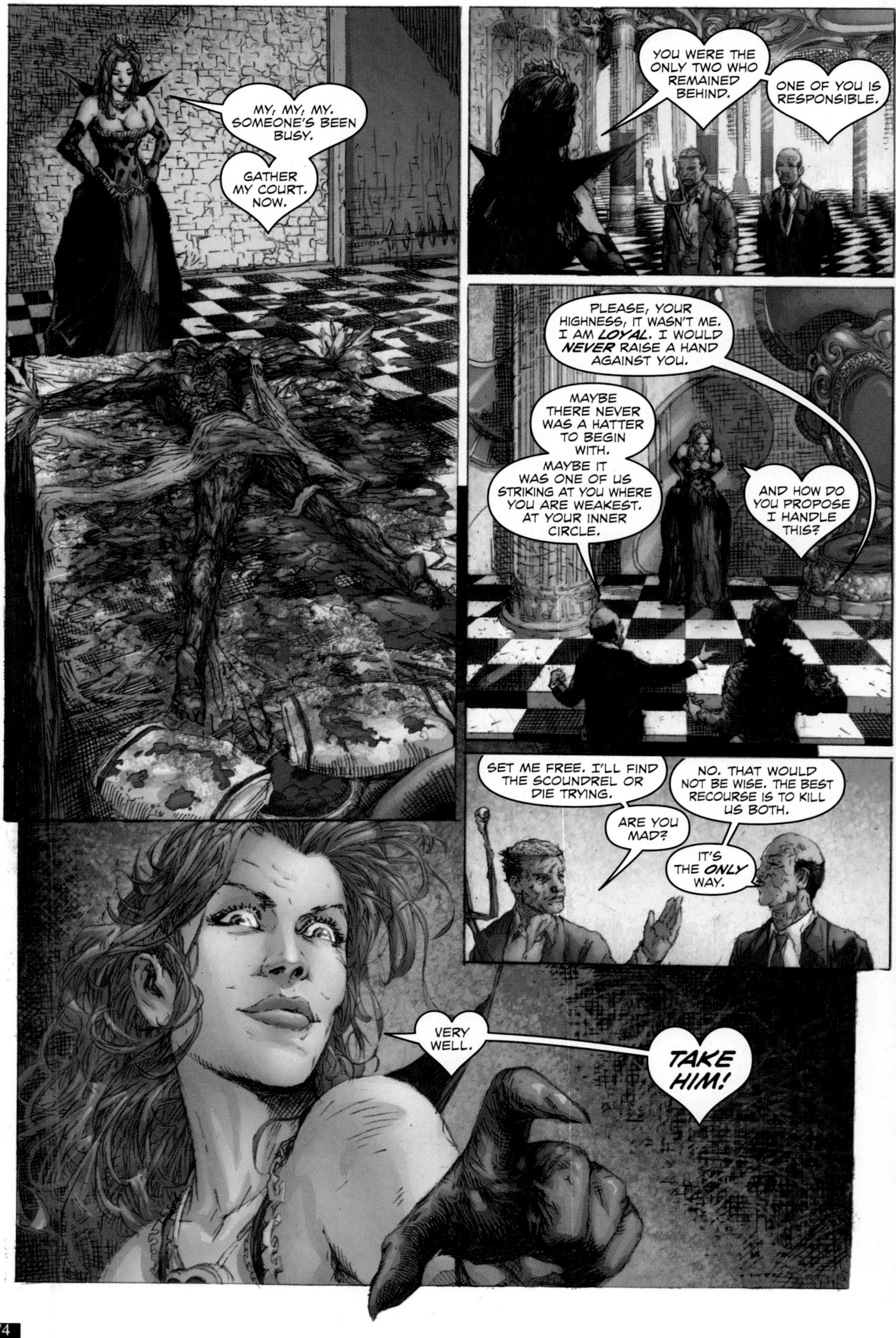

MY, MY, MY. SOMEONE'S BEEN BUSY.
GATHER MY COURT. NOW.
YOU WERE THE ONLY TWO WHO REMAINED BEHIND.
ONE OF YOU IS RESPONSIBLE.
PLEASE, YOUR HIGHNESS, IT WASN'T ME. I AM LOYAL. I WOULD NEVER RAISE A HAND AGAINST YOU.
MAYBE THERE NEVER WAS A HATTER TO BEGIN WITH.
MAYBE IT WAS ONE OF US STRIKING AT YOU WHERE YOU ARE WEAKEST. AT YOUR INNER CIRCLE.
AND HOW DO YOU PROPOSE I HANDLE THIS?
SET ME FREE. I'LL FIND THE SCOUNDREL OR DIE TRYING.
NO. THAT WOULD NOT BE WISE. THE BEST RECOURSE IS TO KILL US BOTH.
ARE YOU MAD?
IT'S THE ONLY WAY.
VERY WELL.
TAKE HIM!

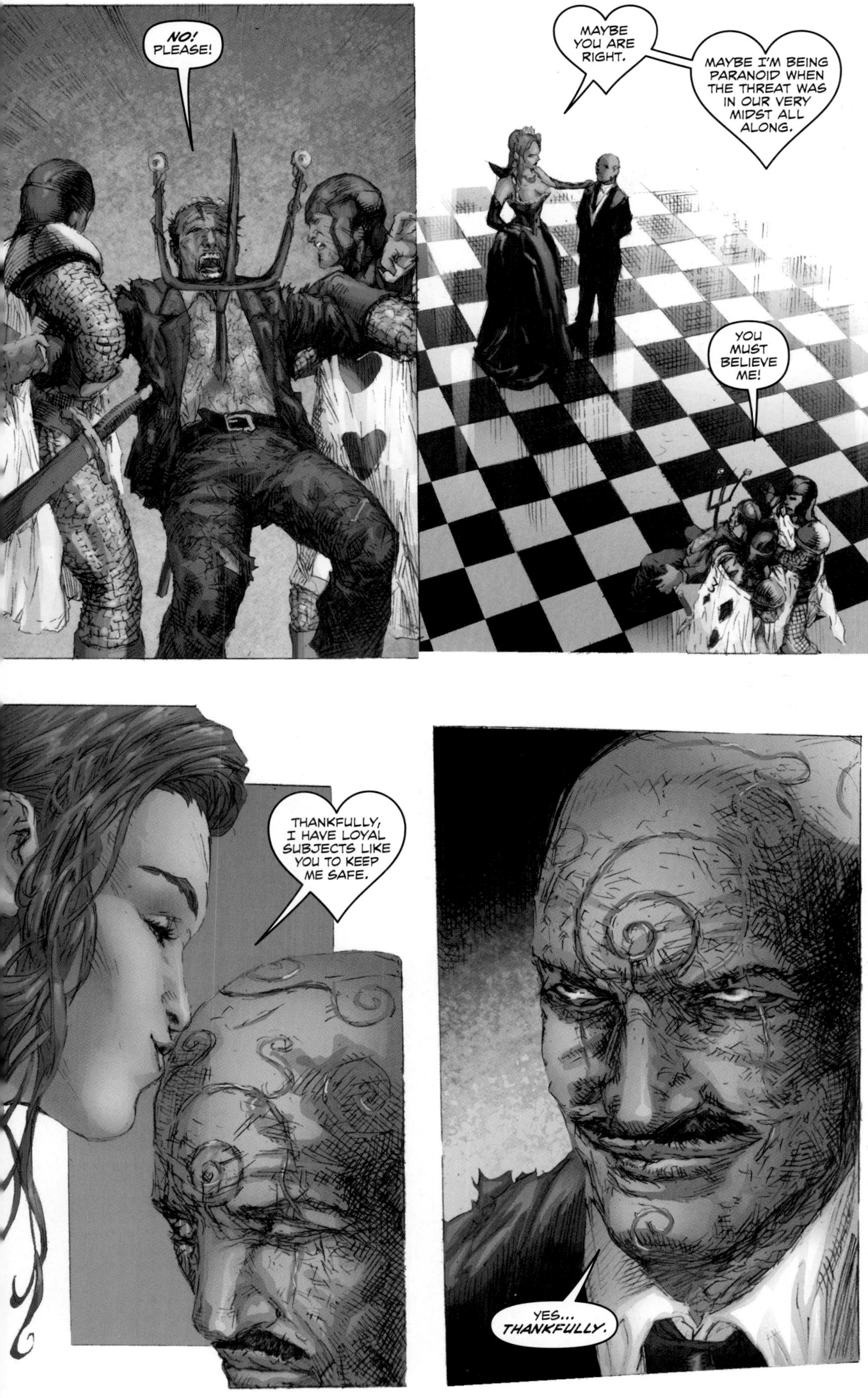
NO! PLEASE!
MAYBE YOU ARE RIGHT.
MAYBE I'M BEING PARANOID WHEN THE THREAT WAS IN OUR VERY MIDST ALL ALONG.
YOU MUST BELIEVE ME!
THANKFULLY, I HAVE LOYAL SUBJECTS LIKE YOU TO KEEP ME SAFE.
YES... THANKFULLY.

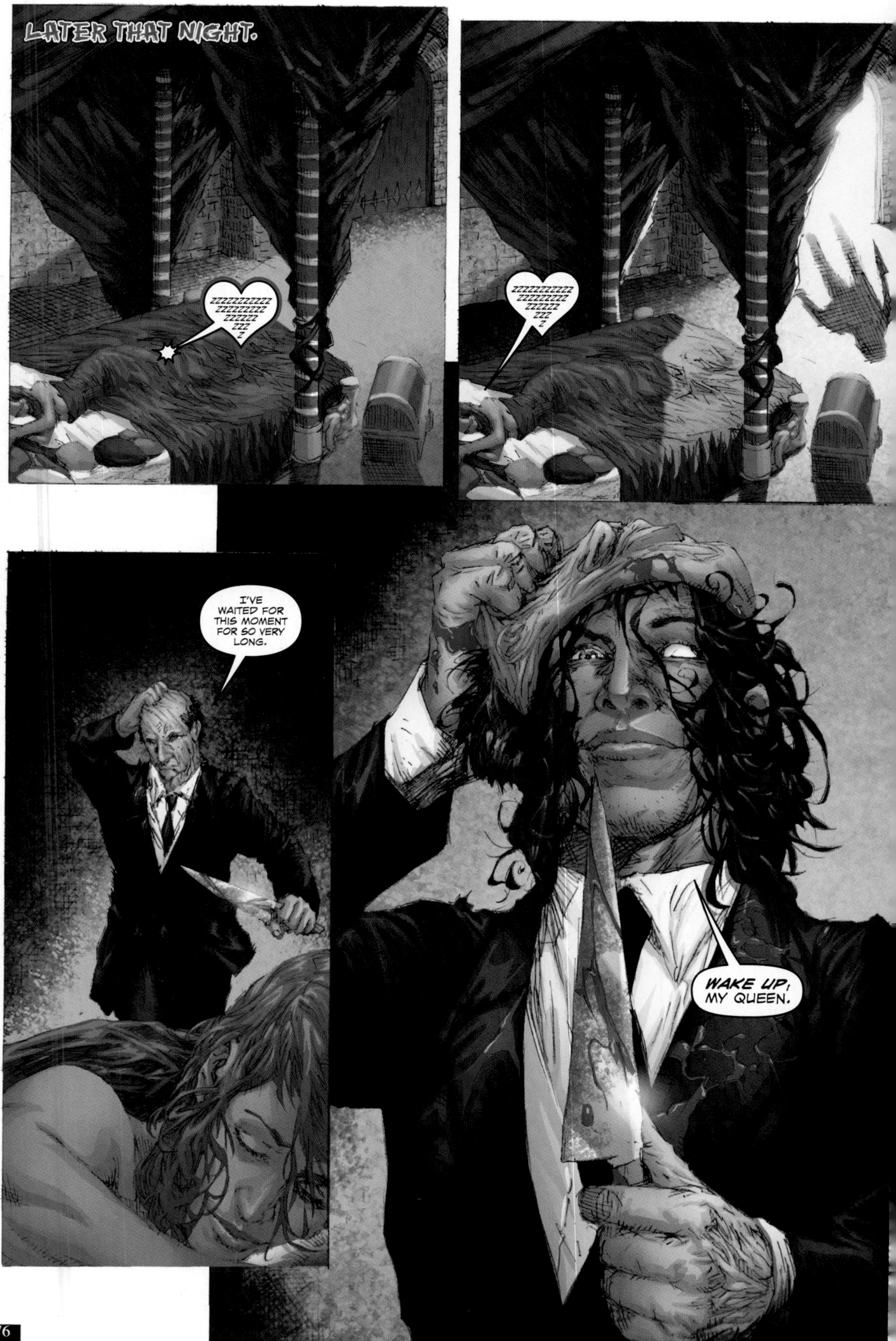
LATER THAT NIGHT.
ZZZZZZZZZZZ ZZZZZZZZZ ZZZZZZ ZZZ Z
ZZZZZZZZZZZ ZZZZZZZZZ ZZZZZZ ZZZ Z
I'VE WAITED FOR THIS MOMENT FOR SO VERY LONG.
WAKE UP, MY QUEEN.

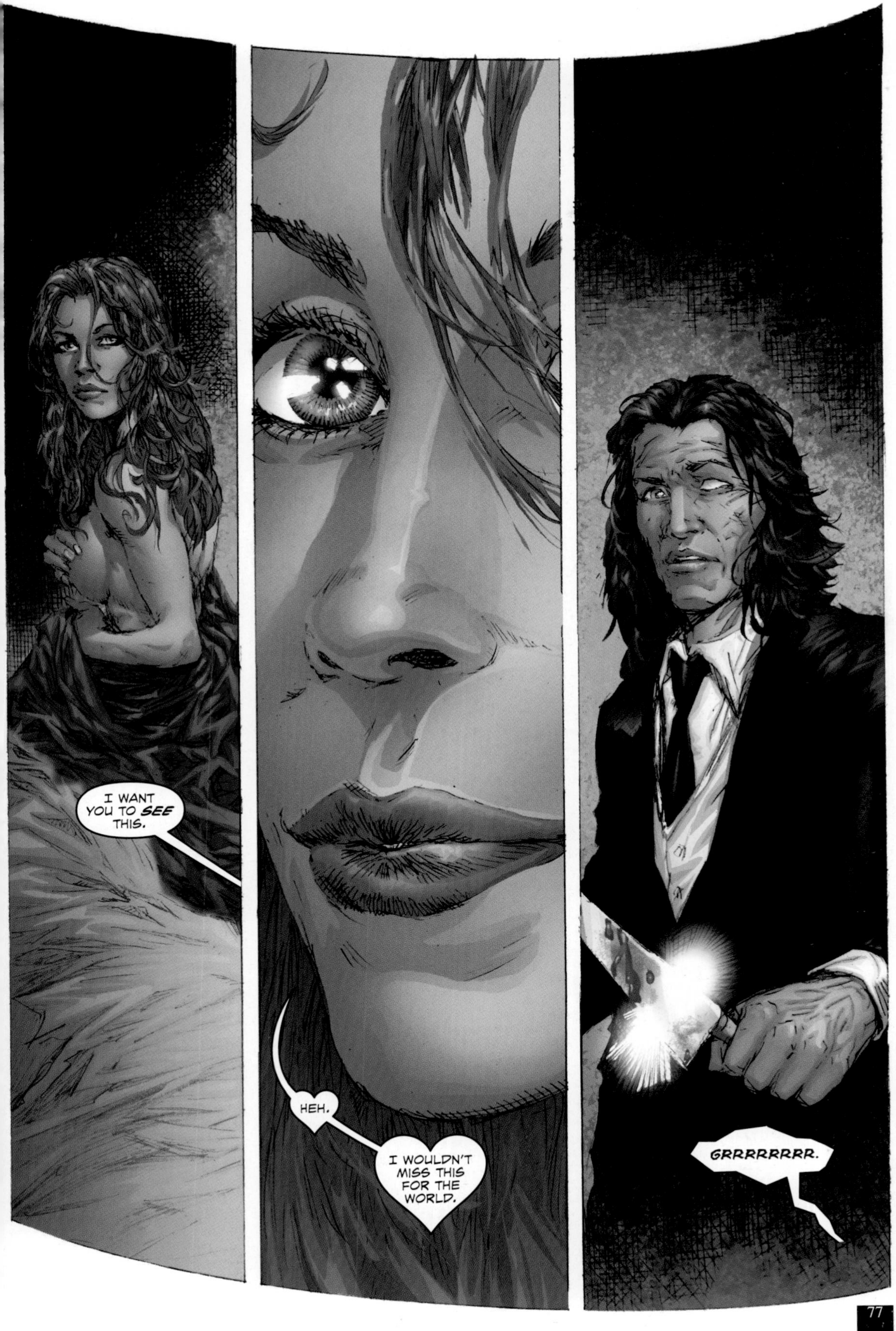

I WANT YOU TO SEE THIS.
HEH.
I WOULDN'T MISS THIS FOR THE WORLD.
GRRRRRRRR.

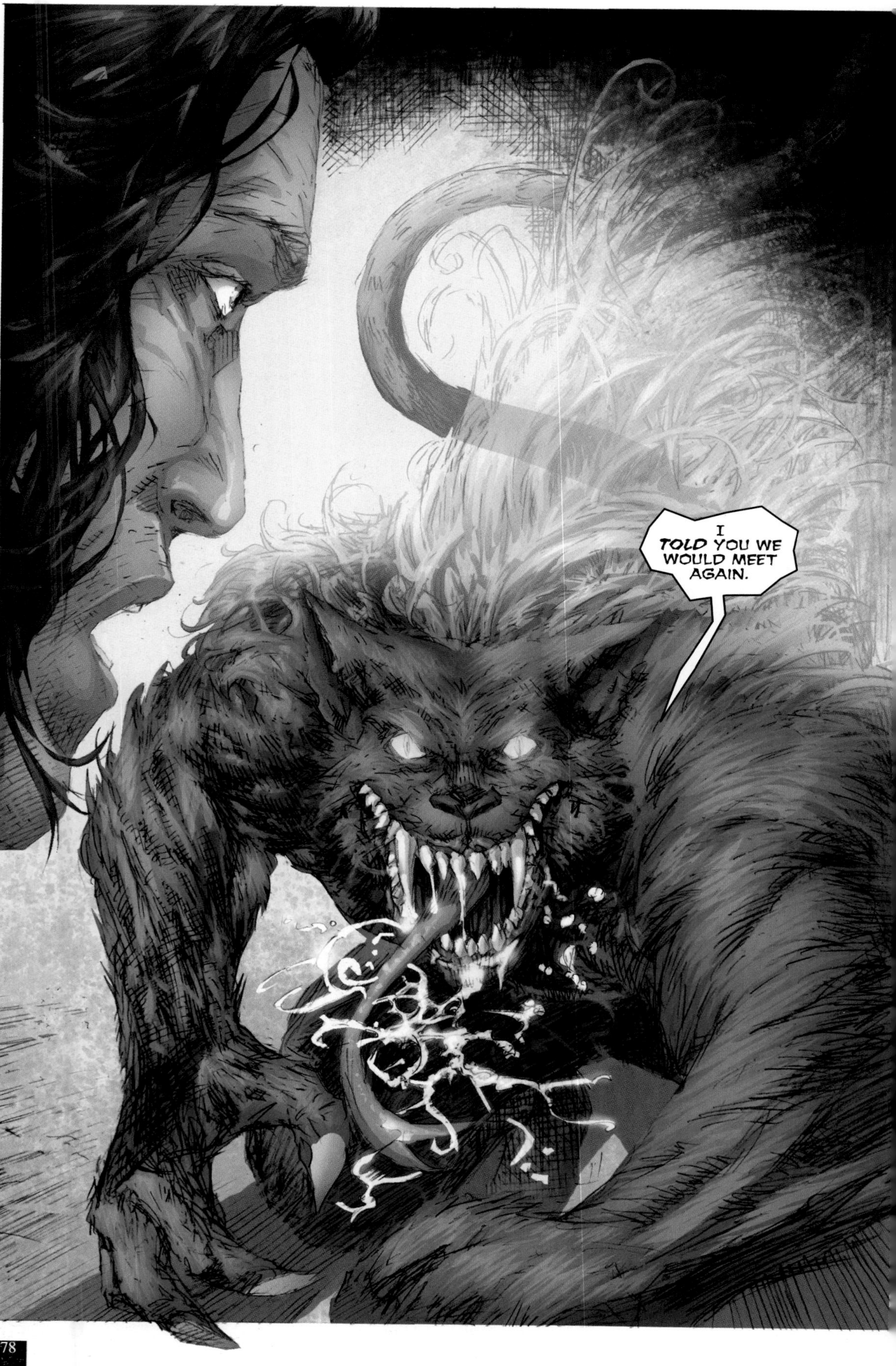
I TOLD YOU WE WOULD MEET AGAIN.

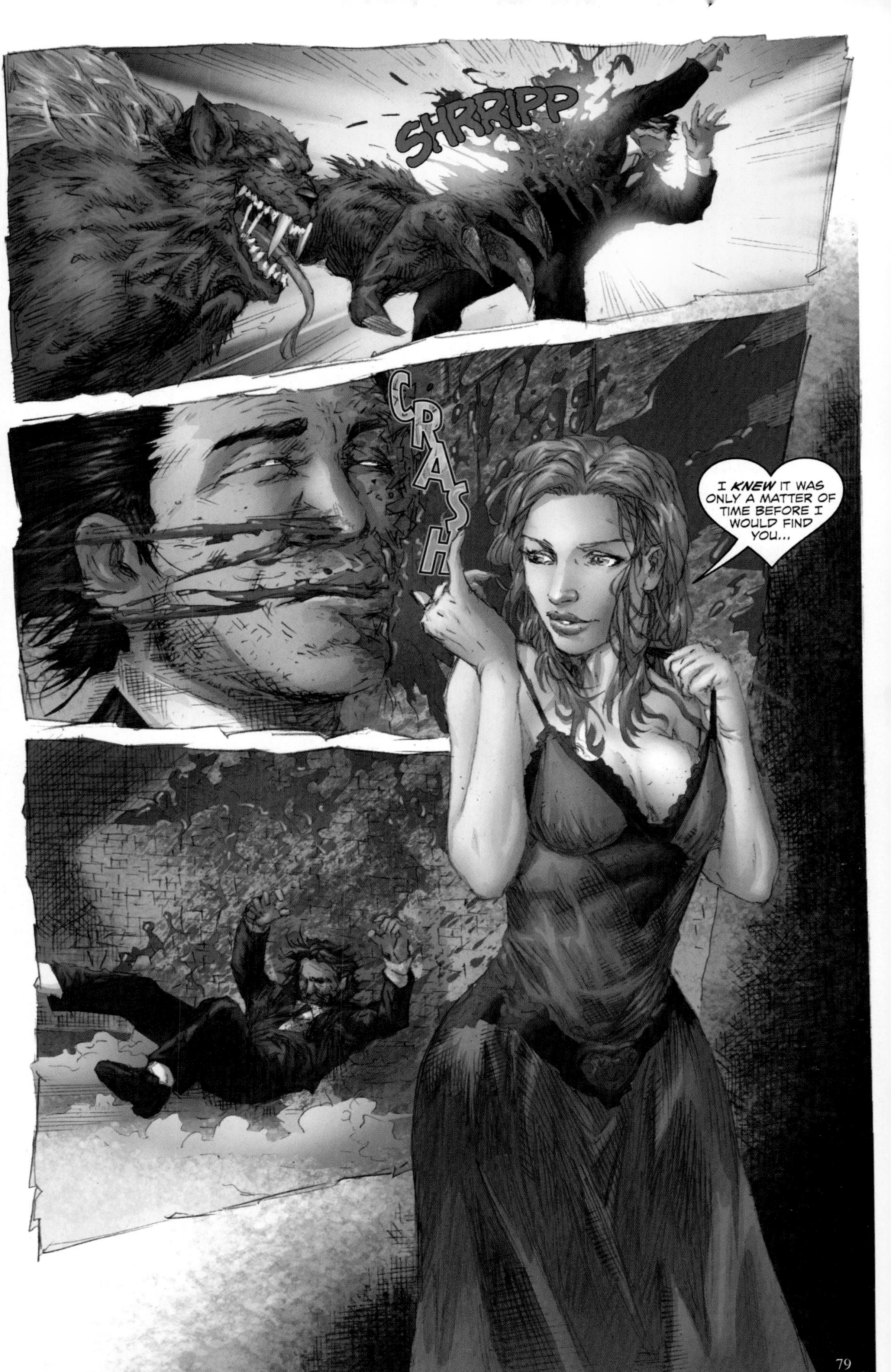
SHRRIPP
CRASH
I KNEW IT WAS ONLY A MATTER OF TIME BEFORE I WOULD FIND YOU...

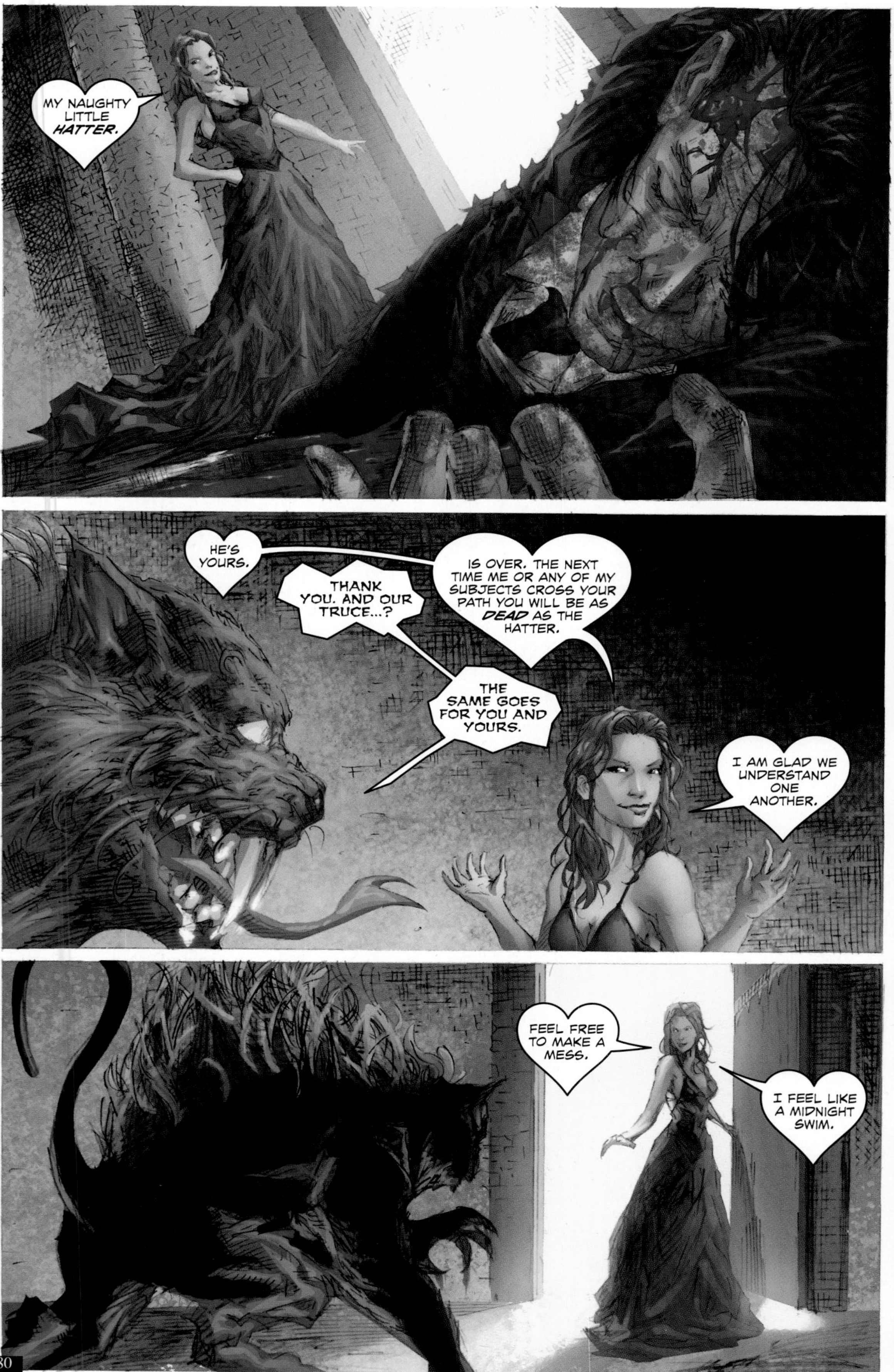
MY NAUGHTY LITTLE *HATTER.*
HE'S YOURS.
THANK YOU. AND OUR TRUCE...?
IS OVER. THE NEXT TIME ME OR ANY OF MY SUBJECTS CROSS YOUR PATH YOU WILL BE AS *DEAD* AS THE HATTER.
THE SAME GOES FOR YOU AND YOURS.
I AM GLAD WE UNDERSTAND ONE ANOTHER.
FEEL FREE TO MAKE A MESS.
I FEEL LIKE A MIDNIGHT SWIM.

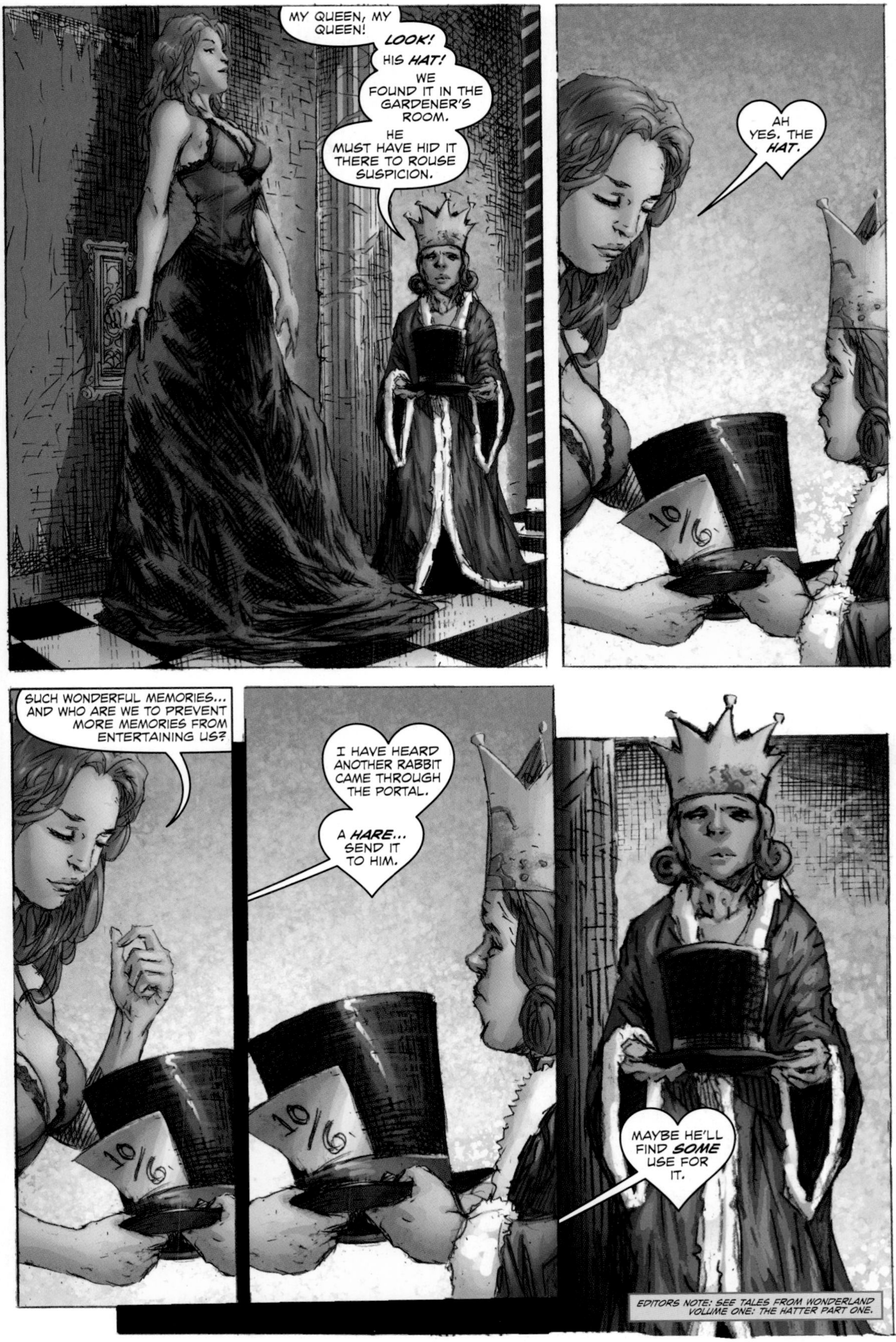
MY QUEEN, MY QUEEN!
LOOK!
HIS HAT!
WE FOUND IT IN THE GARDENER'S ROOM.
HE MUST HAVE HID IT THERE TO ROUSE SUSPICION.
AH YES. THE HAT.
SUCH WONDERFUL MEMORIES... AND WHO ARE WE TO PREVENT MORE MEMORIES FROM ENTERTAINING US?
I HAVE HEARD ANOTHER RABBIT CAME THROUGH THE PORTAL.
A HARE... SEND IT TO HIM.
MAYBE HE'LL FIND SOME USE FOR IT.
EDITORS NOTE: SEE TALES FROM WONDERLAND VOLUME ONE: THE HATTER PART ONE.

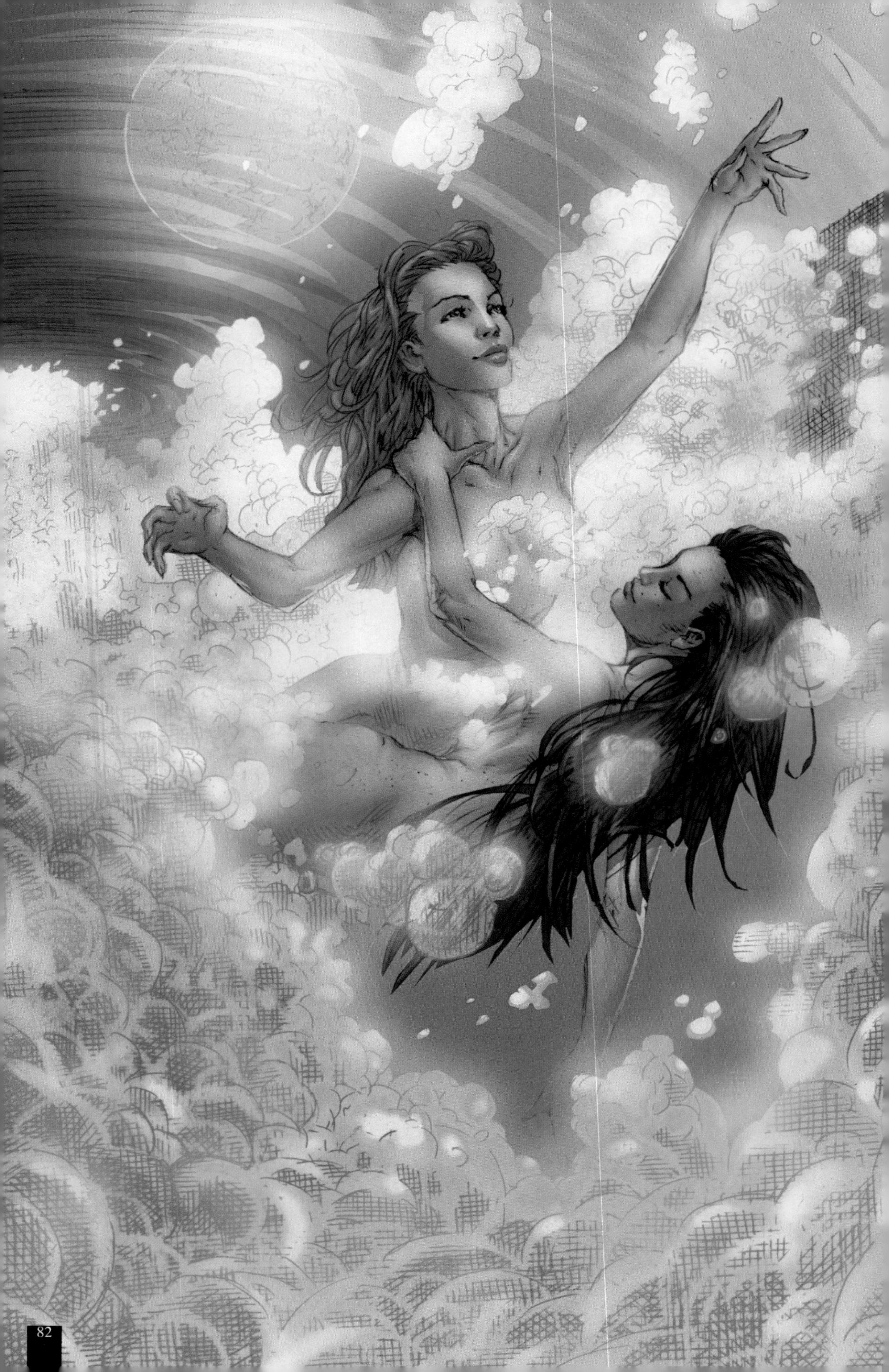

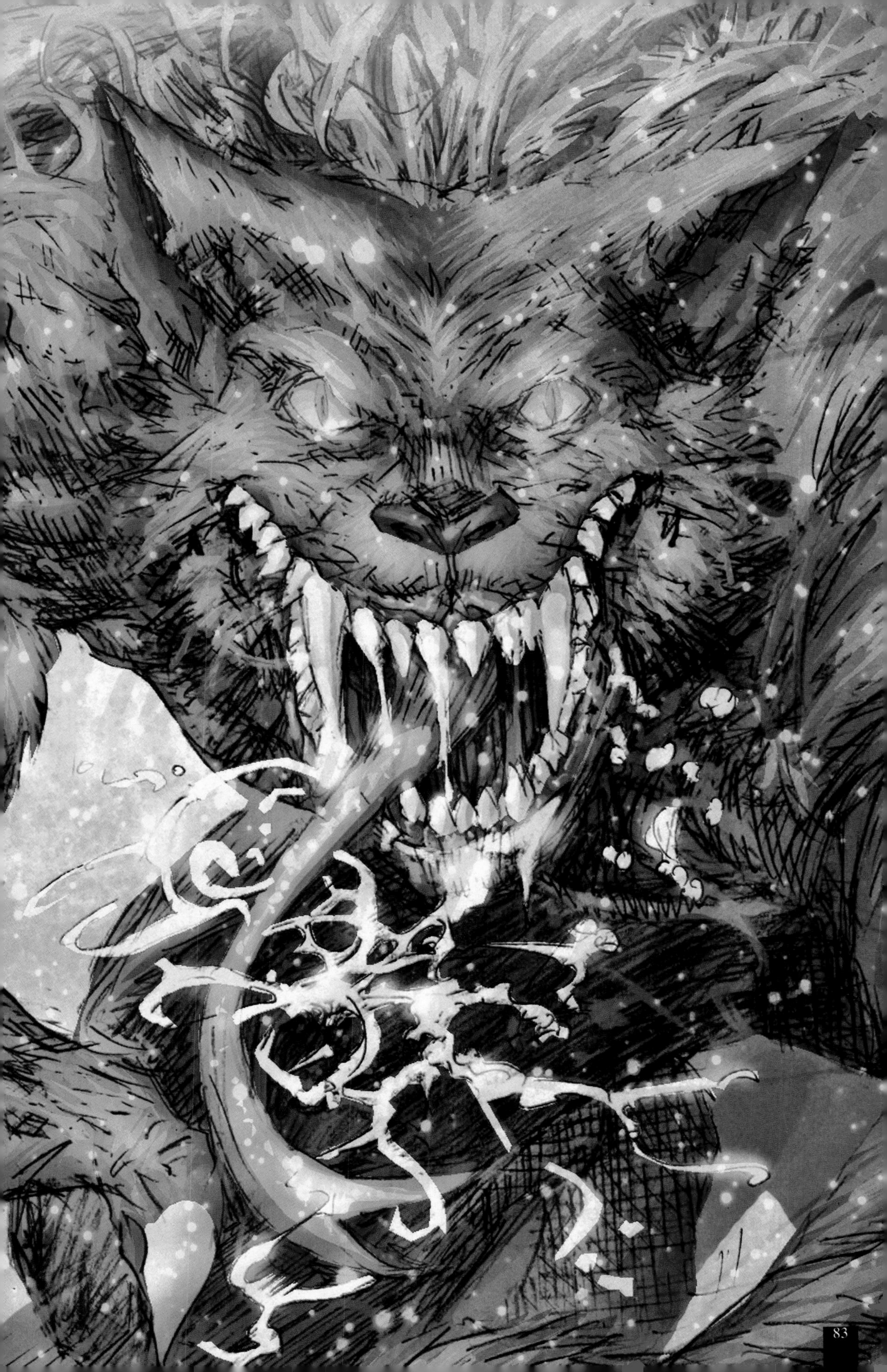

The Redemption

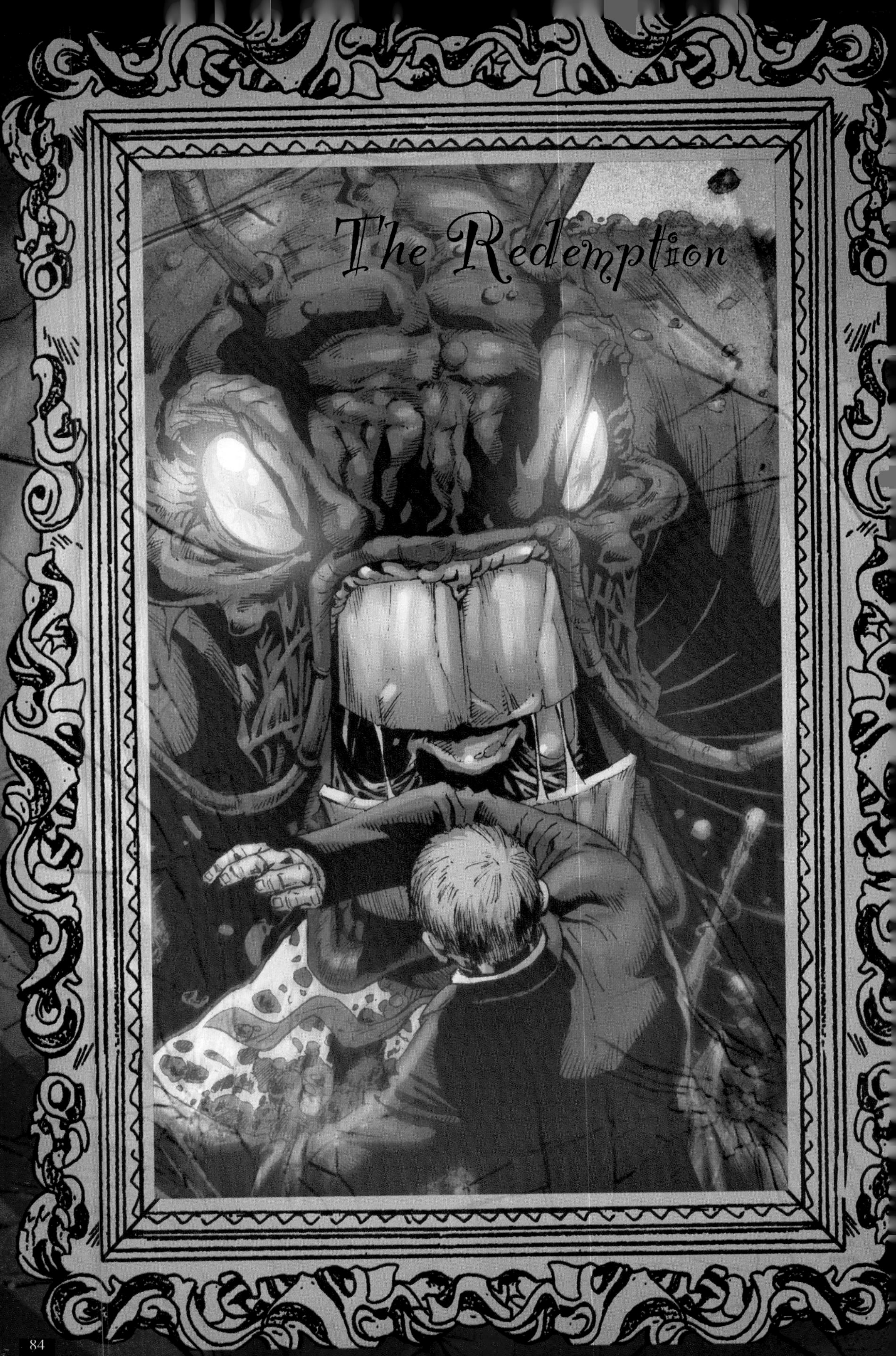

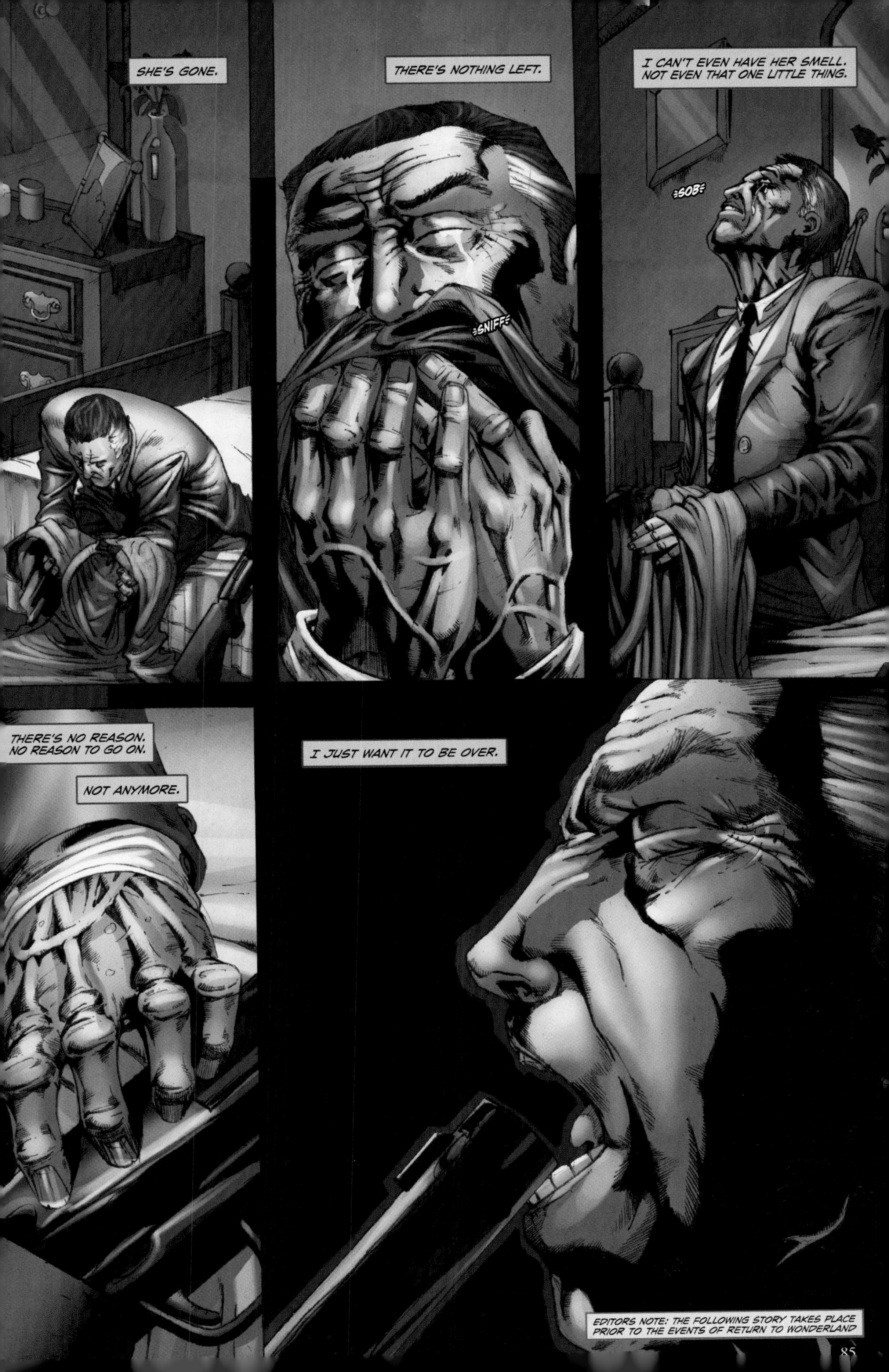
SHE'S GONE.
THERE'S NOTHING LEFT.
SNIFF
I CAN'T EVEN HAVE HER SMELL. NOT EVEN THAT ONE LITTLE THING.
SOB
THERE'S NO REASON. NO REASON TO GO ON.
NOT ANYMORE.
I JUST WANT IT TO BE OVER.
EDITORS NOTE: THE FOLLOWING STORY TAKES PLACE PRIOR TO THE EVENTS OF RETURN TO WONDERLAND

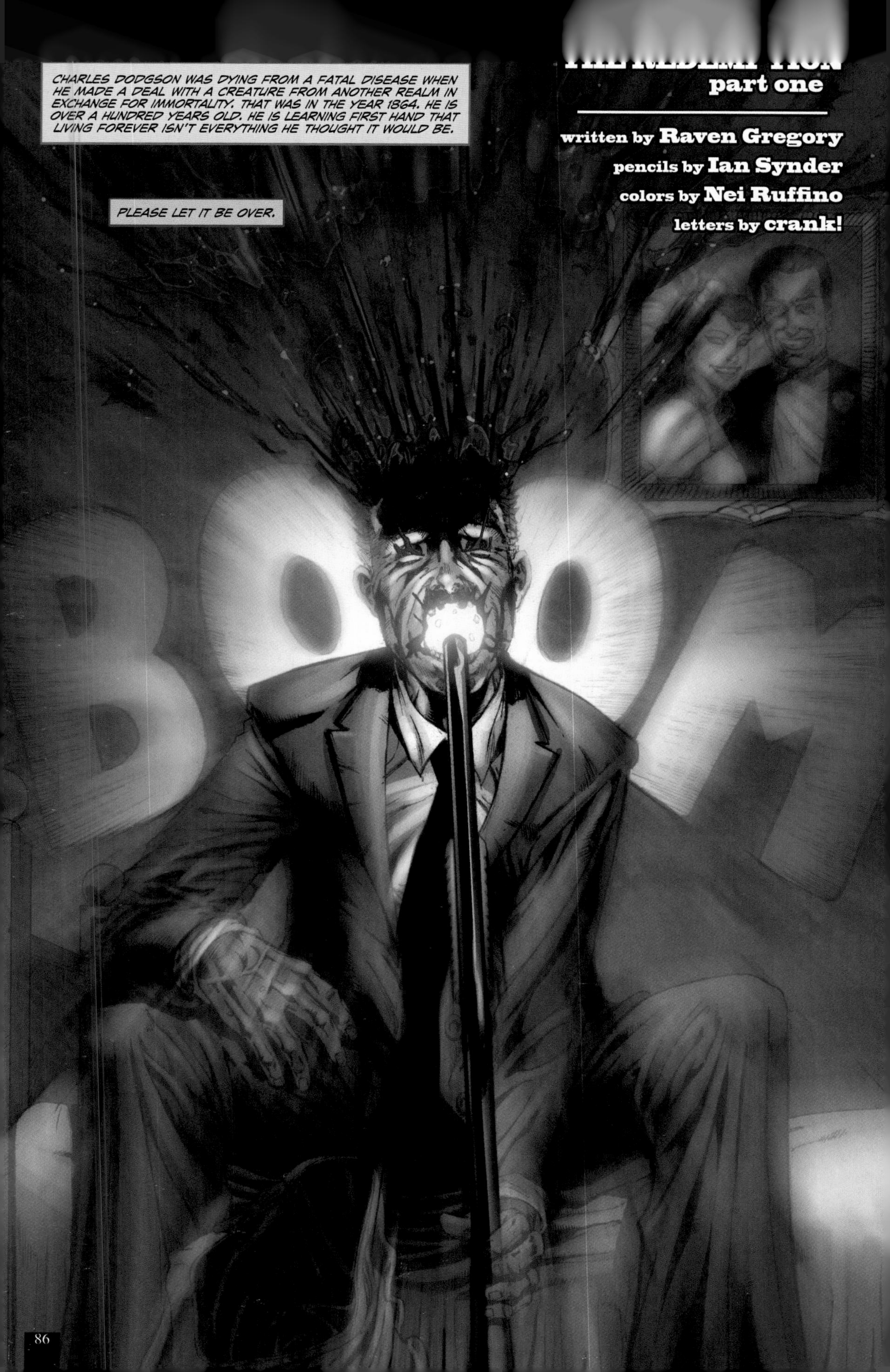

CHARLES DODGSON WAS DYING FROM A FATAL DISEASE WHEN HE MADE A DEAL WITH A CREATURE FROM ANOTHER REALM IN EXCHANGE FOR IMMORTALITY. THAT WAS IN THE YEAR 1864. HE IS OVER A HUNDRED YEARS OLD. HE IS LEARNING FIRST HAND THAT LIVING FOREVER ISN'T EVERYTHING HE THOUGHT IT WOULD BE.
part one
written by Raven Gregory
pencils by Ian Synder
colors by Nei Ruffino
letters by crank!
PLEASE LET IT BE OVER.
BOOM

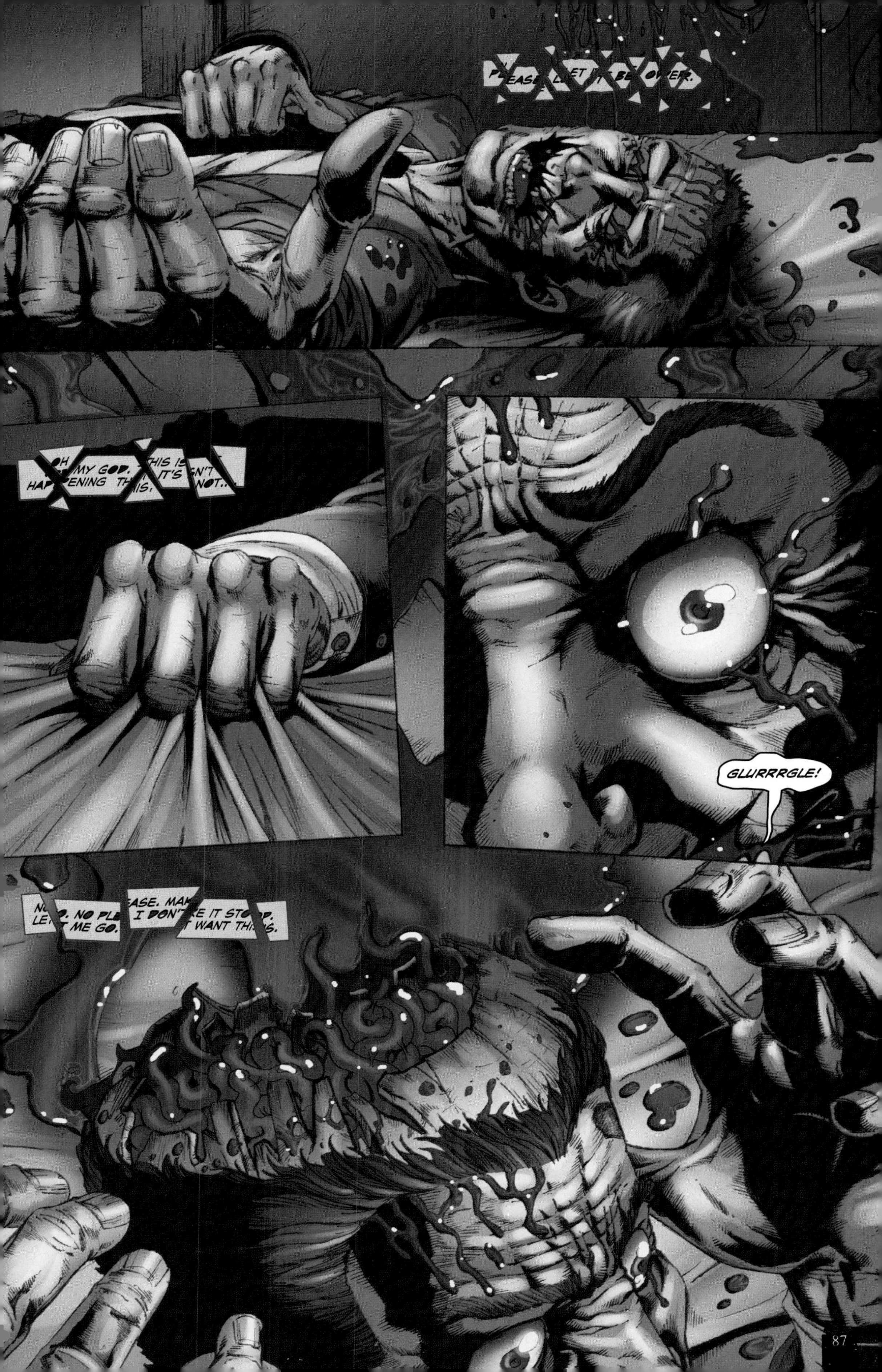
PLEASE LET BE OVER.
OH MY GOD. THIS IS IT'S SN'T HAPPENING TH IS. NOT...
GLURRRGLE!
NO. NO PLE ASE. MAK I DON' E IT STO P. LE ME GO. T WANT THI S.

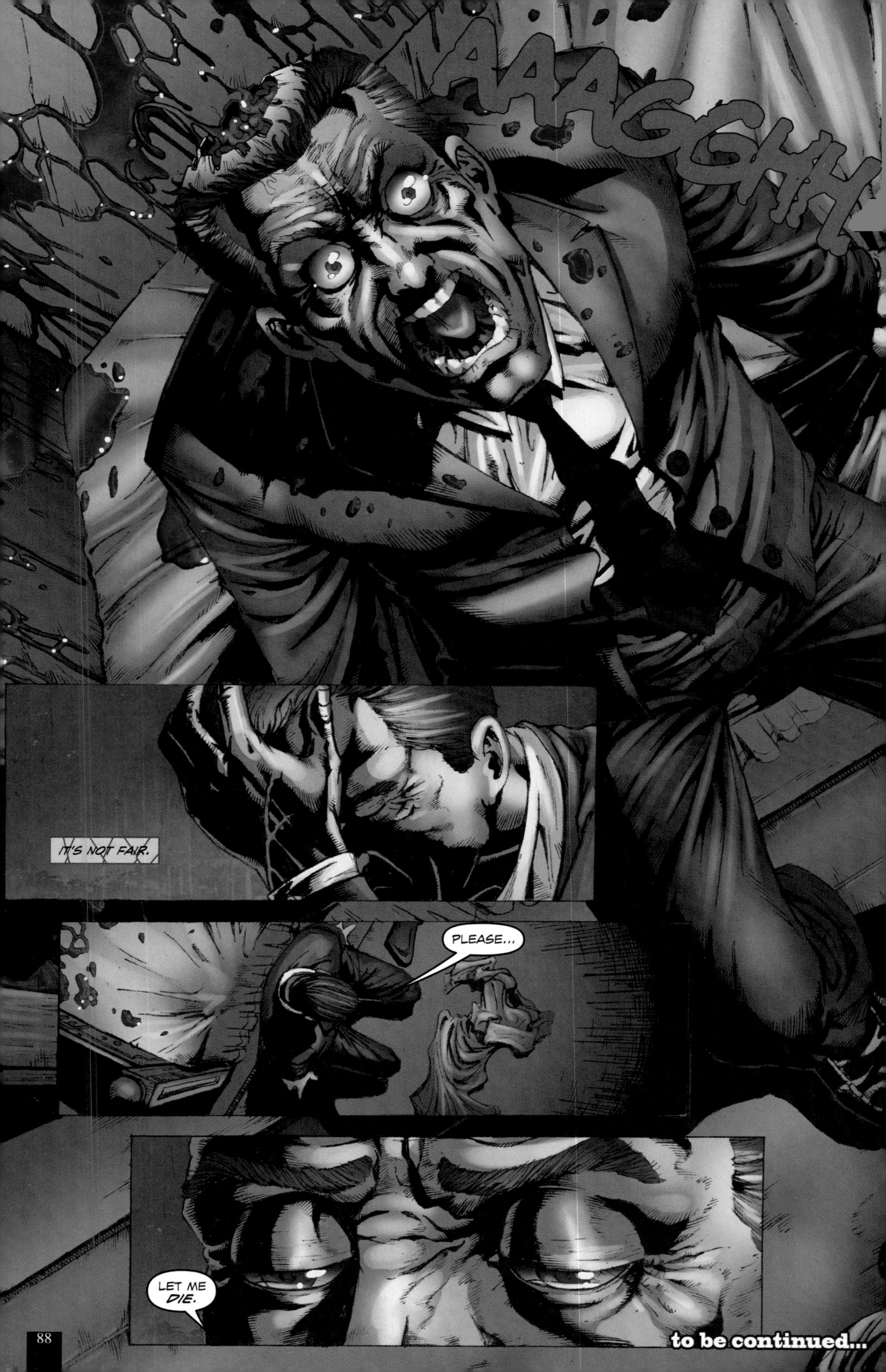
AAAGGHH!
IT'S NOT FAIR.
PLEASE...
LET ME DIE.
to be continued...

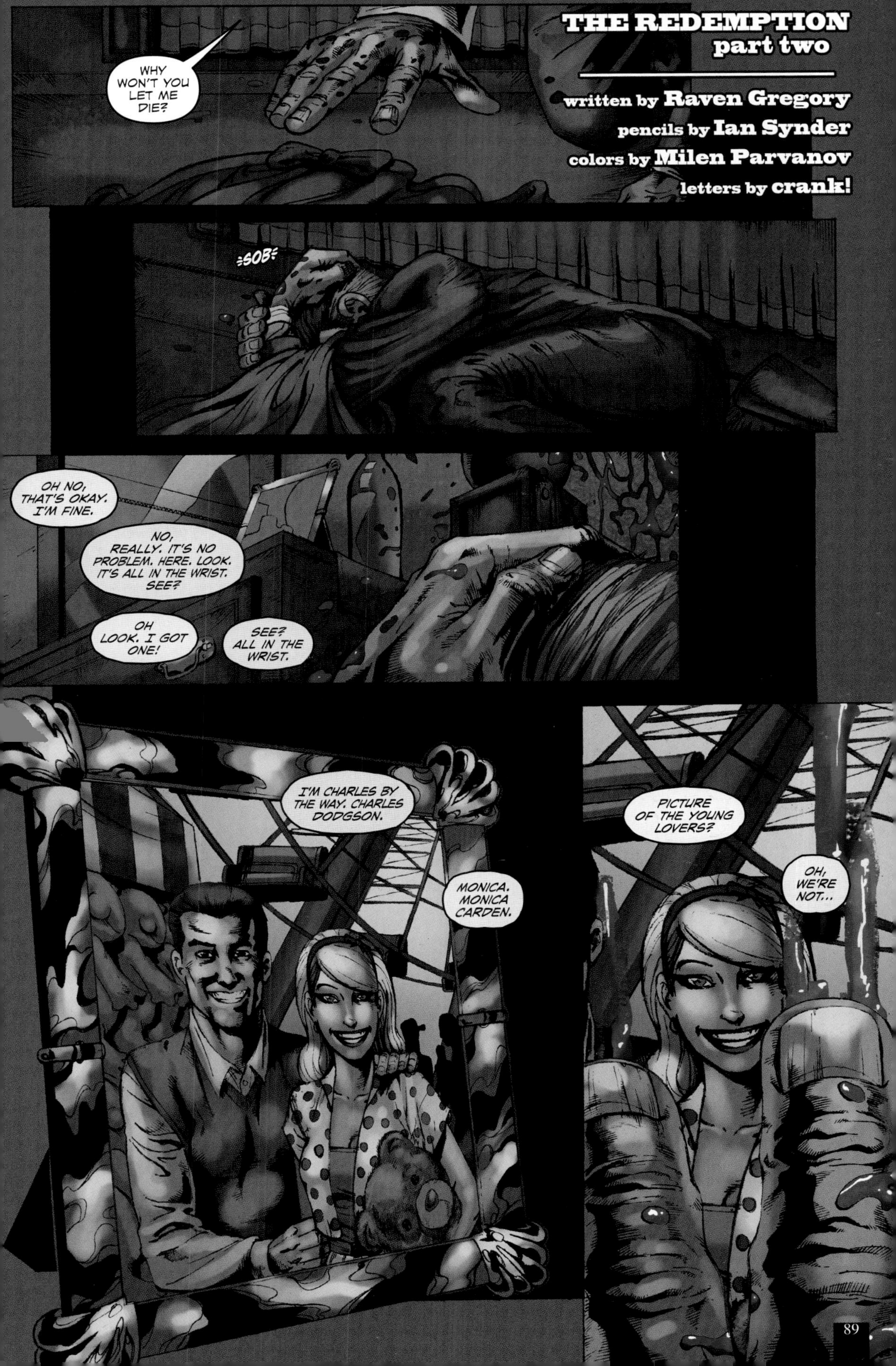
THE REDEMPTION
part two
written by Raven Gregory
pencils by Ian Synder
colors by Milen Parvanov
letters by crank!
WHY WON'T YOU LET ME DIE?
SOB
OH NO, THAT'S OKAY. I'M FINE.
NO, REALLY. IT'S NO PROBLEM. HERE. LOOK. IT'S ALL IN THE WRIST. SEE?
OH LOOK. I GOT ONE!
SEE? ALL IN THE WRIST.
I'M CHARLES BY THE WAY. CHARLES DODGSON.
MONICA. MONICA CARDEN.
PICTURE OF THE YOUNG LOVERS?
OH, WE'RE NOT...

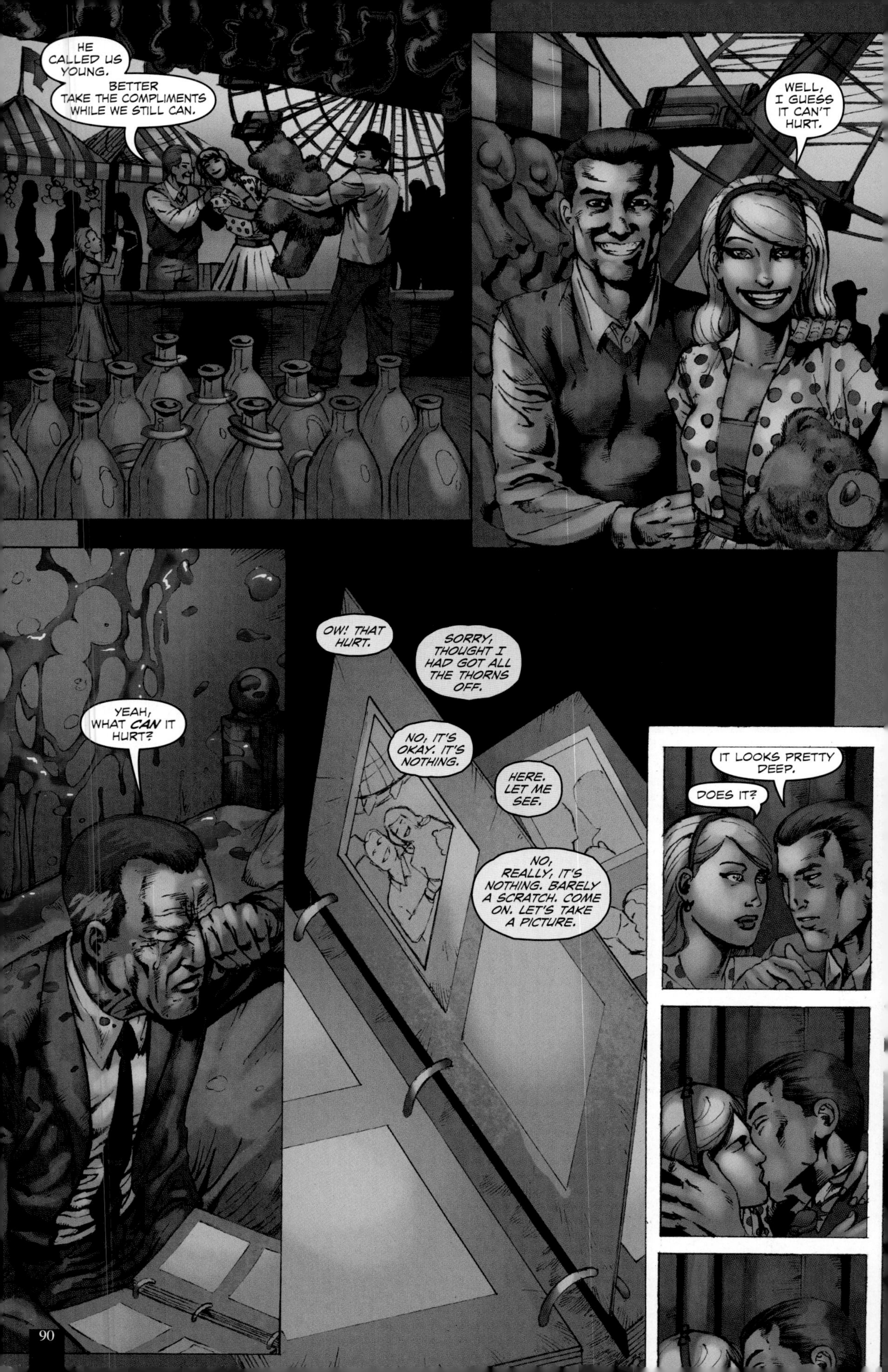
HE CALLED US YOUNG.
BETTER TAKE THE COMPLIMENTS WHILE WE STILL CAN.
WELL, I GUESS IT CAN'T HURT.
YEAH, WHAT CAN IT HURT?
OW! THAT HURT.
SORRY, THOUGHT I HAD GOT ALL THE THORNS OFF.
NO, IT'S OKAY. IT'S NOTHING.
HERE. LET ME SEE.
NO, REALLY, IT'S NOTHING. BARELY A SCRATCH. COME ON. LET'S TAKE A PICTURE.
IT LOOKS PRETTY DEEP.
DOES IT?

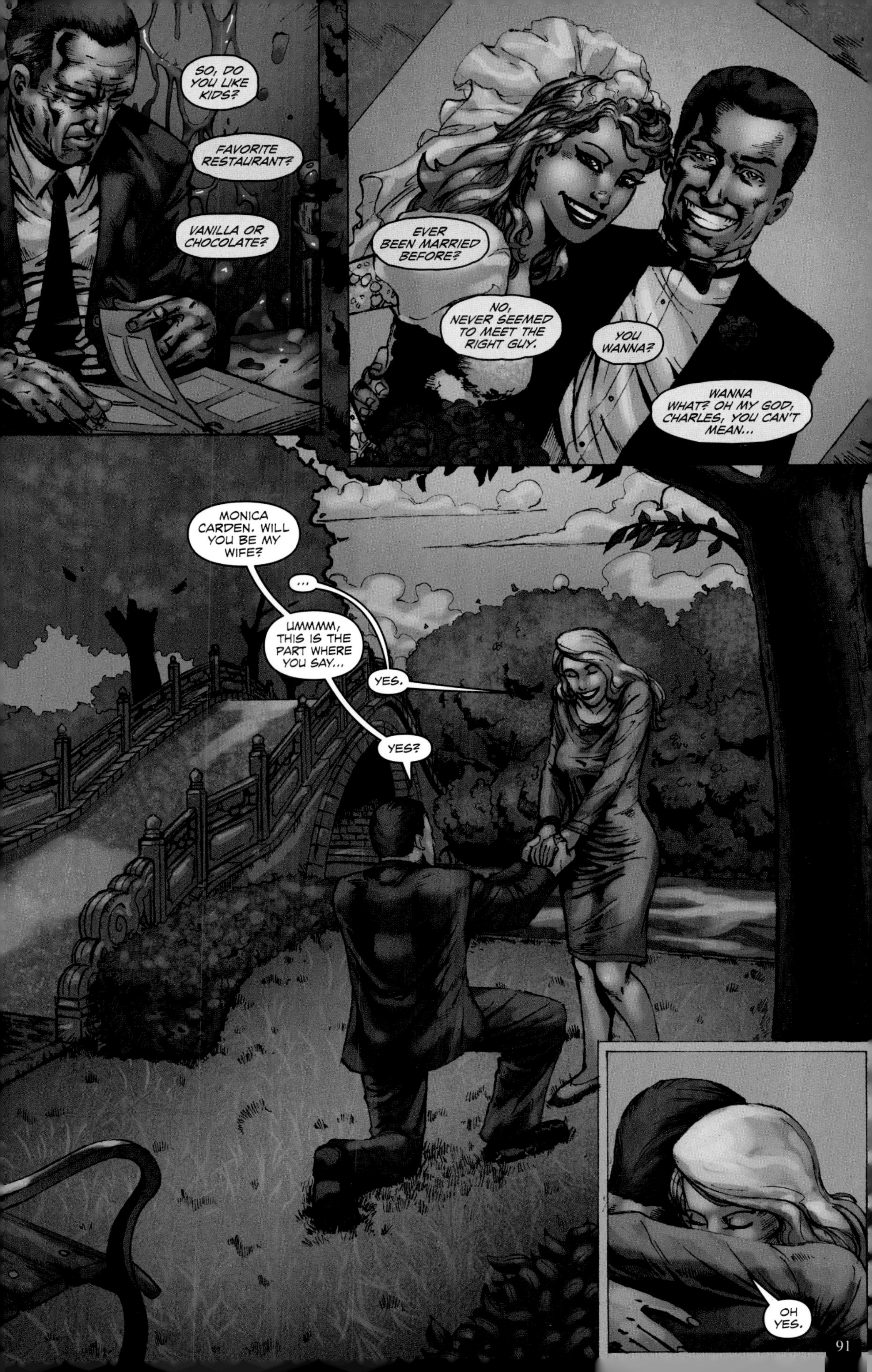
SO, DO YOU LIKE KIDS?
FAVORITE RESTAURANT?
VANILLA OR CHOCOLATE?
EVER BEEN MARRIED BEFORE?
NO, NEVER SEEMED TO MEET THE RIGHT GUY.
YOU WANNA?
WANNA WHAT? OH MY GOD, CHARLES, YOU CAN'T MEAN...
MONICA CARDEN. WILL YOU BE MY WIFE?
...
UMMMM, THIS IS THE PART WHERE YOU SAY...
YES.
YES?
OH YES.

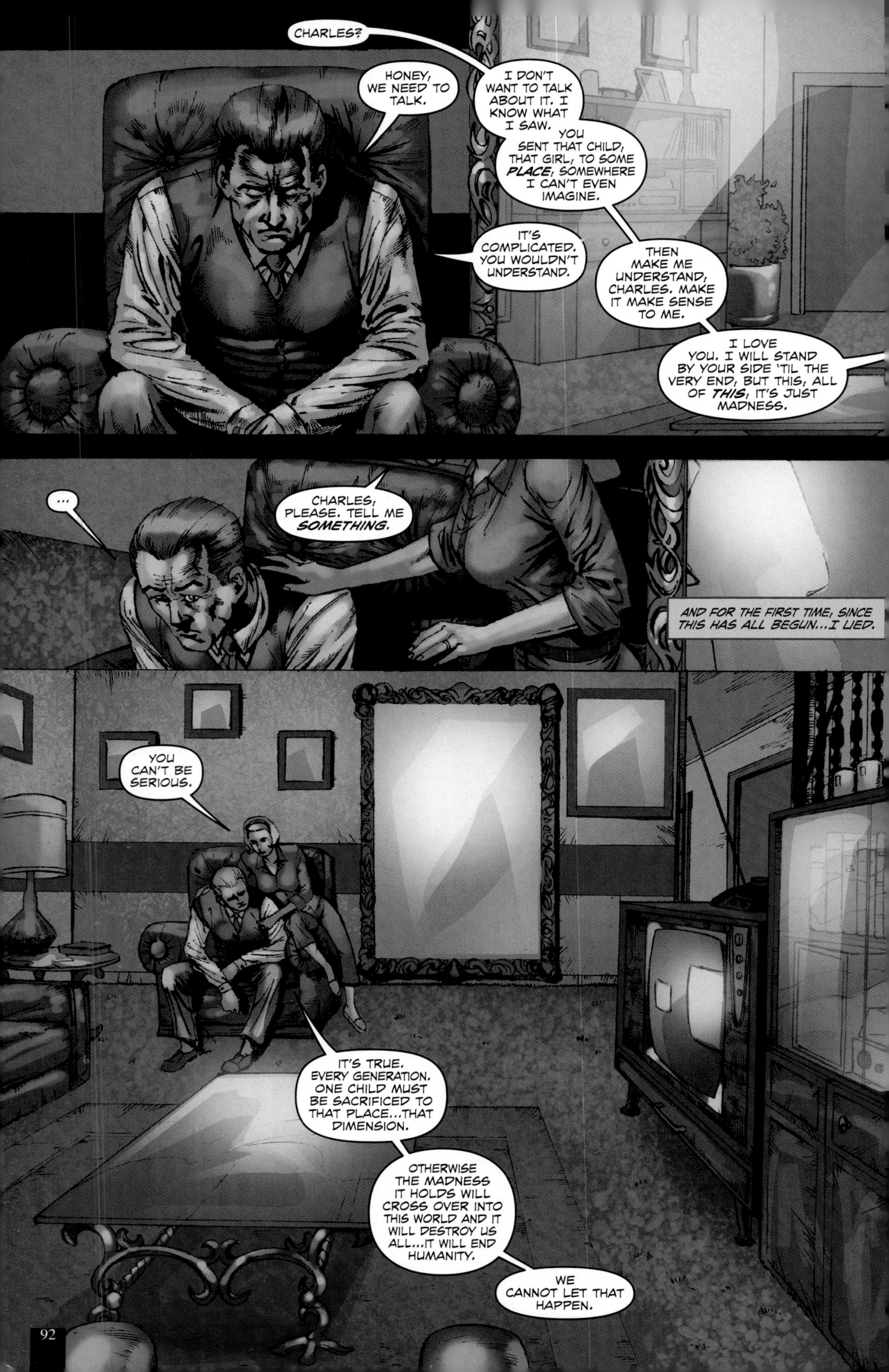
CHARLES?
HONEY, WE NEED TO TALK.
I DON'T WANT TO TALK ABOUT IT. I KNOW WHAT I SAW.
YOU SENT THAT CHILD, THAT GIRL, TO SOME PLACE, SOMEWHERE I CAN'T EVEN IMAGINE.
IT'S COMPLICATED. YOU WOULDN'T UNDERSTAND.
THEN MAKE ME UNDERSTAND, CHARLES. MAKE IT MAKE SENSE TO ME.
I LOVE YOU. I WILL STAND BY YOUR SIDE 'TIL THE VERY END, BUT THIS, ALL OF THIS, IT'S JUST MADNESS.
...
CHARLES, PLEASE. TELL ME SOMETHING.
AND FOR THE FIRST TIME, SINCE THIS HAS ALL BEGUN...I LIED.
YOU CAN'T BE SERIOUS.
IT'S TRUE. EVERY GENERATION. ONE CHILD MUST BE SACRIFICED TO THAT PLACE...THAT DIMENSION.
OTHERWISE THE MADNESS IT HOLDS WILL CROSS OVER INTO THIS WORLD AND IT WILL DESTROY US ALL...IT WILL END HUMANITY.
WE CANNOT LET THAT HAPPEN.

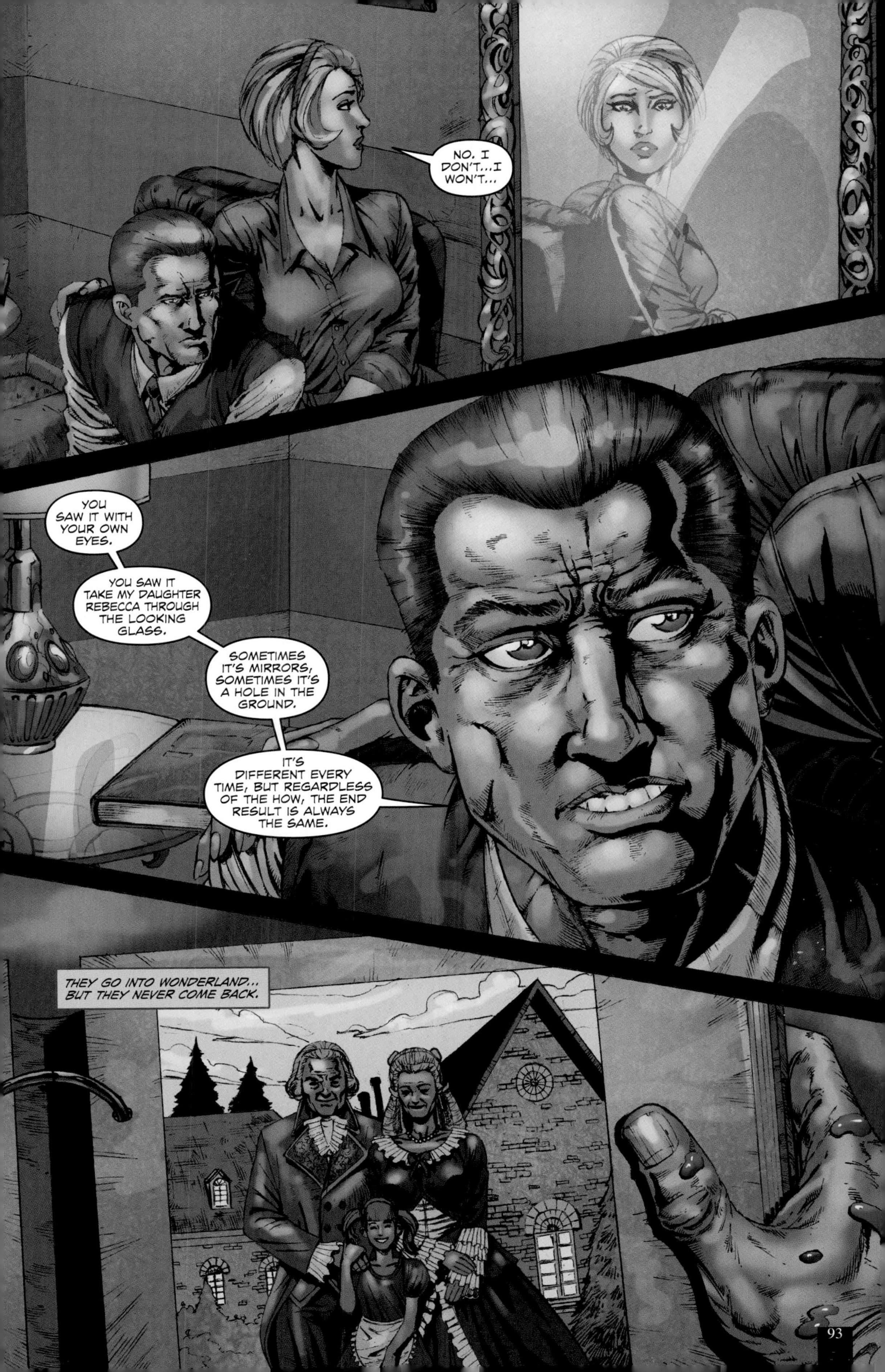
NO. I DON'T...I WON'T...
YOU SAW IT WITH YOUR OWN EYES.
YOU SAW IT TAKE MY DAUGHTER REBECCA THROUGH THE LOOKING GLASS.
SOMETIMES IT'S MIRRORS, SOMETIMES IT'S A HOLE IN THE GROUND.
IT'S DIFFERENT EVERY TIME, BUT REGARDLESS OF THE HOW, THE END RESULT IS ALWAYS THE SAME.
THEY GO INTO WONDERLAND... BUT THEY NEVER COME BACK.

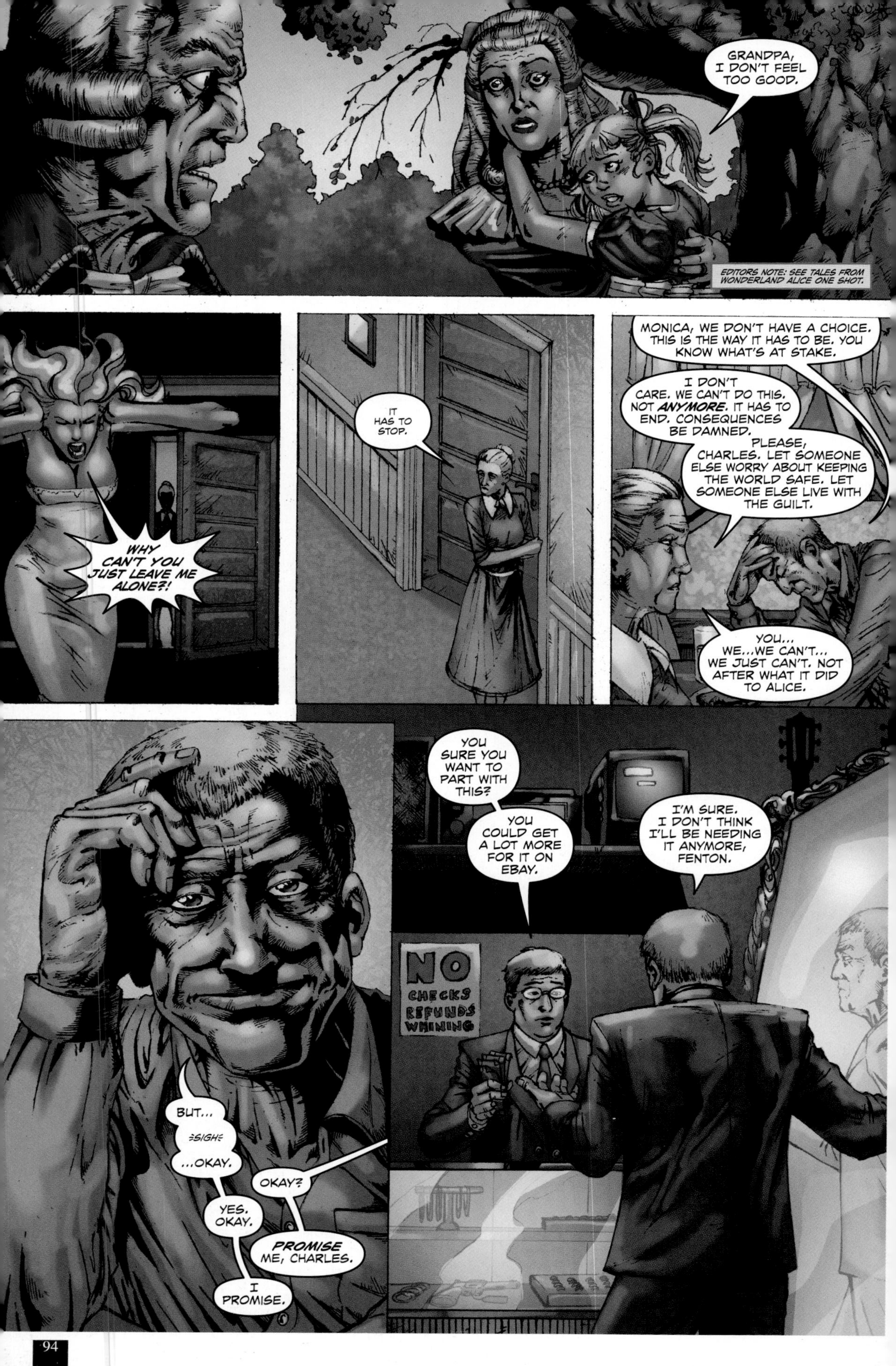
GRANDPA, I DON'T FEEL TOO GOOD.
EDITORS NOTE: SEE TALES FROM WONDERLAND ALICE ONE SHOT.
WHY CAN'T YOU JUST LEAVE ME ALONE?!
IT HAS TO STOP.
MONICA, WE DON'T HAVE A CHOICE. THIS IS THE WAY IT HAS TO BE. YOU KNOW WHAT'S AT STAKE.
I DON'T CARE. WE CAN'T DO THIS. NOT ANYMORE. IT HAS TO END. CONSEQUENCES BE DAMNED.
PLEASE, CHARLES. LET SOMEONE ELSE WORRY ABOUT KEEPING THE WORLD SAFE. LET SOMEONE ELSE LIVE WITH THE GUILT.
YOU... WE...WE CAN'T... WE JUST CAN'T. NOT AFTER WHAT IT DID TO ALICE.
BUT...
=SIGH=
...OKAY.
OKAY?
YES. OKAY.
PROMISE ME, CHARLES.
I PROMISE.
YOU SURE YOU WANT TO PART WITH THIS?
YOU COULD GET A LOT MORE FOR IT ON EBAY.
I'M SURE. I DON'T THINK I'LL BE NEEDING IT ANYMORE, FENTON.
NO
CHECKS
REFUNDS
WHINING

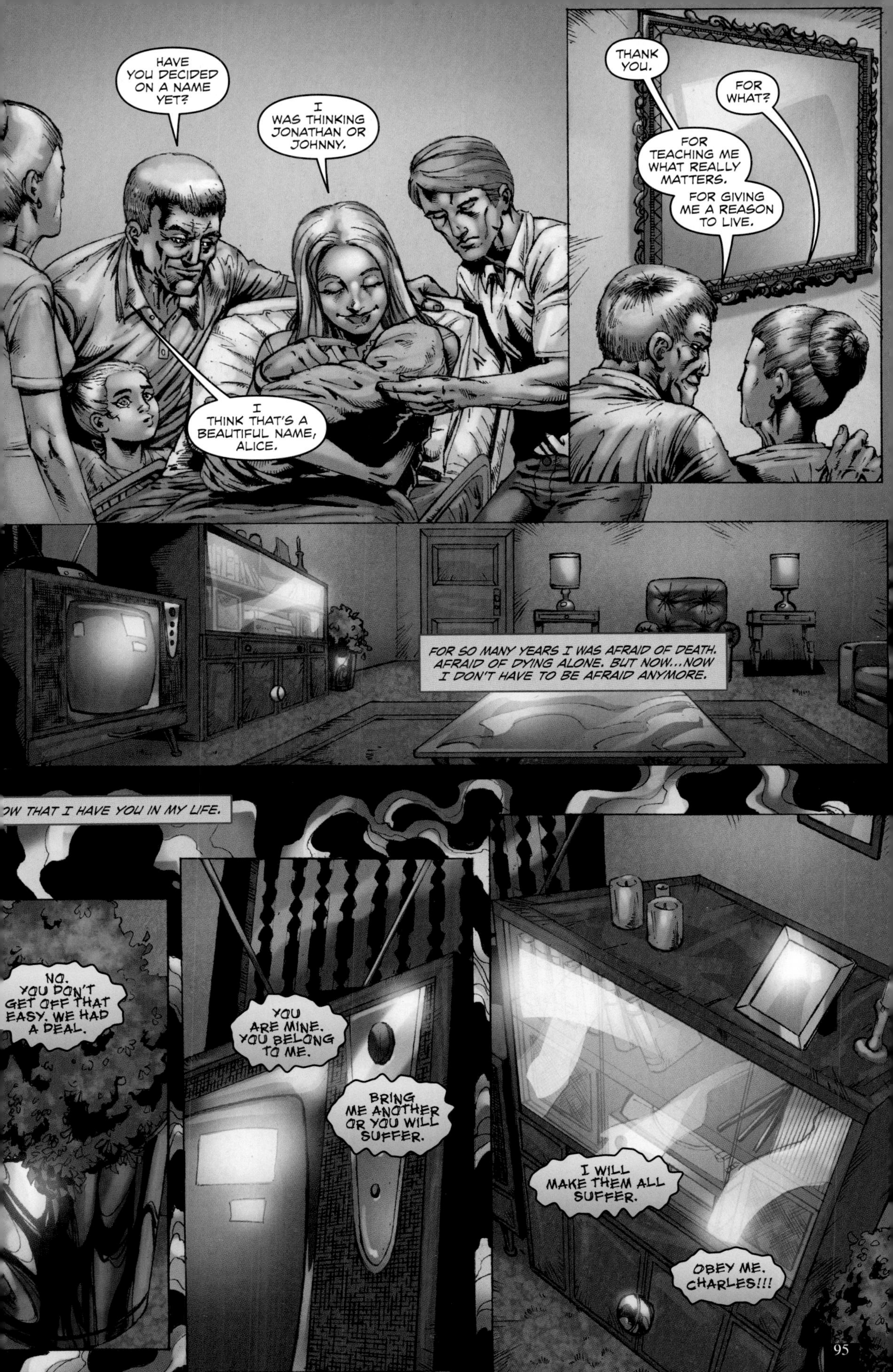

HAVE YOU DECIDED ON A NAME YET?
I WAS THINKING JONATHAN OR JOHNNY.
I THINK THAT'S A BEAUTIFUL NAME, ALICE.
THANK YOU.
FOR WHAT?
FOR TEACHING ME WHAT REALLY MATTERS.
FOR GIVING ME A REASON TO LIVE.
FOR SO MANY YEARS I WAS AFRAID OF DEATH. AFRAID OF DYING ALONE. BUT NOW...NOW I DON'T HAVE TO BE AFRAID ANYMORE.
OW THAT I HAVE YOU IN MY LIFE.
NO. YOU DON'T GET OFF THAT EASY. WE HAD A DEAL.
YOU ARE MINE. YOU BELONG TO ME.
BRING ME ANOTHER OR YOU WILL SUFFER.
I WILL MAKE THEM ALL SUFFER.
OBEY ME. CHARLES!!!

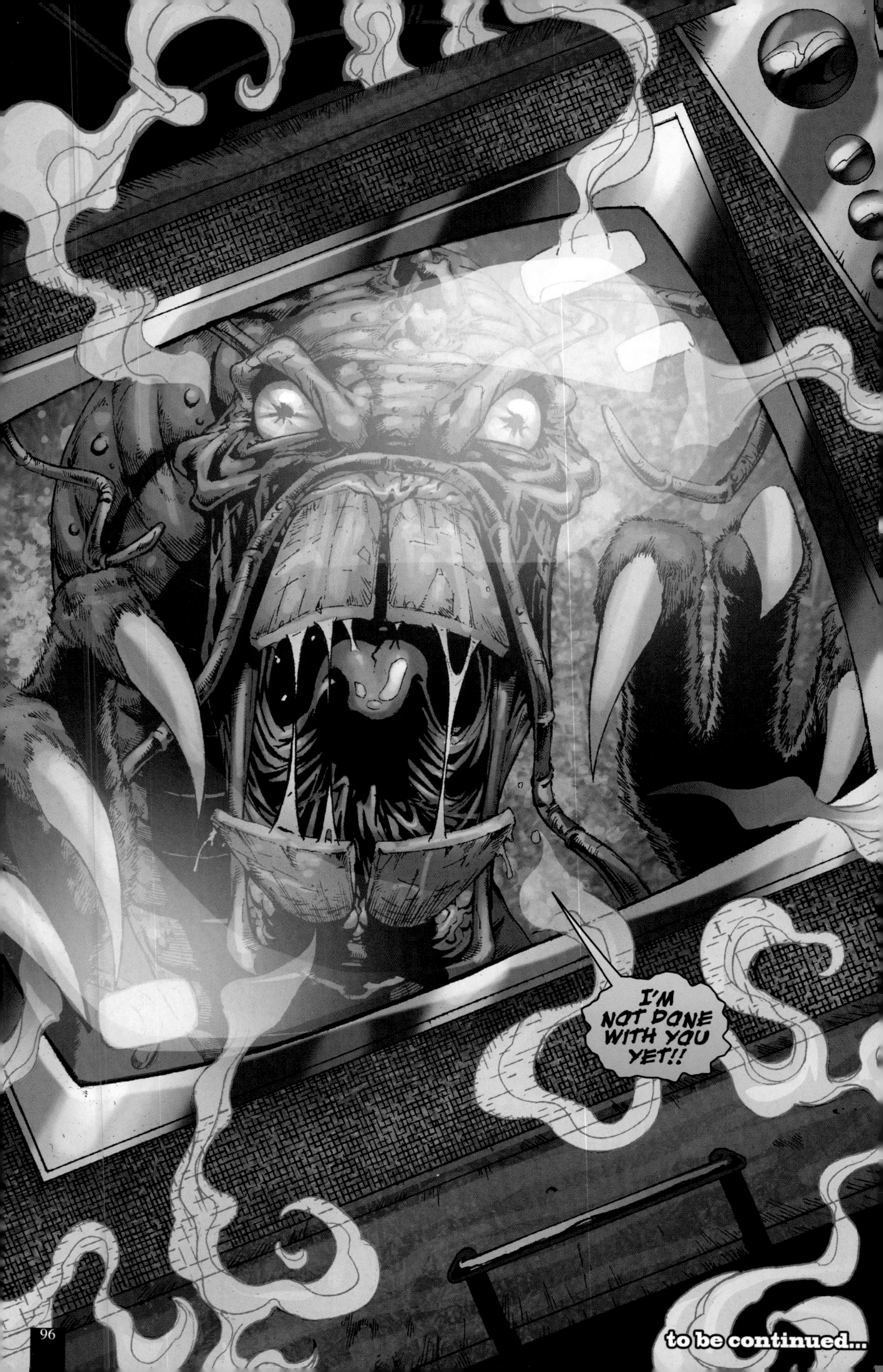
I'M NOT DONE WITH YOU YET!!
to be continued...

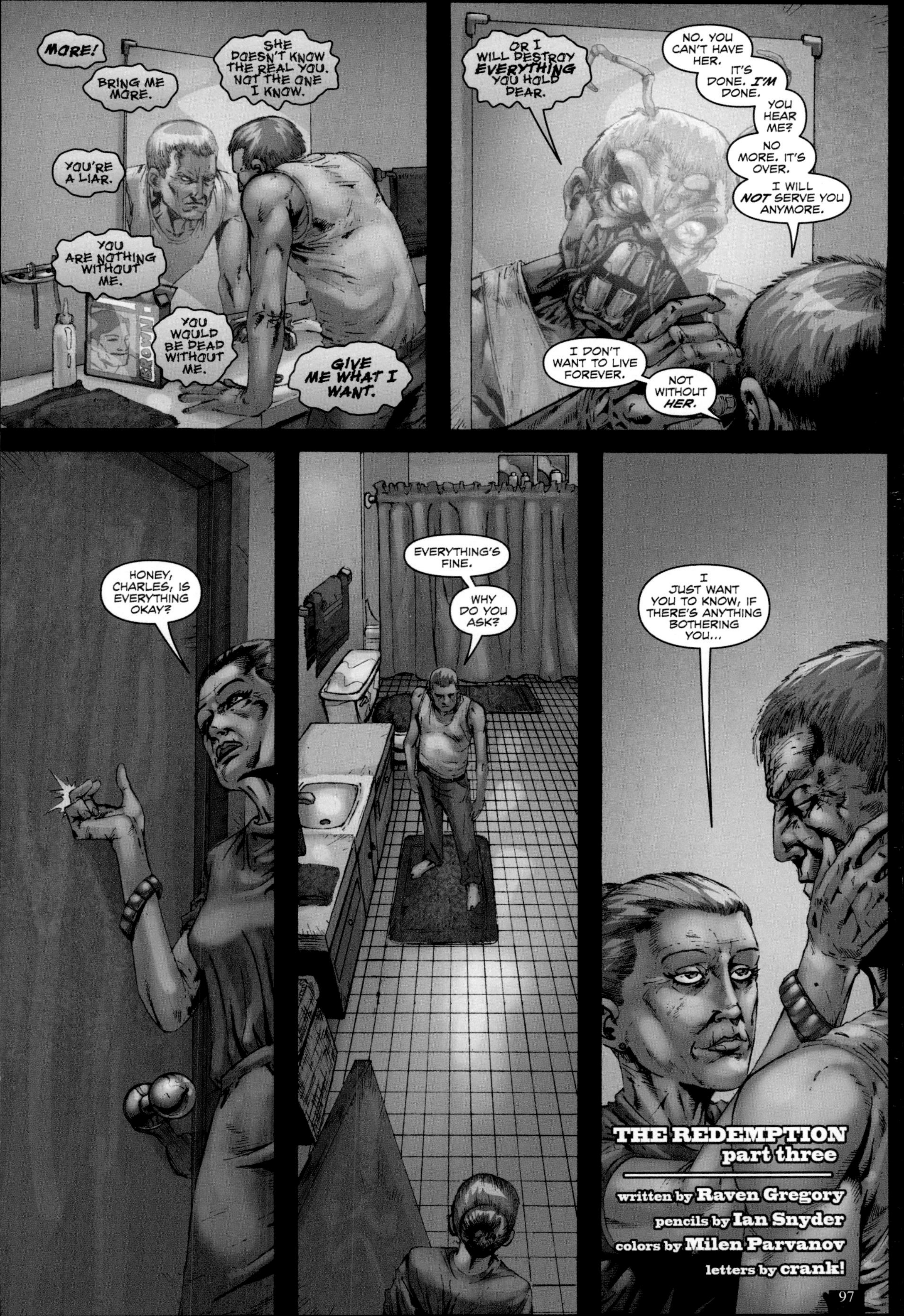
MORE!
BRING ME MORE.
SHE DOESN'T KNOW THE REAL YOU. NOT THE ONE I KNOW.
YOU'RE A LIAR.
YOU ARE NOTHING WITHOUT ME.
YOU WOULD BE DEAD WITHOUT ME.
GIVE ME WHAT I WANT.
OR I WILL DESTROY EVERYTHING YOU HOLD DEAR.
NO. YOU CAN'T HAVE HER.
IT'S DONE. I'M DONE.
YOU HEAR ME?
NO MORE. IT'S OVER.
I WILL NOT SERVE YOU ANYMORE.
I DON'T WANT TO LIVE FOREVER.
NOT WITHOUT HER.
HONEY, CHARLES, IS EVERYTHING OKAY?
EVERYTHING'S FINE.
WHY DO YOU ASK?
I JUST WANT YOU TO KNOW, IF THERE'S ANYTHING BOTHERING YOU...
THE REDEMPTION part three
written by Raven Gregory
pencils by Ian Snyder
colors by Milen Parvanov
letters by crank!

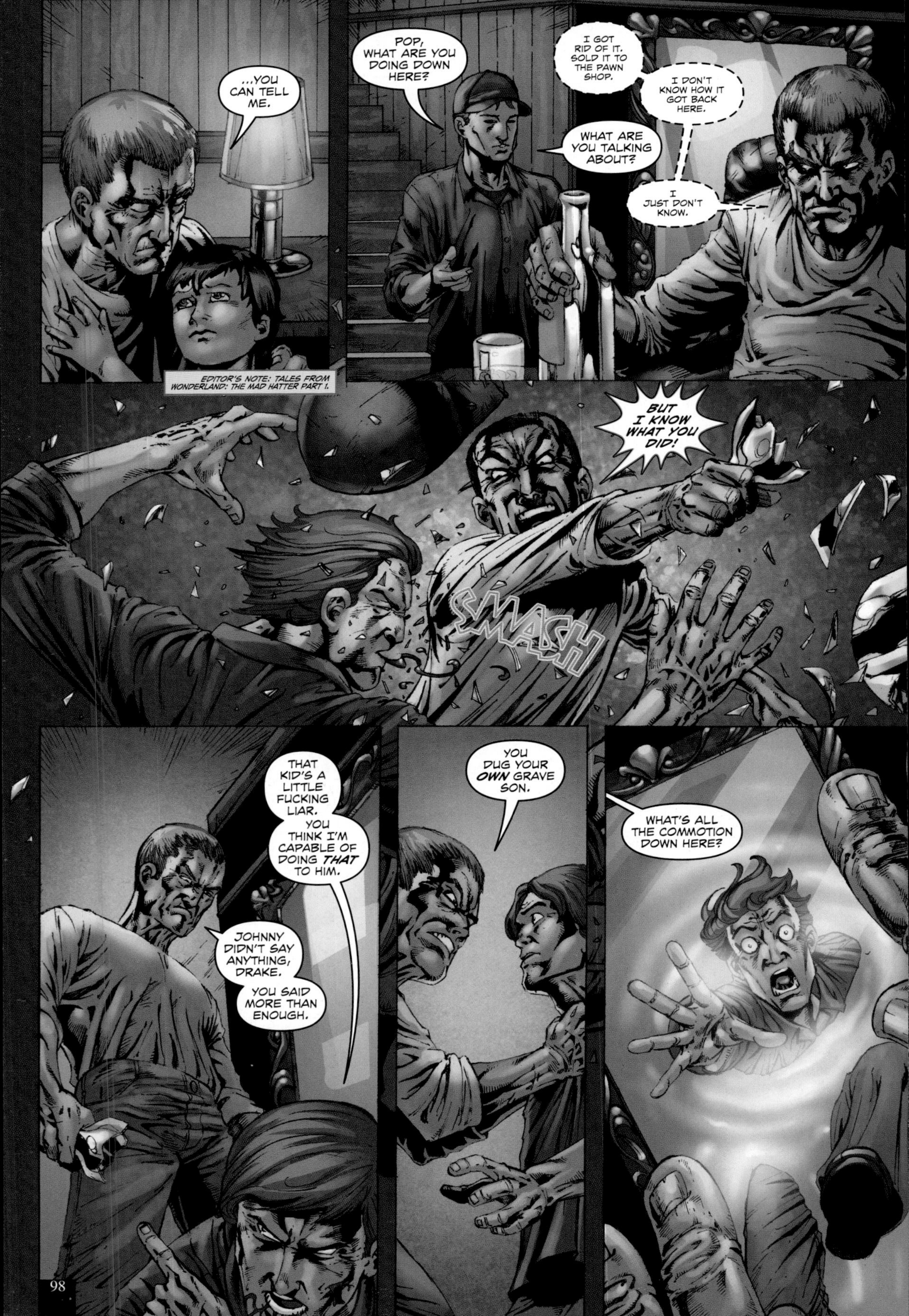

...YOU CAN TELL ME.
POP, WHAT ARE YOU DOING DOWN HERE?
I GOT RID OF IT. SOLD IT TO THE PAWN SHOP.
I DON'T KNOW HOW IT GOT BACK HERE.
WHAT ARE YOU TALKING ABOUT?
I JUST DON'T KNOW.
EDITOR'S NOTE: TALES FROM WONDERLAND: THE MAD HATTER PART 1.
BUT I KNOW WHAT YOU DID!
SMASH
THAT KID'S A LITTLE FUCKING LIAR.
YOU THINK I'M CAPABLE OF DOING THAT TO HIM.
JOHNNY DIDN'T SAY ANYTHING, DRAKE.
YOU SAID MORE THAN ENOUGH.
YOU DUG YOUR OWN GRAVE SON.
WHAT'S ALL THE COMMOTION DOWN HERE?

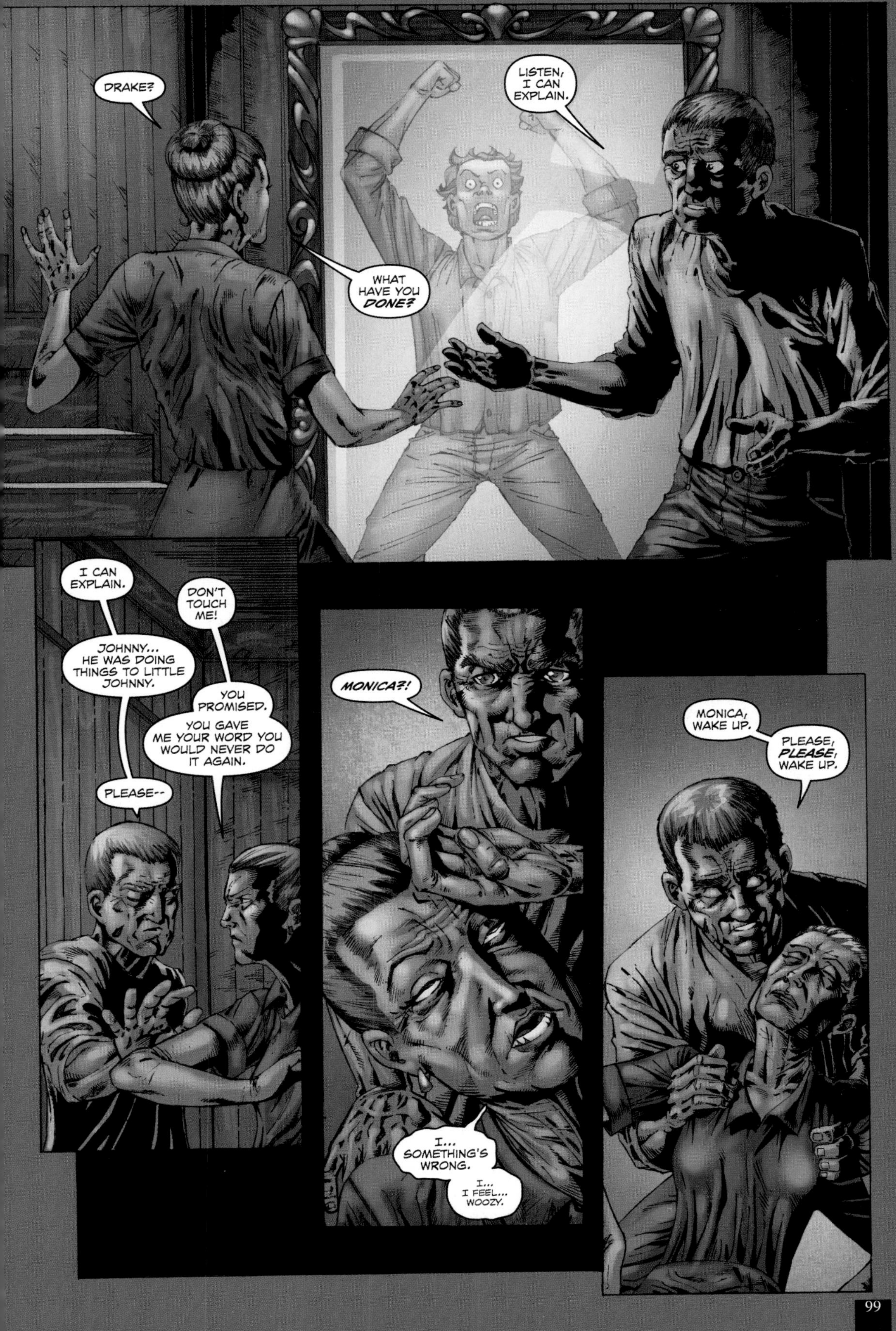
DRAKE?
LISTEN, I CAN EXPLAIN.
WHAT HAVE YOU DONE?
I CAN EXPLAIN.
DON'T TOUCH ME!
JOHNNY... HE WAS DOING THINGS TO LITTLE JOHNNY.
YOU PROMISED. YOU GAVE ME YOUR WORD YOU WOULD NEVER DO IT AGAIN.
PLEASE--
MONICA?!
I... SOMETHING'S WRONG.
I... I FEEL... WOOZY.
MONICA, WAKE UP.
PLEASE, PLEASE, WAKE UP.

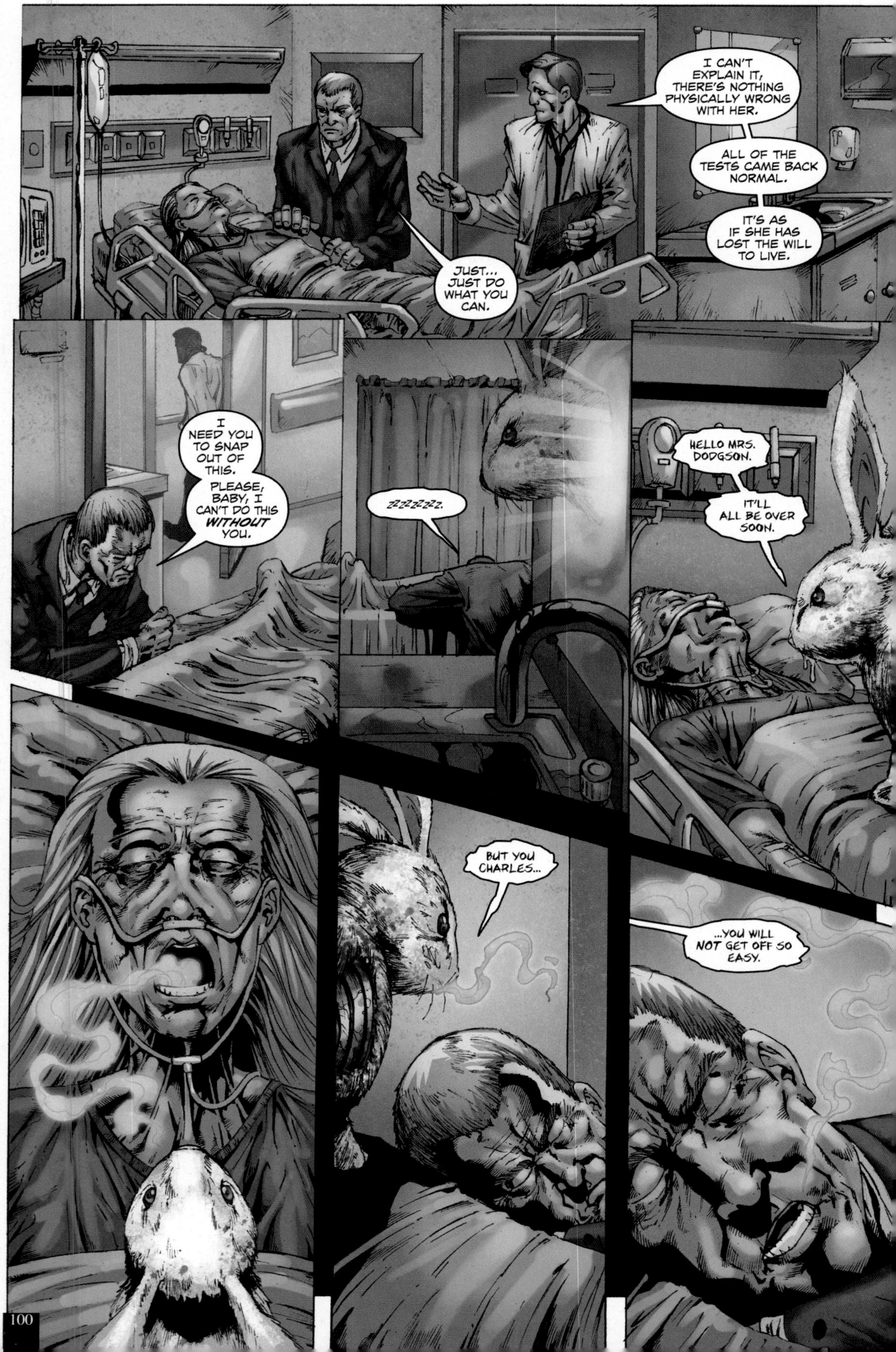
I CAN'T EXPLAIN IT, THERE'S NOTHING PHYSICALLY WRONG WITH HER.
ALL OF THE TESTS CAME BACK NORMAL.
IT'S AS IF SHE HAS LOST THE WILL TO LIVE.
JUST... JUST DO WHAT YOU CAN.
I NEED YOU TO SNAP OUT OF THIS.
PLEASE, BABY, I CAN'T DO THIS *WITHOUT* YOU.
ZZZZZZZZZ.
HELLO MRS. DODGSON.
IT'LL ALL BE OVER SOON.
BUT YOU CHARLES...
...YOU WILL *NOT* GET OFF SO EASY.

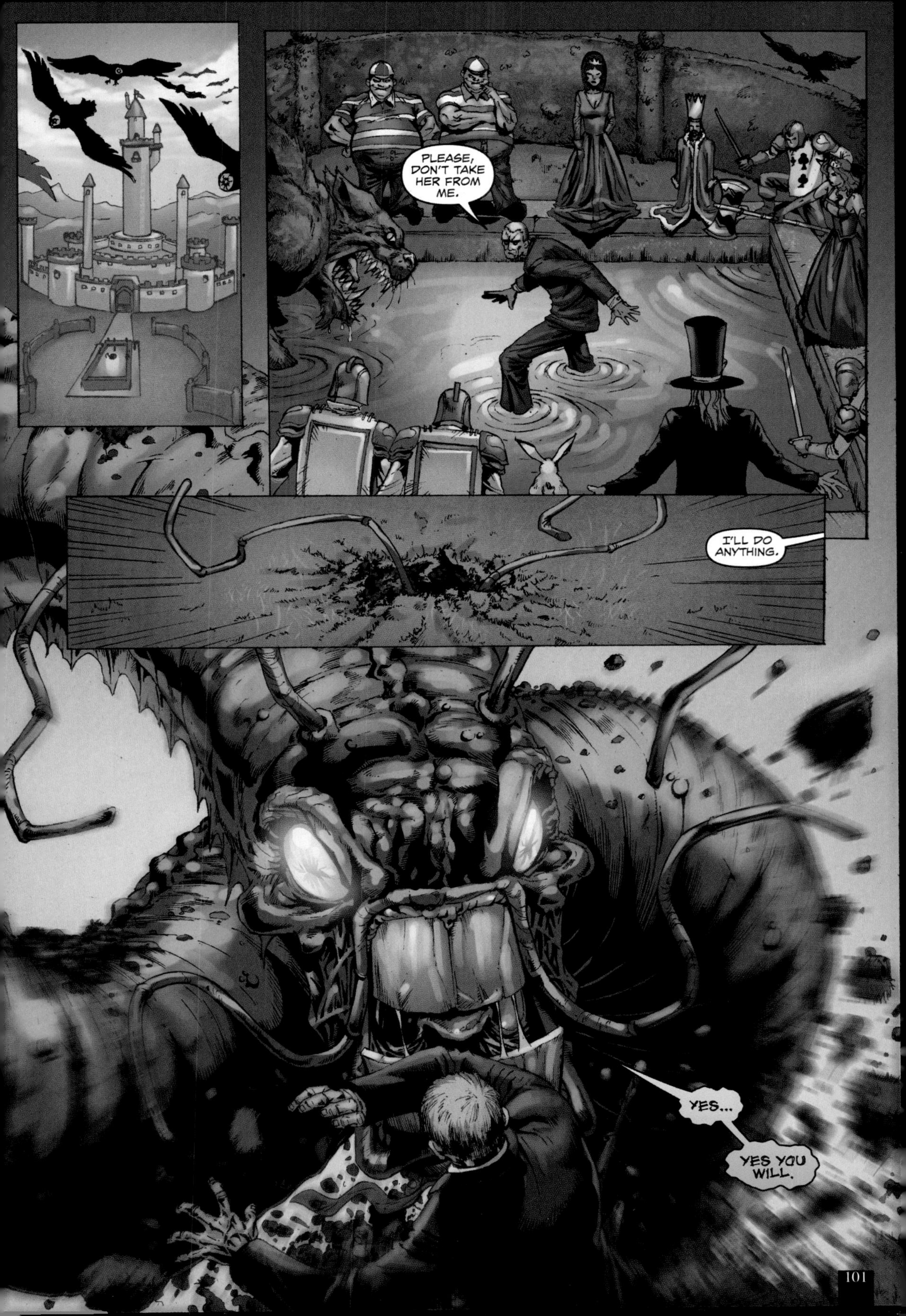
PLEASE, DON'T TAKE HER FROM ME.
I'LL DO ANYTHING.
YES...
YES YOU WILL.

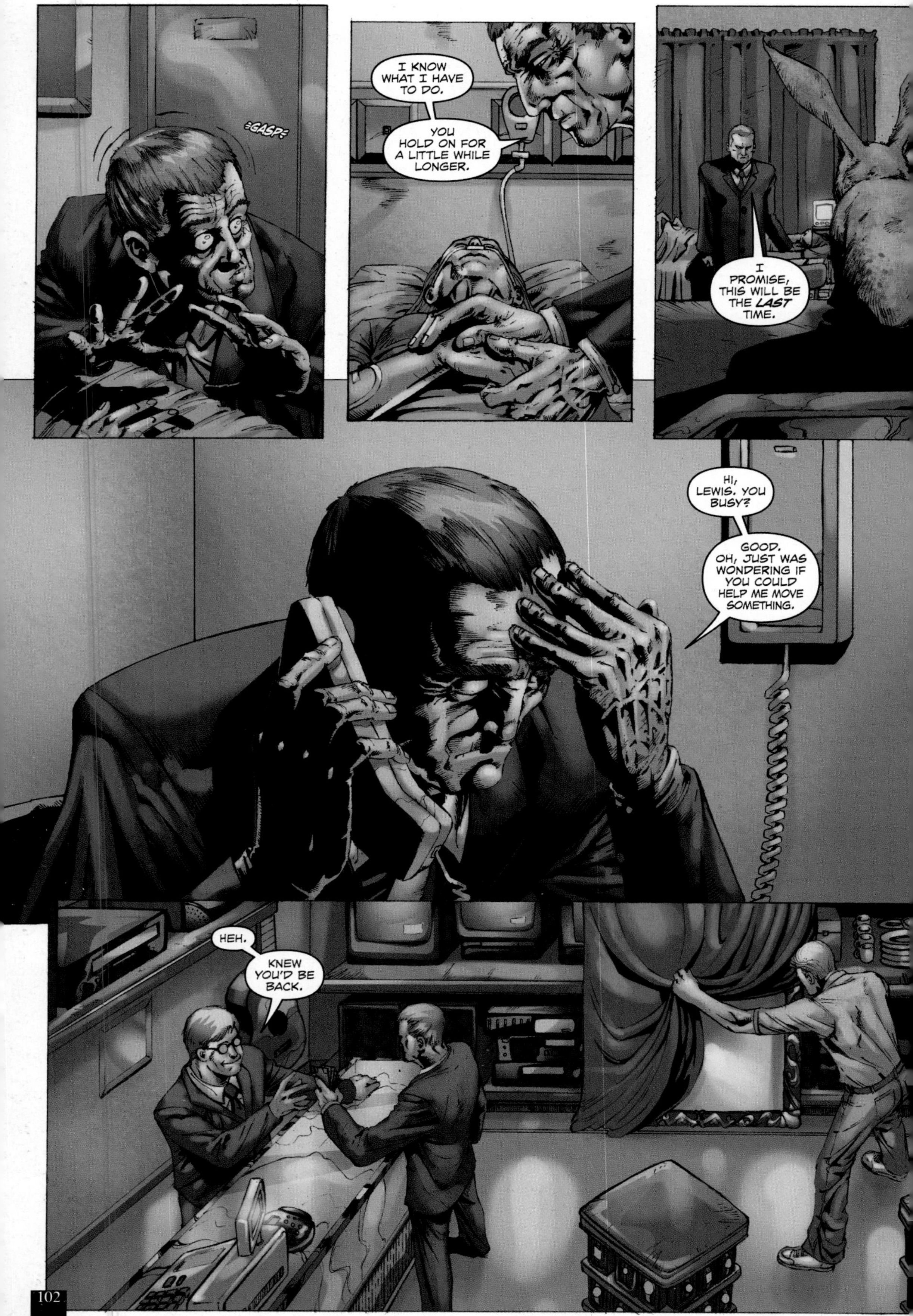

GASP
I KNOW WHAT I HAVE TO DO.
YOU HOLD ON FOR A LITTLE WHILE LONGER.
I PROMISE, THIS WILL BE THE *LAST* TIME.
HI, LEWIS. YOU BUSY?
GOOD. OH, JUST WAS WONDERING IF YOU COULD HELP ME MOVE SOMETHING.
HEH.
KNEW YOU'D BE BACK.

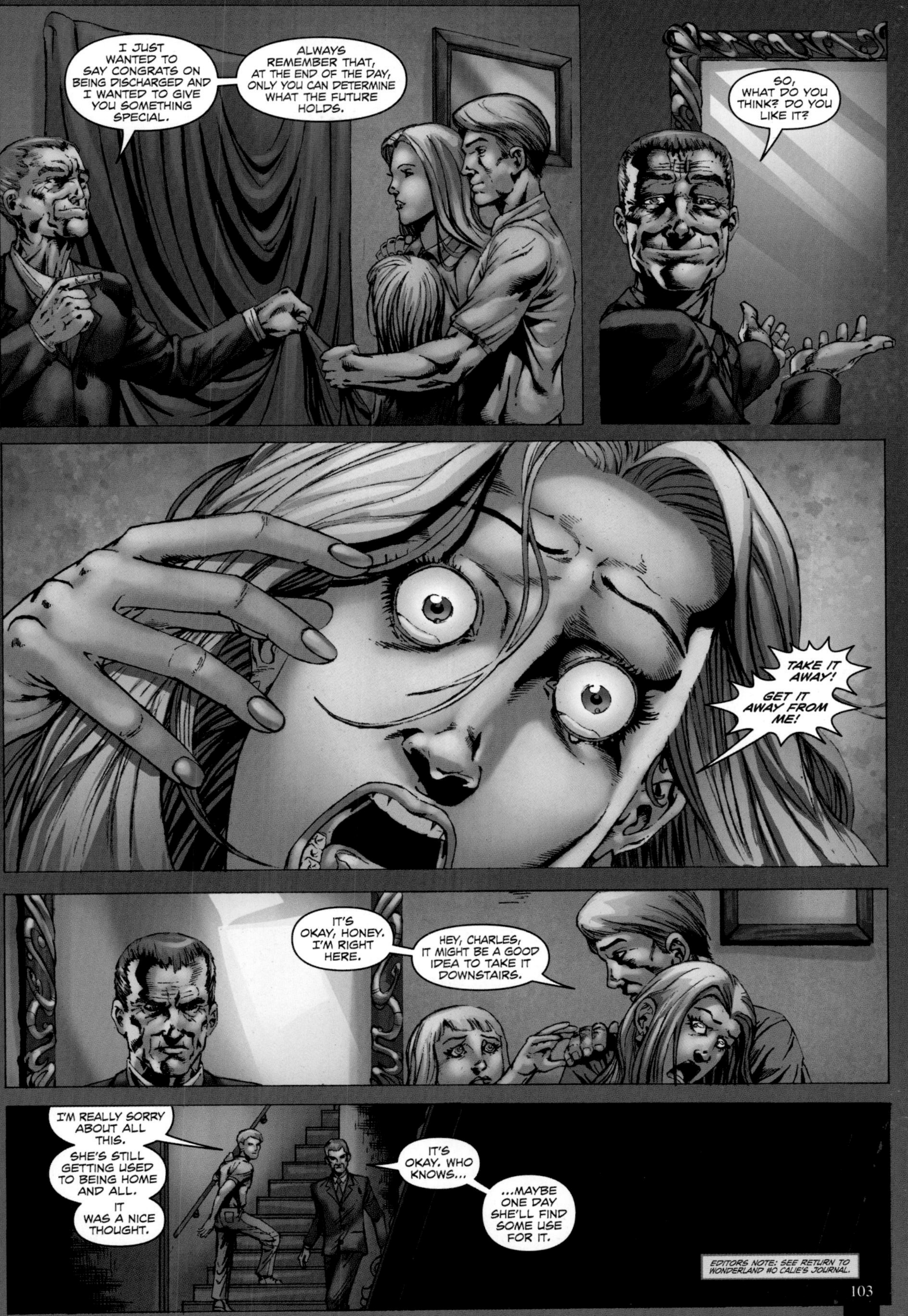
I JUST WANTED TO SAY CONGRATS ON BEING DISCHARGED AND I WANTED TO GIVE YOU SOMETHING SPECIAL.
ALWAYS REMEMBER THAT, AT THE END OF THE DAY, ONLY YOU CAN DETERMINE WHAT THE FUTURE HOLDS.
SO, WHAT DO YOU THINK? DO YOU LIKE IT?
TAKE IT AWAY! GET IT AWAY FROM ME!
IT'S OKAY, HONEY. I'M RIGHT HERE.
HEY, CHARLES, IT MIGHT BE A GOOD IDEA TO TAKE IT DOWNSTAIRS.
I'M REALLY SORRY ABOUT ALL THIS.
SHE'S STILL GETTING USED TO BEING HOME AND ALL.
IT WAS A NICE THOUGHT.
IT'S OKAY. WHO KNOWS...
...MAYBE ONE DAY SHE'LL FIND SOME USE FOR IT.
EDITORS NOTE: SEE RETURN TO WONDERLAND #0 CALIE'S JOURNAL.

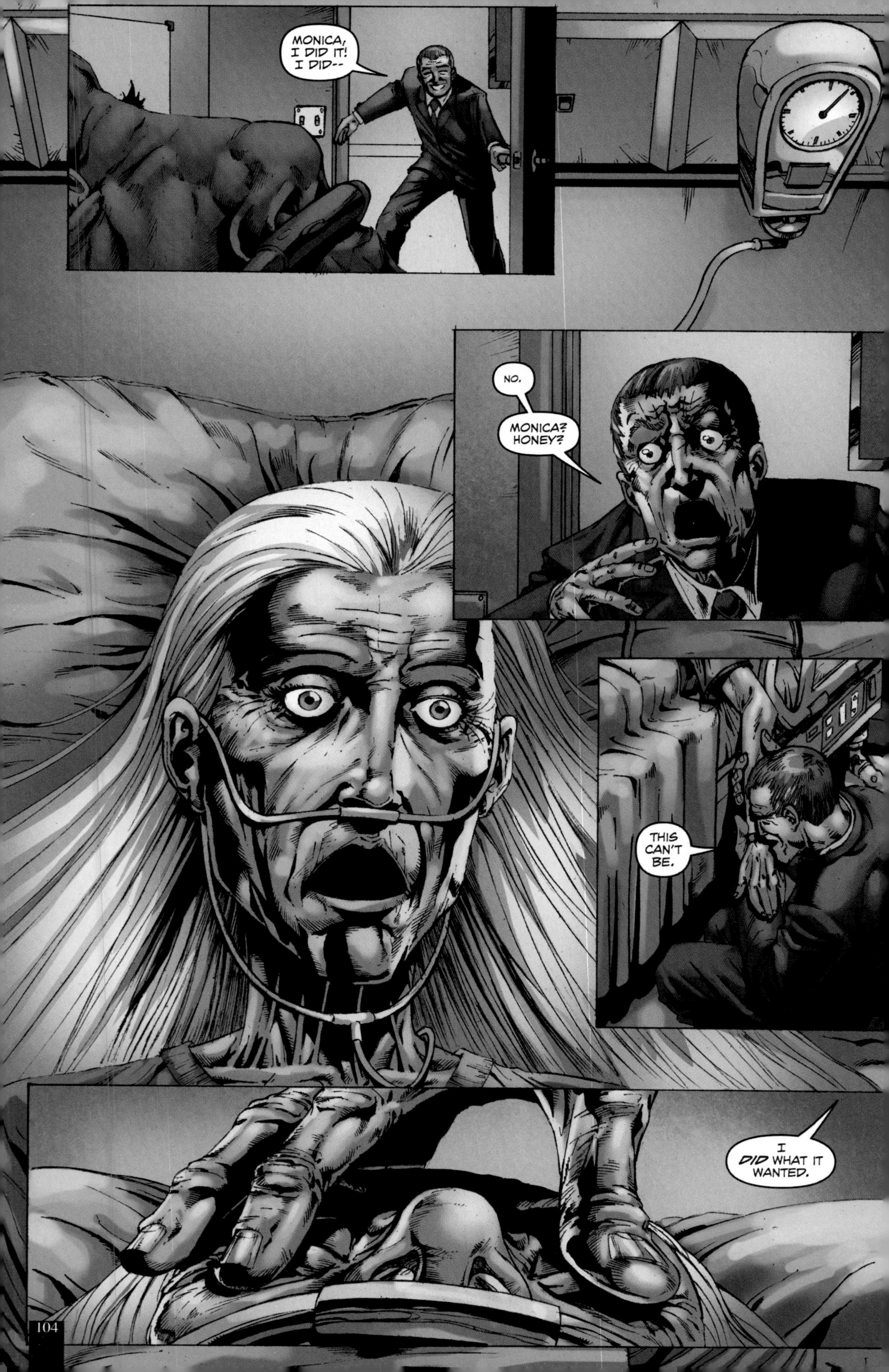
MONICA, I DID IT! I DID--
NO.
MONICA? HONEY?
THIS CAN'T BE.
I *DID* WHAT IT WANTED.

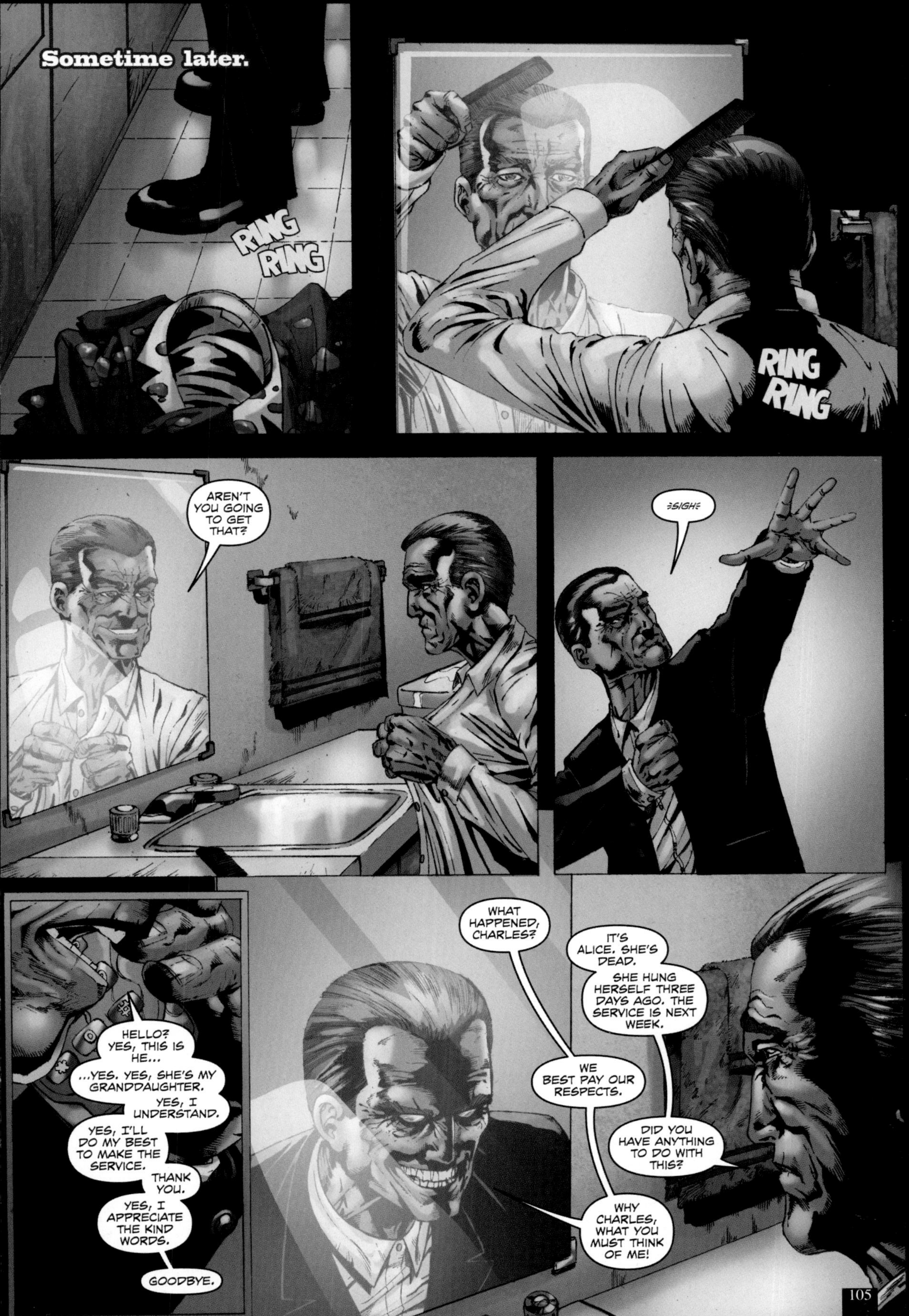

Sometime later.
RING RING
RING RING
AREN'T YOU GOING TO GET THAT?
≈SIGH≈
HELLO? YES, THIS IS HE...
...YES. YES, SHE'S MY GRANDDAUGHTER.
YES, I UNDERSTAND.
YES, I'LL DO MY BEST TO MAKE THE SERVICE.
THANK YOU.
YES, I APPRECIATE THE KIND WORDS.
GOODBYE.
WHAT HAPPENED, CHARLES?
IT'S ALICE. SHE'S DEAD.
SHE HUNG HERSELF THREE DAYS AGO. THE SERVICE IS NEXT WEEK.
WE BEST PAY OUR RESPECTS.
DID YOU HAVE ANYTHING TO DO WITH THIS?
WHY CHARLES, WHAT YOU MUST THINK OF ME!

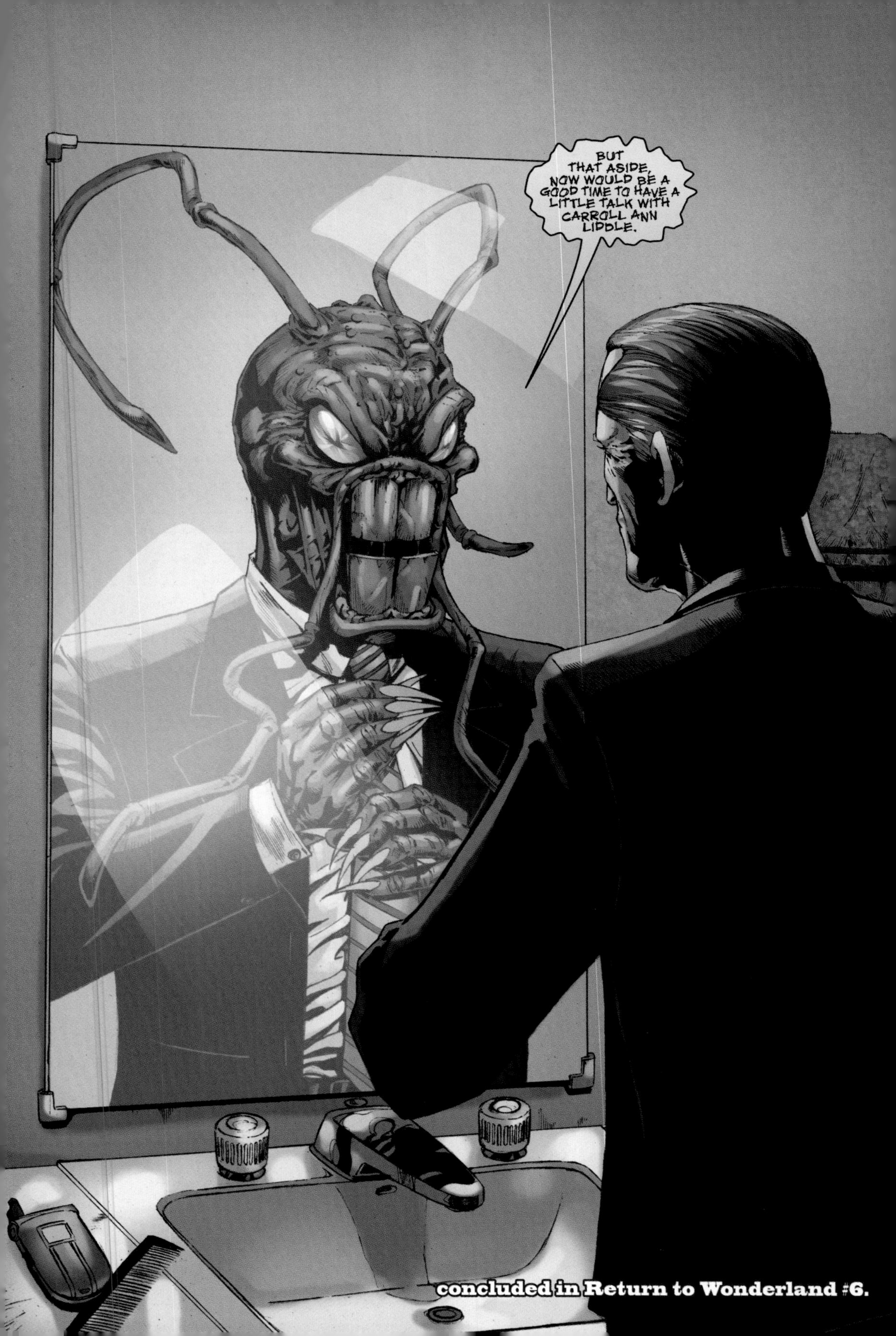
BUT THAT ASIDE, NOW WOULD BE A GOOD TIME TO HAVE A LITTLE TALK WITH CARROLL ANN LIDDLE.

concluded in Return to Wonderland #6.

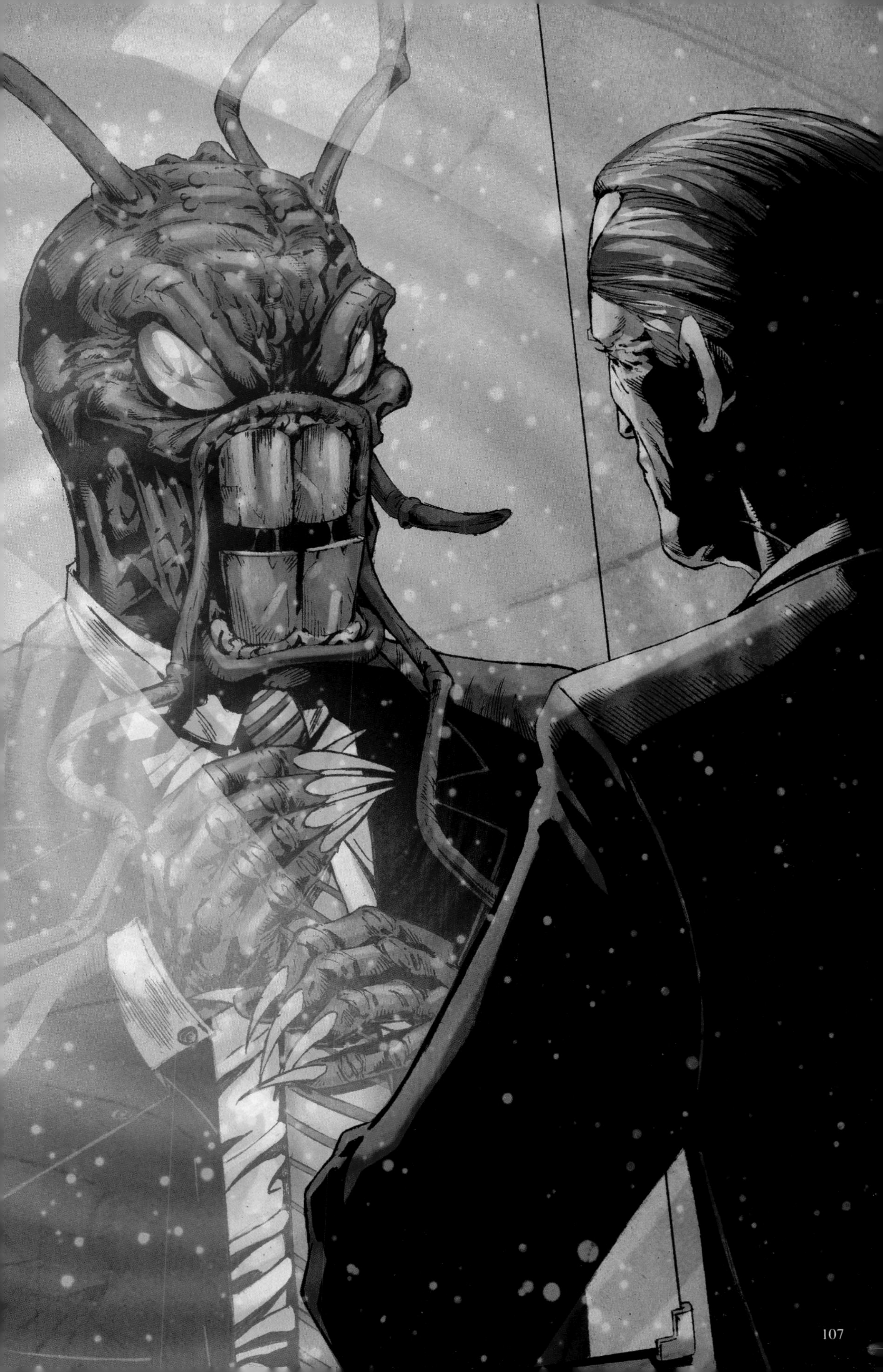

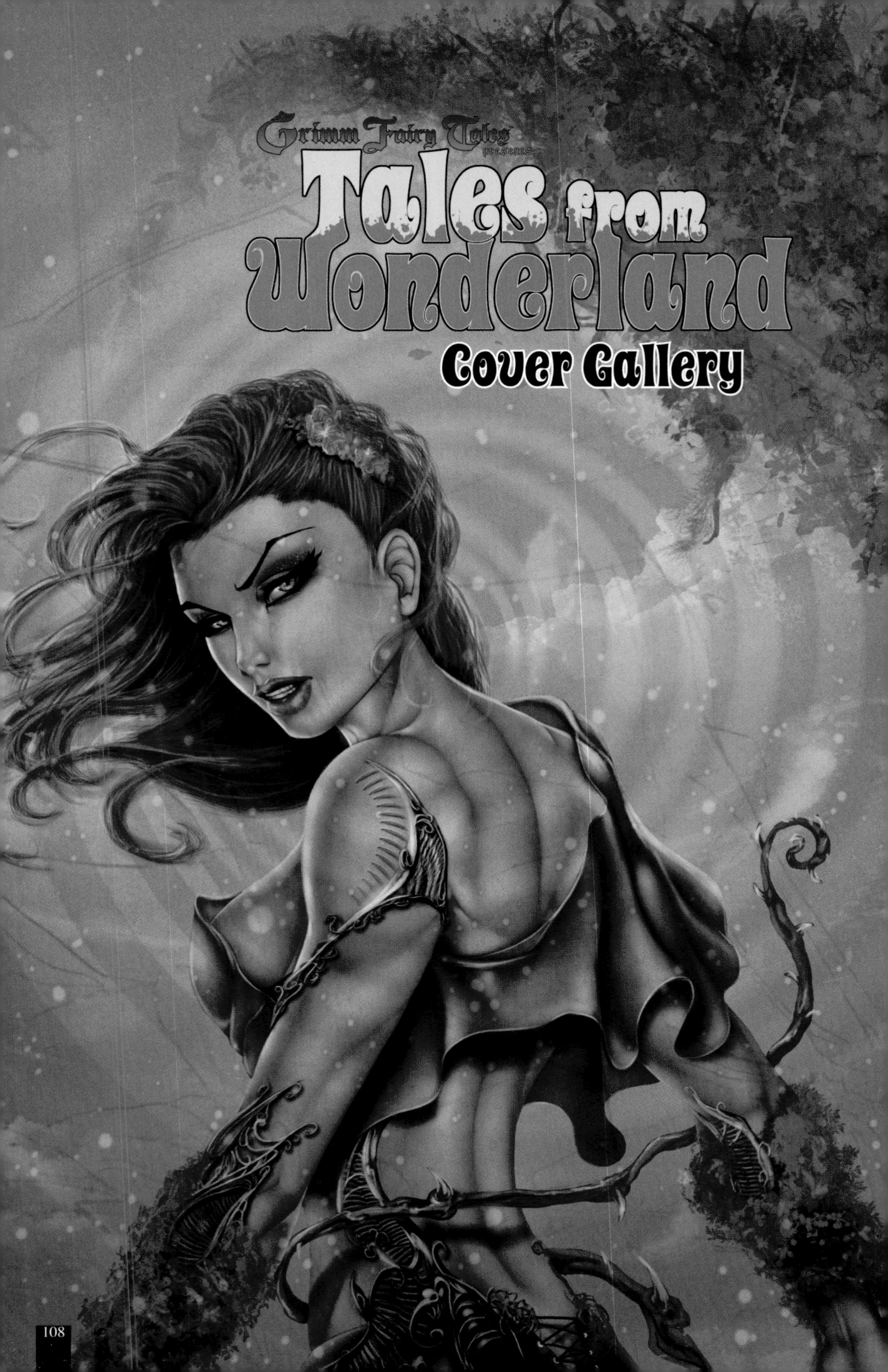
Grimm Fairy Tales presents
Tales from Wonderland
Cover Gallery

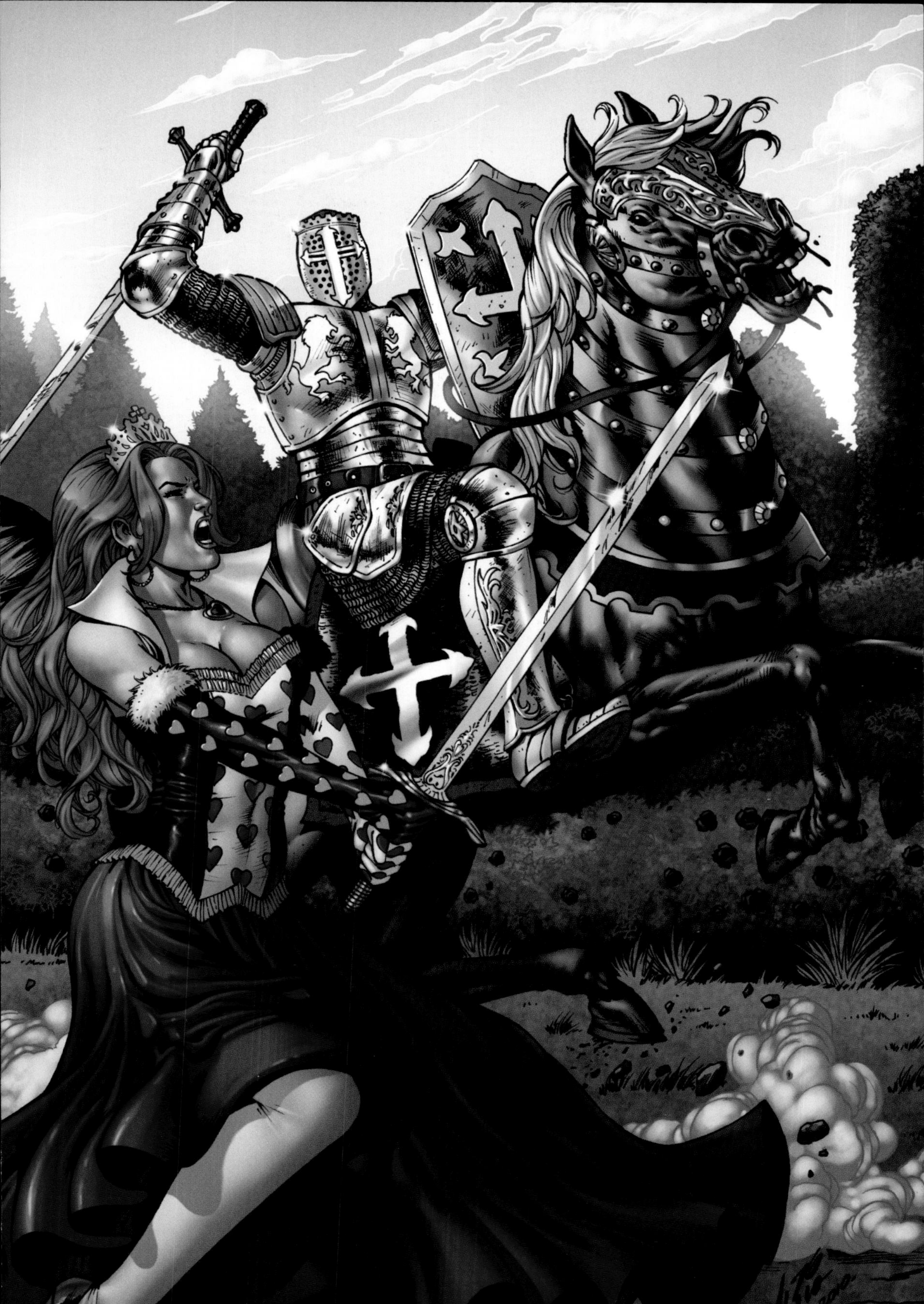

Tales from Wonderland: The White Knight • Cover A
Cover by Al Rio • Colors by Jose Cano

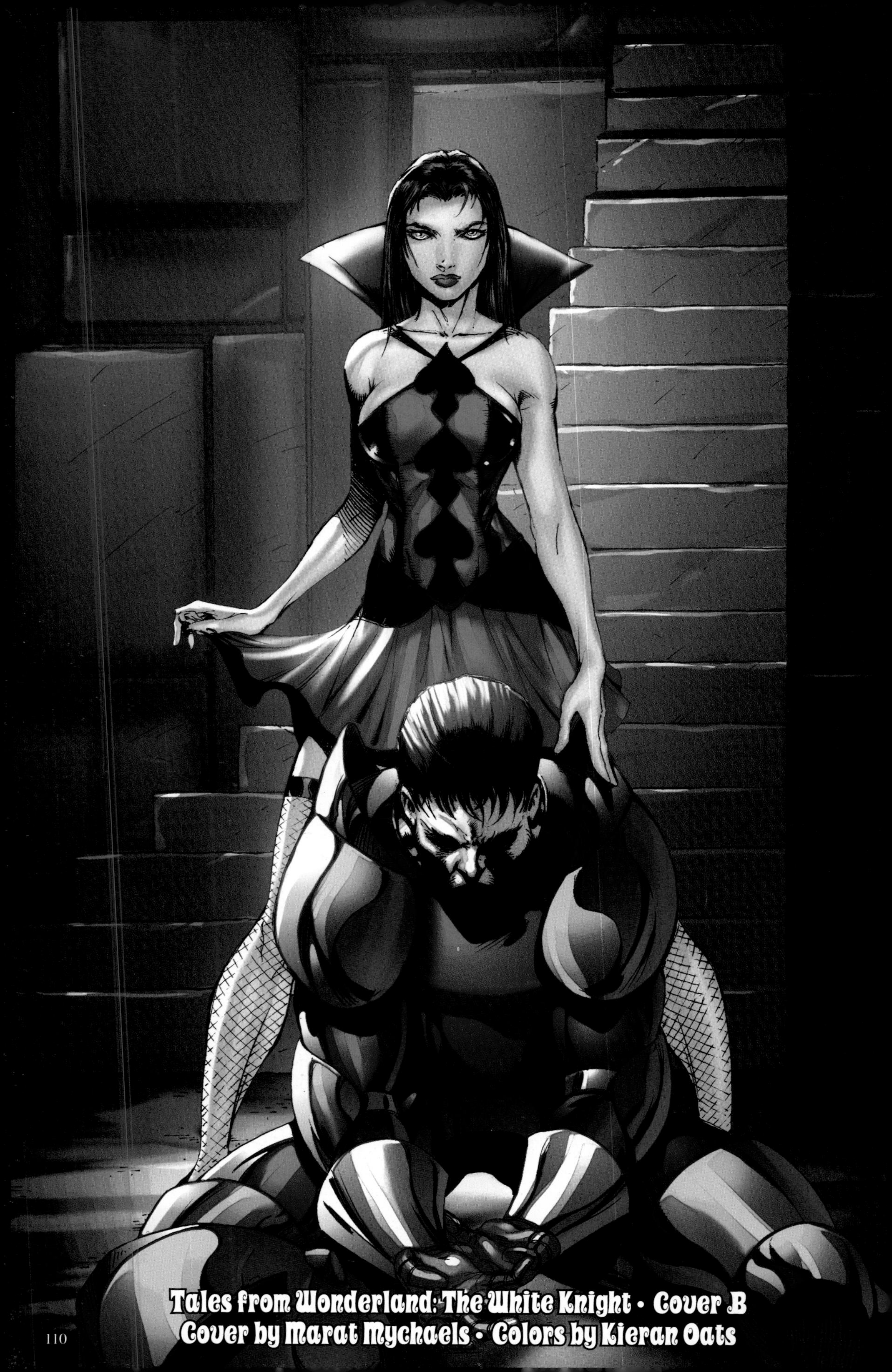

Tales from Wonderland: The White Knight • Cover B
Cover by Marat Mychaels • Colors by Kieran Oats

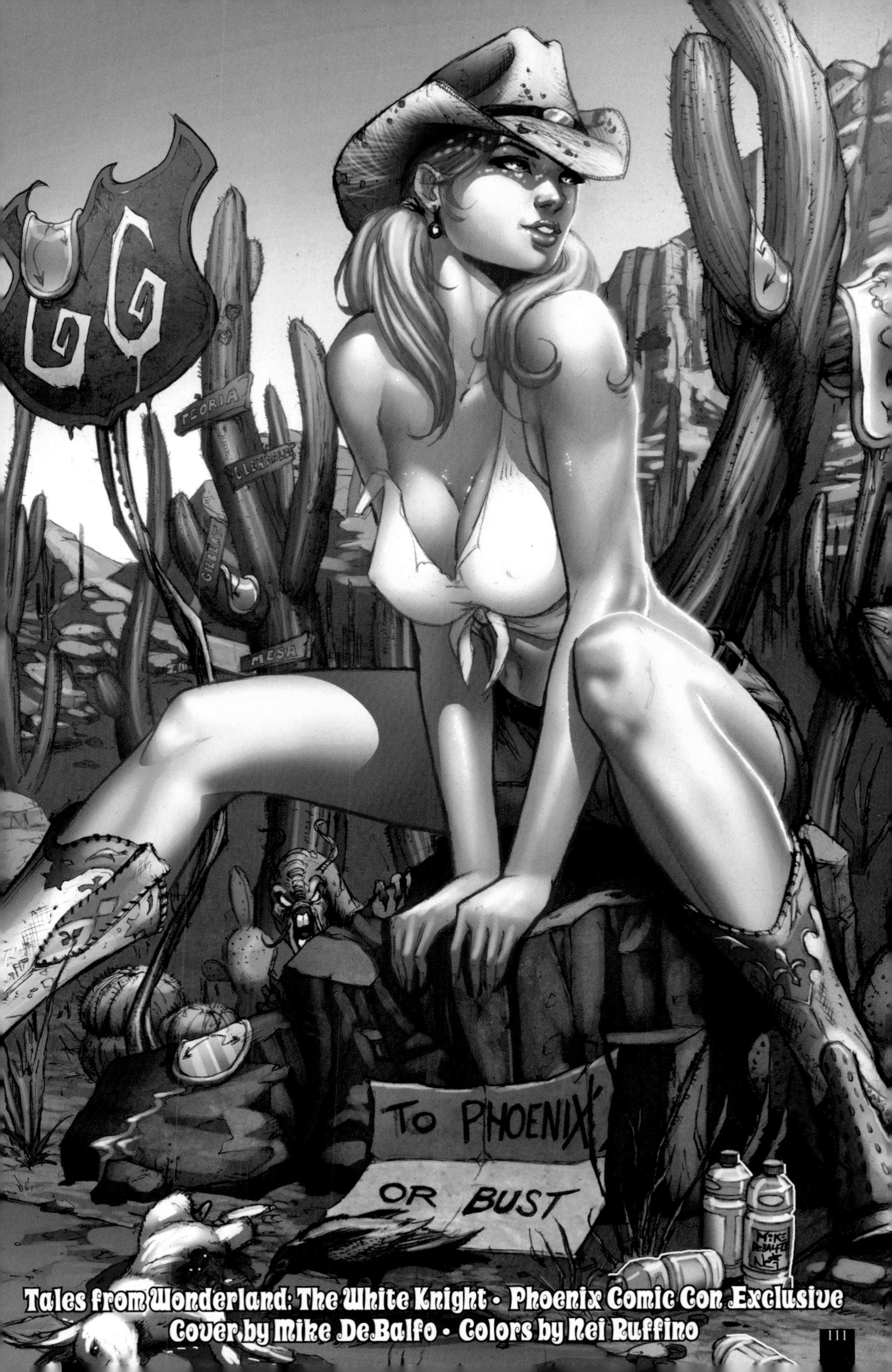
PEORIA
GLENDALE
GILBERT
MESA
TO PHOENIX
OR BUST

Tales from Wonderland: The White Knight • Phoenix Comic Con Exclusive
Cover by Mike DeBalfo • Colors by Nei Ruffino

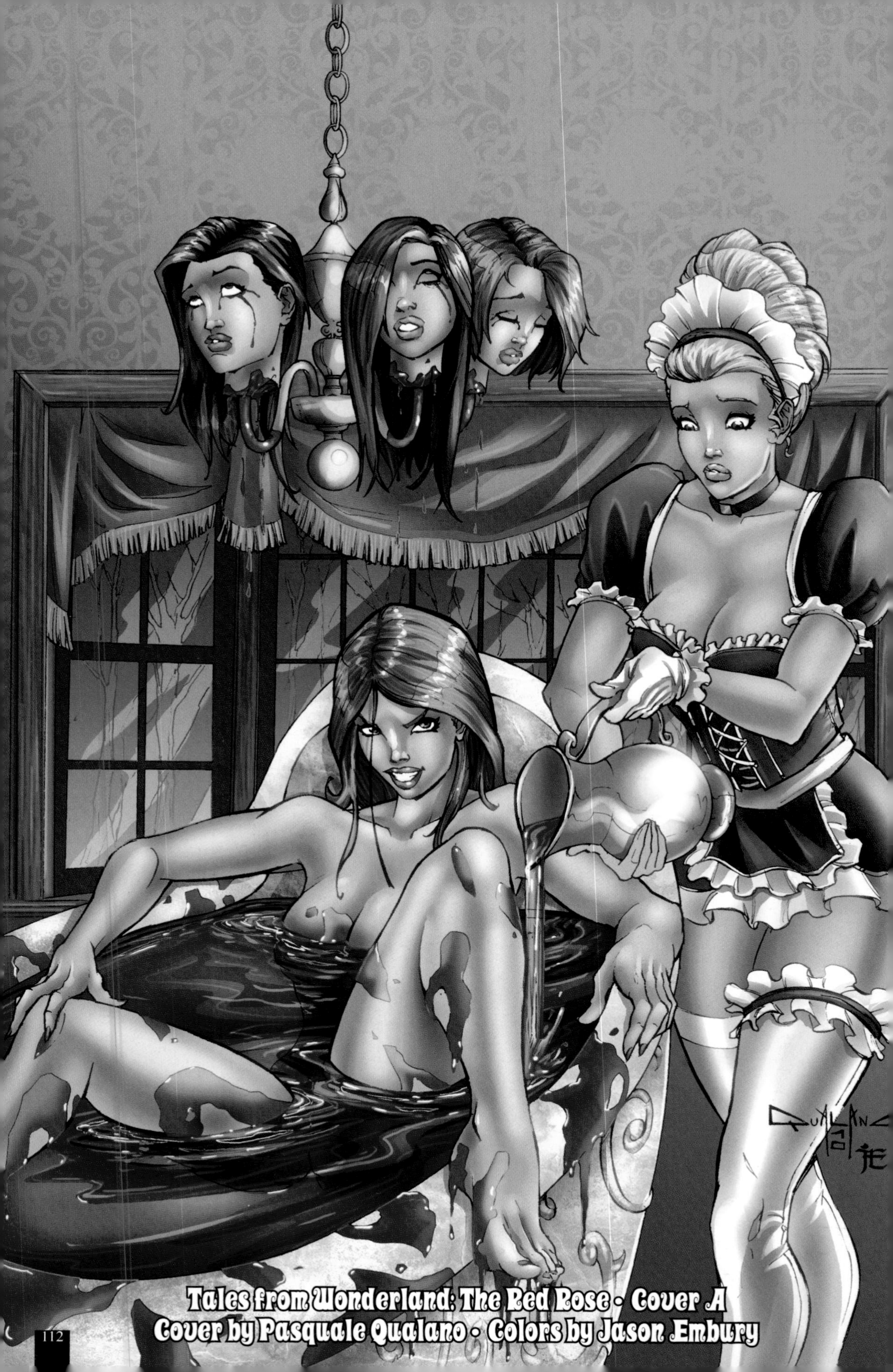

Tales from Wonderland: The Red Rose - Cover A
Cover by Pasquale Qualano - Colors by Jason Embury

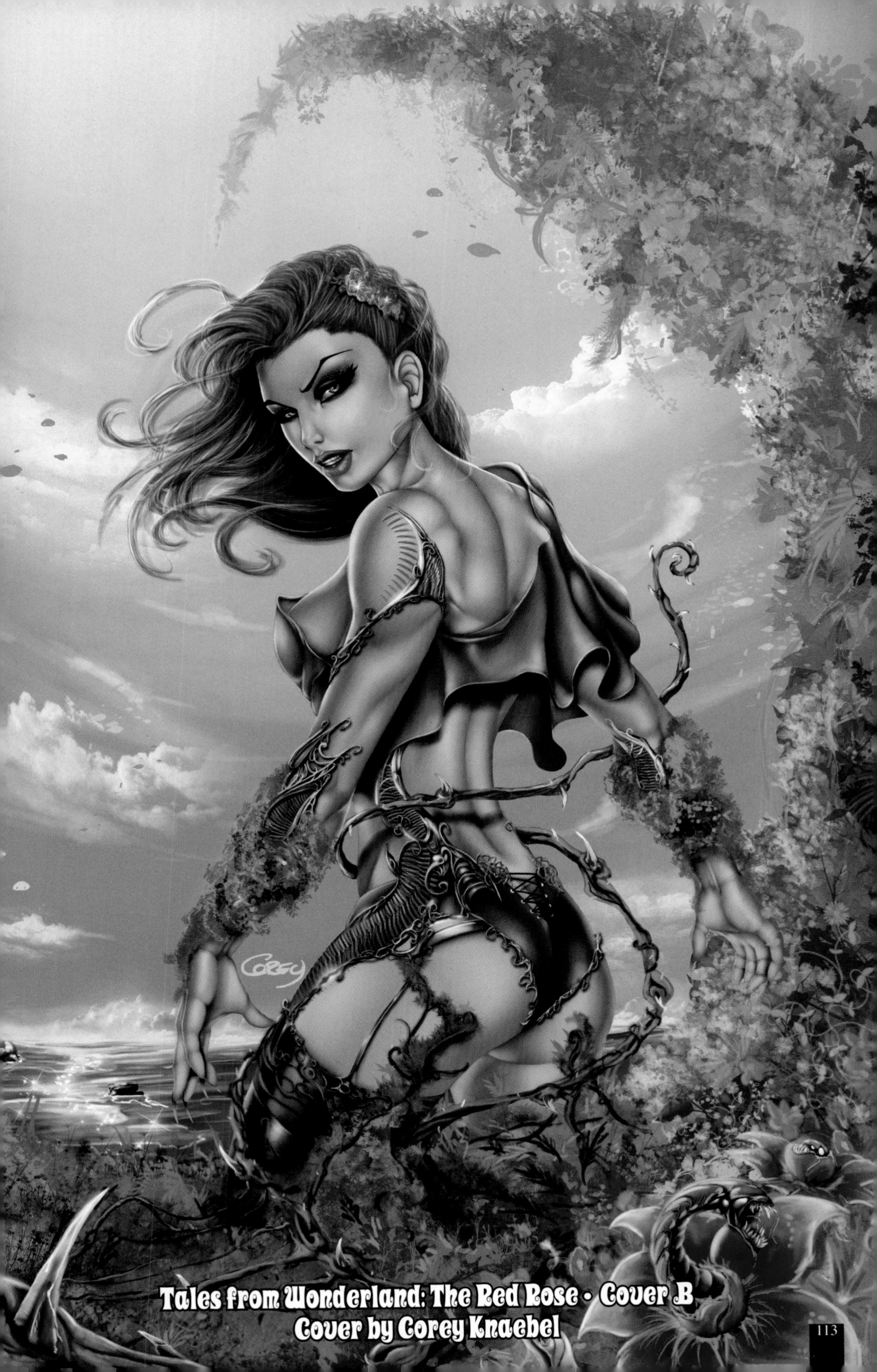
COREY

Tales from Wonderland: The Red Rose • Cover B
Cover by Corey Knaebel

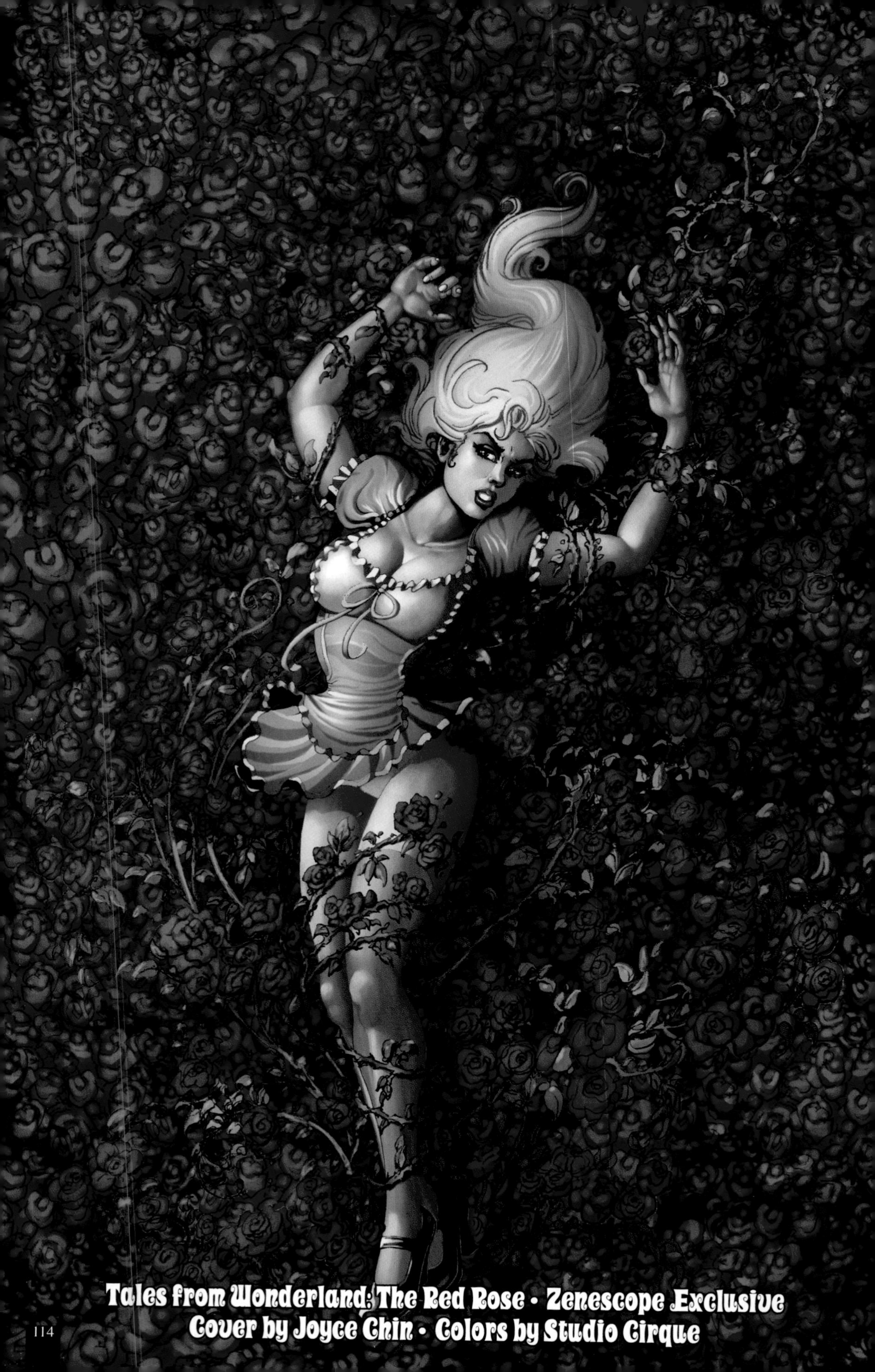

Tales from Wonderland: The Red Rose • Zenescope Exclusive
Cover by Joyce Chin • Colors by Studio Cirque

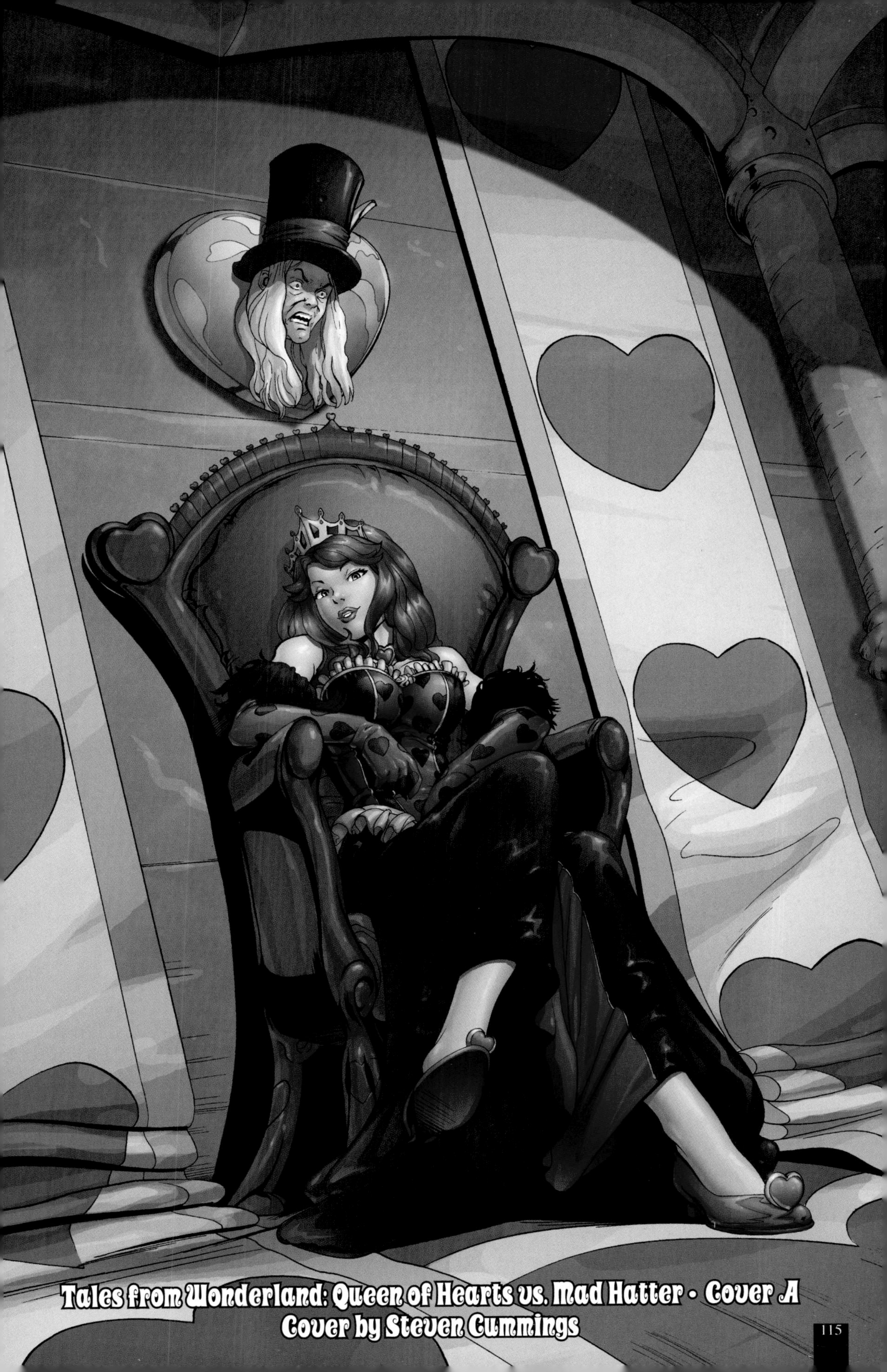

Tales from Wonderland: Queen of Hearts vs. Mad Hatter • Cover A
Cover by Steven Cummings

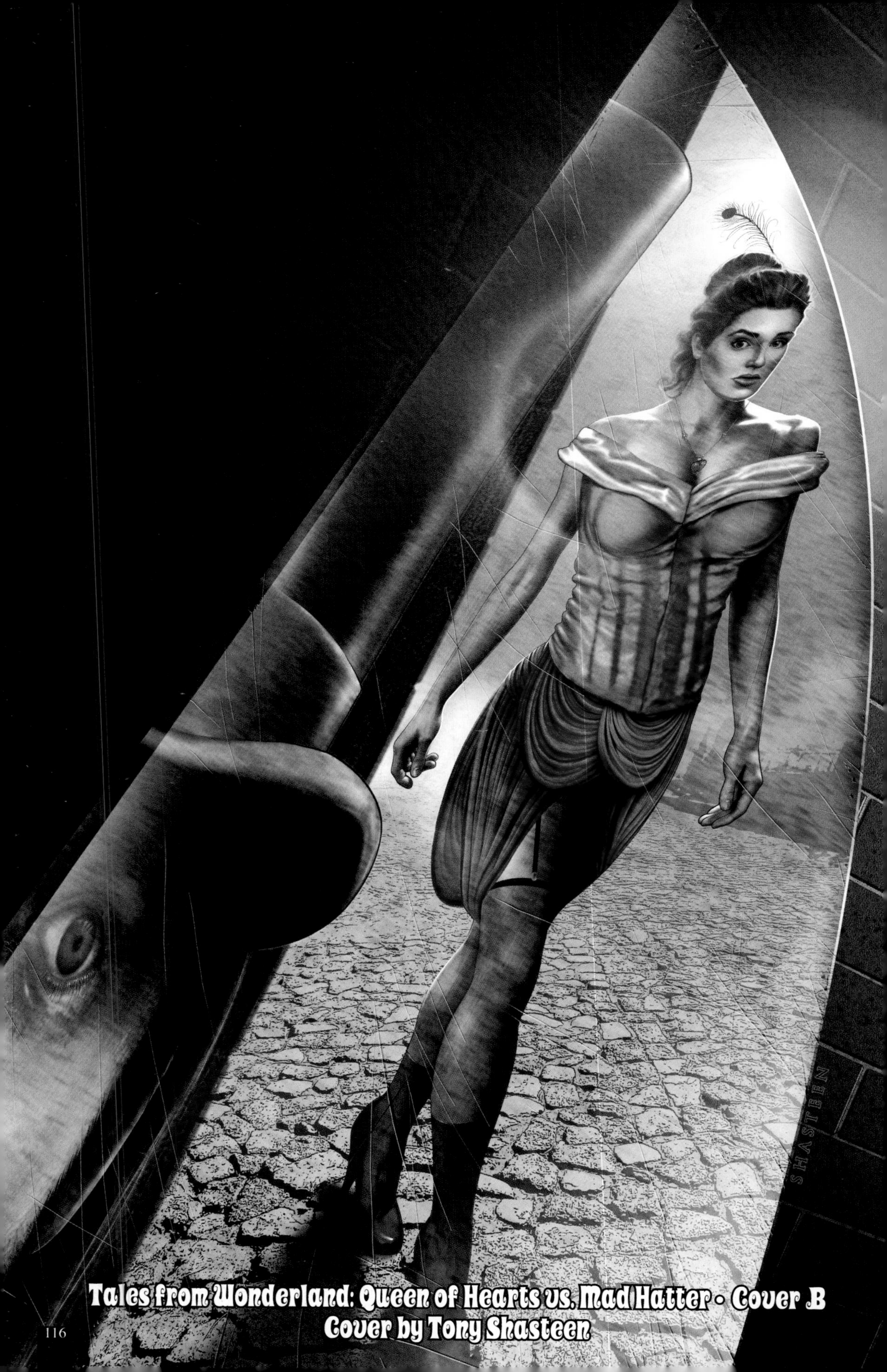
SHASTEEN

Tales from Wonderland: Queen of Hearts vs. Mad Hatter • Cover B
Cover by Tony Shasteen

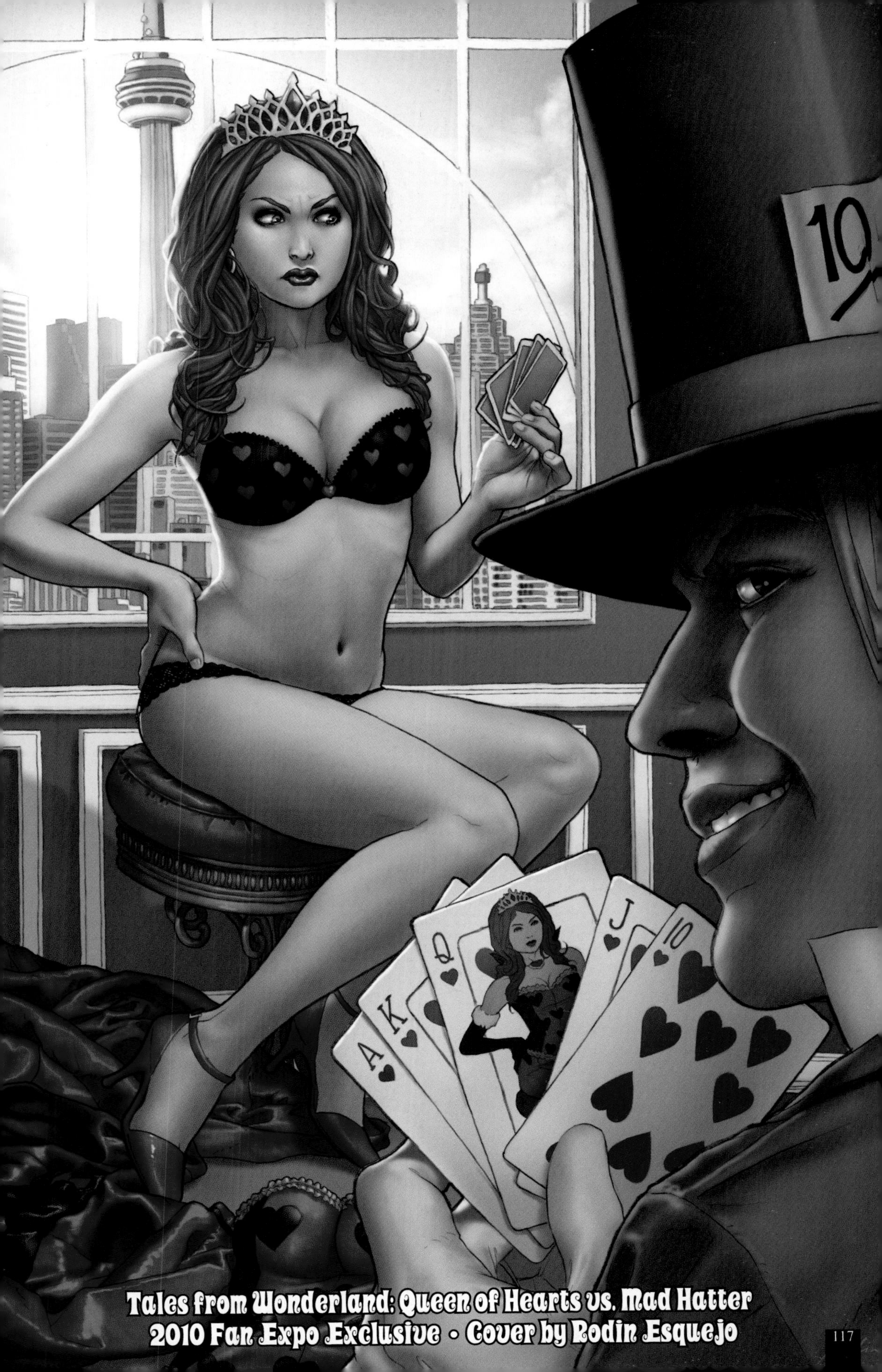

Tales from Wonderland: Queen of Hearts vs. Mad Hatter
2010 Fan Expo Exclusive • Cover by Rodin Esquejo

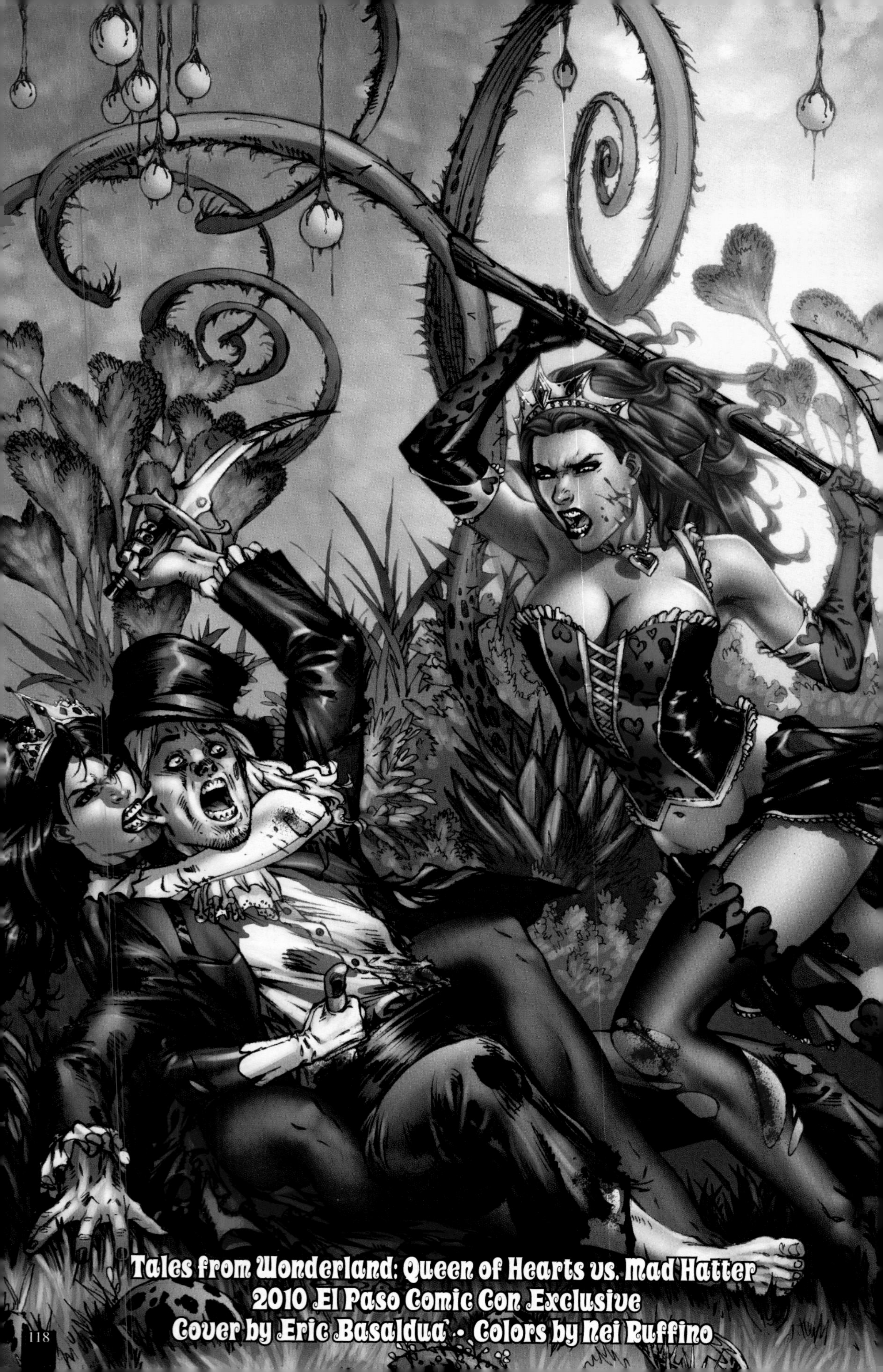

Tales from Wonderland: Queen of Hearts vs. Mad Hatter
2010 El Paso Comic Con Exclusive
Cover by Eric Basaldua · Colors by Nei Ruffino

Tales from Wonderland

volume three

Also from Zenescope Entertainment...

Check out this sneak peek of Zenescope's
CHARMED comic book series in stores now!

This special BOOK of SHADOWS
preview recaps the entire CHARMED
television series and showcases some
artwork from issue #1 of the hit series.
Also, be sure to look for the CHARMED
trade paperback in stores this winter!

Based on the television show created by:
Constance M. Burge

Charmed #0: Book of Shadows
Written by Paul Ruditis
Edited by Ralph Tedesco & Raven Gregory
Design and production by David Seidman
Original Book of Shadows artwork created by:
Derek Baron, Dan Haberkorn, and Carol Wood

Additional Book of Shadows artwork created by:
Dave Hoover and David Seidman

Select Book of Shadows text taken from the following episodes:
"Something Wicca This Way Comes" • Written by Constance M. Burge
"The Truth is Out There ... And it Hurts" • Written by Zack Estrin & Chris Levinson
"The Witch is Back" • Written by Sheryl J. Anderson
"That Old Black Magic" • Written by Vivian Mayhew & Valerie Mayhew
"Magic Hour" • Written by Chris Levinson & Zack Estrin
"All Halliwell's Eve" • Written by Sheryl J. Anderson
"Blinded by the Whitelighter" • Written by Nell Scovell
"Pre-Witched" • Written by Chris Levinson & Zack Estrin
"Charmed Again" • Written by Brad Kern
"Hell Hath No Fury" • Written by Krista Vernoff
"Charmed and Dangerous" • Written by Monica Breen and Alison Schapker
"Lucky Charmed" • Written by Curtis Kheel
"Extreme Makeover: World Edition" • Written by Cameron Litvak
"Kill Billie Vol. 2" • Written by Brad Kern
"Forever Charmed" • Written by Brad Kern

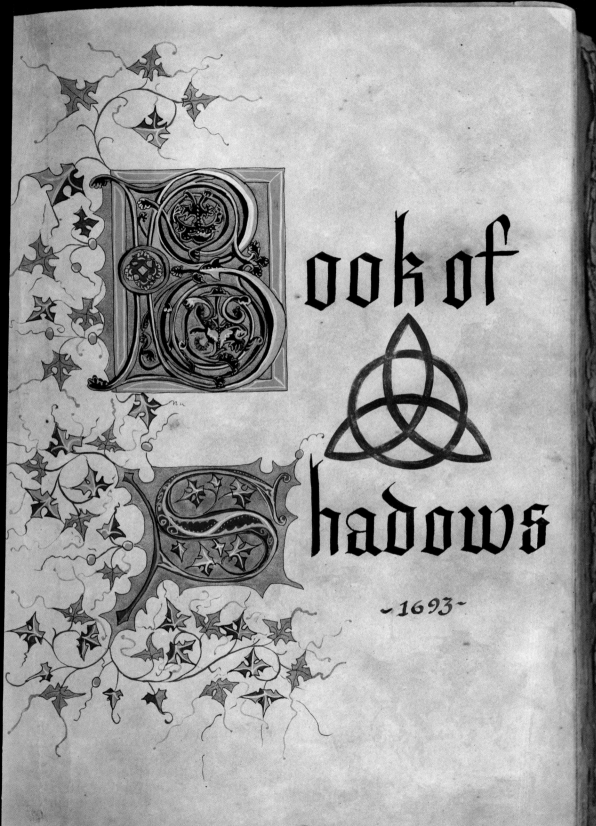

Book of Shadows

~1693~

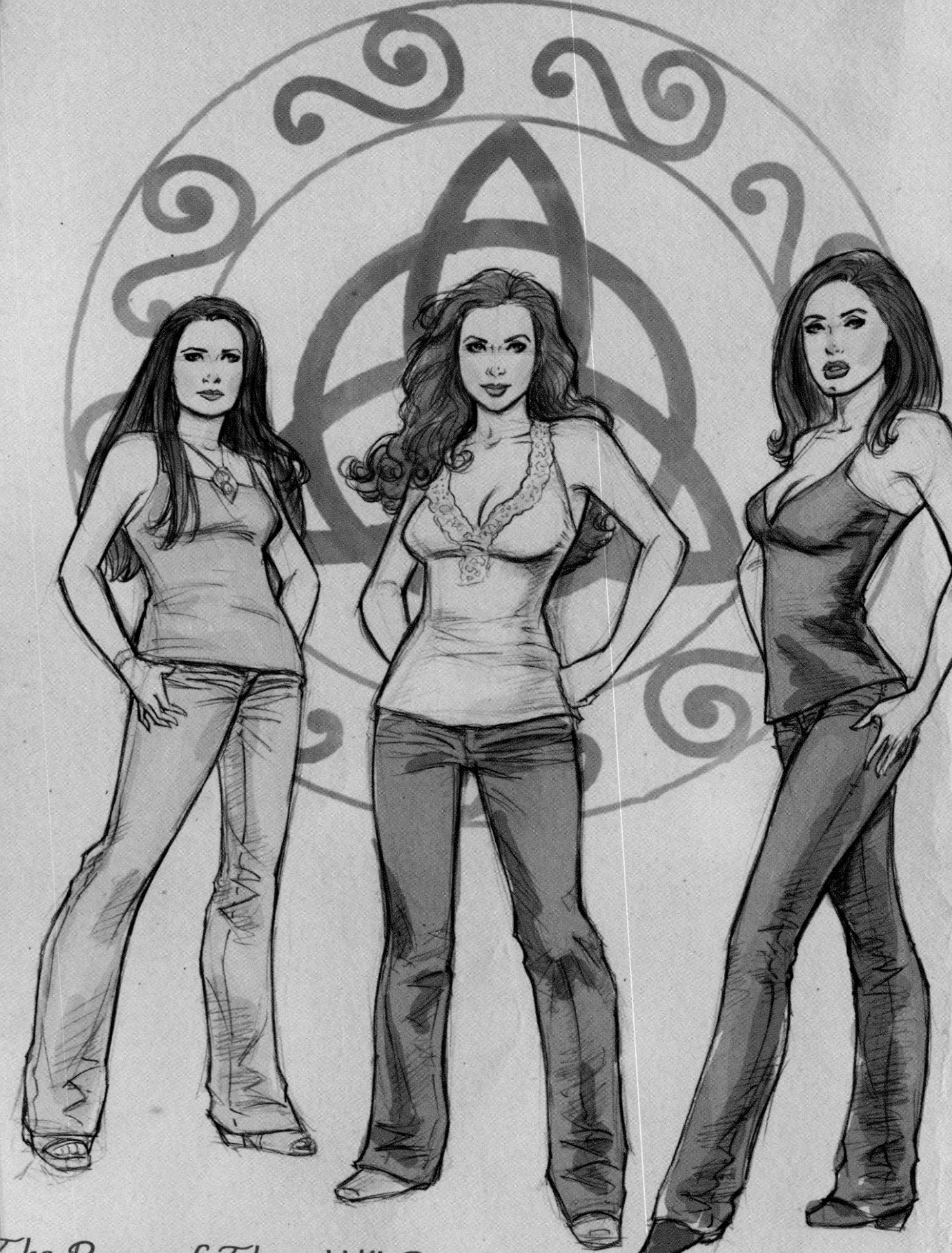

The Power of Three Will Set You Free

The Warren line of witches descends from Melinda Warren, a victim of the Salem Witch Trials in the seventeenth century. As Melinda was burned at the stake she vowed that each generation of Warren witches would grow stronger, culminating in the arrival of three sisters. These sisters would be the most powerful good witches the world has ever known. They would destroy all kinds of evil and be known as The Charmed Ones.

The Charmed Ones

ear now the words
of the witches

The secrets we hid in the night.

The oldest of spells are invoked
here.

The great gift of magic
is sought.

In this night and in this hour,

I call upon the ancient
power.

Bring your power to
we sisters three!

We want the power!

Give us the power!

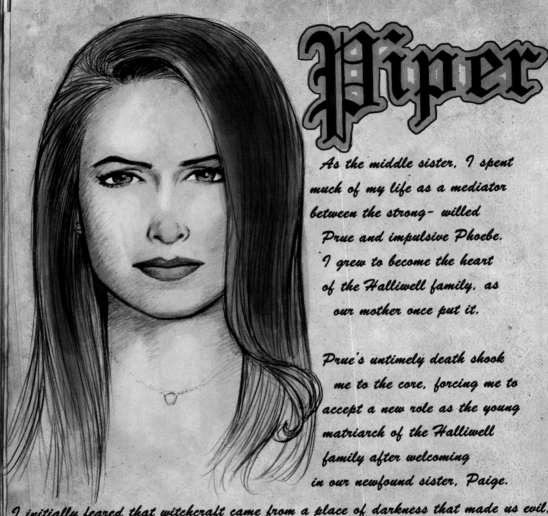

Piper

As the middle sister, I spent much of my life as a mediator between the strong- willed Prue and impulsive Phoebe. I grew to become the heart of the Halliwell family, as our mother once put it.

Prue's untimely death shook me to the core, forcing me to accept a new role as the young matriarch of the Halliwell family after welcoming in our newfound sister, Paige.

I initially feared that witchcraft came from a place of darkness that made us evil, but I quickly learned that we were a powerful force for good. The first of my powers to be revealed was the ability to freeze people and objects through molecular immobilization. That ability grew into speeding the molecules to the point of combustion, which proved an easier way to take out low-level demons. I studied to be a chef, managed a restaurant, and eventually opened the nightclub, P3, with the help of my sisters. My cooking skills also made me a natural at brewing potions, if I do say so myself.

Leo Wyatt

Soon after my powers reawakened I met a guardian angel in the form of Whitelighter Leo Wyatt. Leo died heroically in World War Two and was rewarded with an offer to work for the side of good instead of moving on to the afterlife. Though romance between a Whitelighter and his charge was forbidden, Leo and I fell in love and married. The fates and our own stubbornness threw many obstacles into our course of love, but we stuck it out, started a family, and look forward to growing old together.

I spent much of my life searching for my place in the world. After a brief time in New York, I returned home to the strained relationship with my sister, Prue. Ever the impetuous one, I proudly take the blame for chanting the incantation that activated the power of The Charmed Ones. With the help of our magical sisterhood, Prue and I healed our rift before her tragic death.

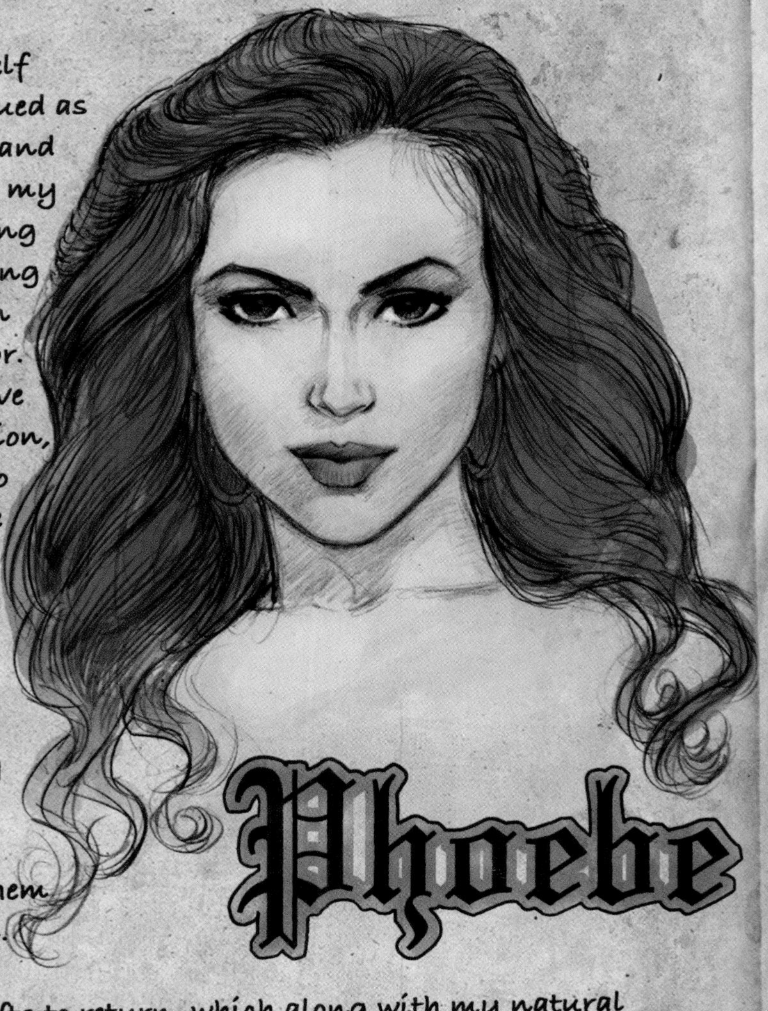

Phoebe

My journey for self discovery continued as I finished college and eventually found my passion, stumbling into a career writing an advice column for The Bay Mirror. My primary active power is premonition, with the ability to see into the future as well as the past. For a time, I also possessed the powers of levitation and empathy, but my active magic was stripped from me when I exploited them for personal gain. Premonition was the first of my gifts to return, which along with my natural spell-writing talent, still makes me a powerful force for good.

I have had two great loves in my life beginning with the half-human, Cole Turner. Cole was torn in two by his demon half, Belthazor, when we met. Though he escaped Belthazor's grasp, our relationship ended in tragedy when he could not overcome the darkness still within him.

Coop -

Several men followed Cole, but none of them could fill the hole in my heart until the Elders assigned a Cupid named Coop to help me find love again. What neither of us realized was that the Elders had always intended for Coop to be that love.

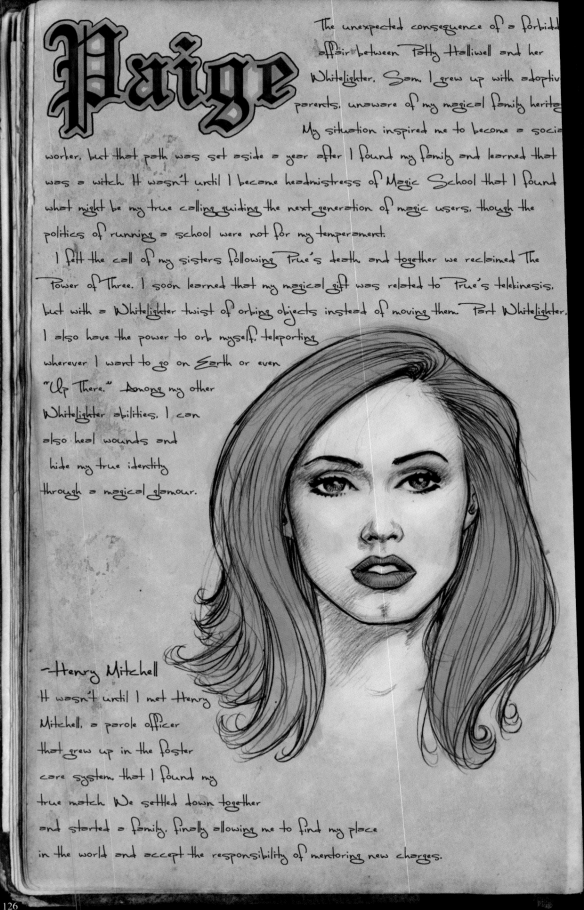

Paige

The unexpected consequence of a forbidden affair between Patty Halliwell and her Whitelighter, Sam, I grew up with adoptive parents, unaware of my magical family heritage.

My situation inspired me to become a social worker, but that path was set aside a year after I found my family and learned that I was a witch. It wasn't until I became headmistress of Magic School that I found what might be my true calling, guiding the next generation of magic users, though the politics of running a school were not for my temperament.

I felt the call of my sisters following Prue's death and together we reclaimed The Power of Three. I soon learned that my magical gift was related to Prue's telekinesis, but with a Whitelighter twist of orbing objects instead of moving them. Part Whitelighter, I also have the power to orb myself, teleporting wherever I want to go on Earth or even "Up There." Among my other Whitelighter abilities, I can also heal wounds and hide my true identity through a magical glamour.

—Henry Mitchell

It wasn't until I met Henry Mitchell, a parole officer that grew up in the foster care system, that I found my true match. We settled down together and started a family, finally allowing me to find my place in the world and accept the responsibility of mentoring new charges.

In Memoriam

Prue Halliwell

Prue Halliwell was the firstborn Charmed One. After our mother died, Prue took on a maternal role when we moved in with our Grams. At first, Prue was skeptical of the magic and Phoebe's leap-before-looking approach to gaining our powers, but she came to fully embrace our heritage. Prue always had an interest in history, having worked with antiquities in her job at Buckland Auction House before returning to her passion for photography.

She was not a stranger to loss, having to let her first true love, Andy Trudeau, die in the fight against evil. Prue's powers of telekinesis and astral projection grew over time, but even those were not enough to save her when the Source's assassin, Shax, took her from our family at far too young an age.

COLE TURNER

Each of The Charmed Ones has dated darkness over the years, but no one from the side of evil had more of an affect on our family than Cole Turner. His half-demon side, Belthazor was in constant battle with the human half, Cole, when I, Phoebe, fell in love with him. Our tumultuous relationship led to a marriage performed in a dark ceremony, even though our love was pure. Unfortunately, that love was not enough to save Cole when his darkness took control and we were forced to vanquish him for good.

Witches

Wiccan Rede: And it harm none, do what ye will

Witches, like mortals, can be either good or evil, but only the good witches serve as protectors of the Innocent. Traditionally, Witches are born with a primary active power, such as telekinesis, but their powers grow as they age. Often, their supernatural abilities are exhibited in early childhood, though it is not unusual for a person to grow into adulthood before her or his capabilities are realized. In addition to their active powers, Witches can also cast spells and create potions to amplify their magic. They live by the rule that they are not to use their magic for personal gain. Witches must decide within the first forty-eight hours of their powers awakening if they will travel the path of good or evil.

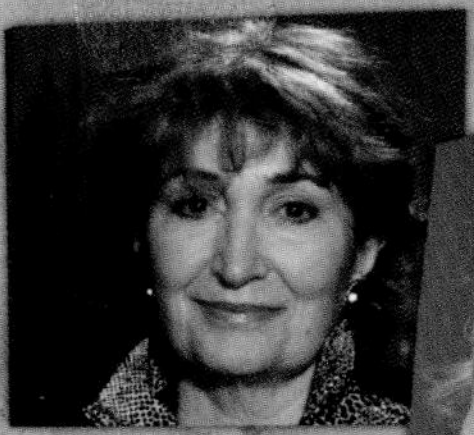

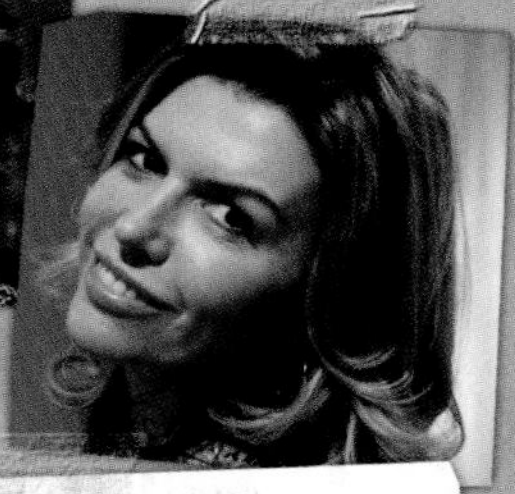

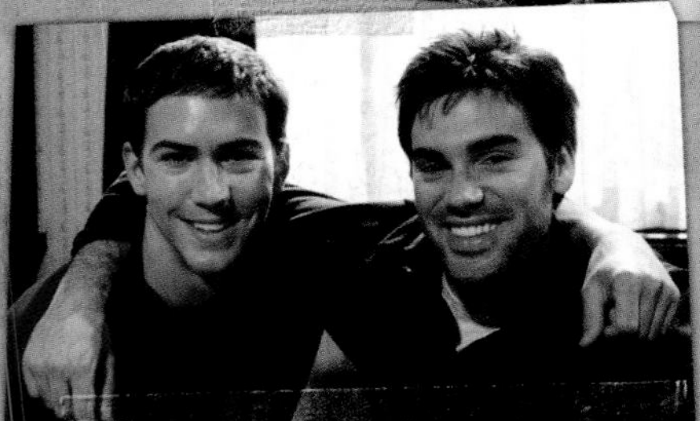

The Warren Witches

The powerful line of witches descended from Melinda Warren, a seventeenth century witch that was burned at the stake. The Warren Witches grew stronger with each generation until Patricia Halliwell gave birth to The Charmed Ones, a trio of sisters prophesied to be the most powerful witches the world has ever known. The line continues with their offspring, beginning with Piper's sons, Wyatt and Chris, who have journeyed from the future on occasion to help the current generation.

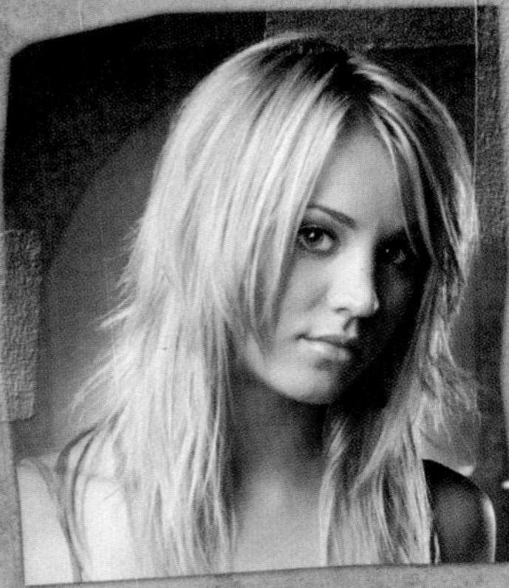

Billie Jenkins

Billie Jenkins was a protege of The Charmed Ones and aided in the fight against evil while they were in hiding. She continued to train with the sisters after their existence was revealed to the world and became a strong force for good. Billie turned to the side of evil after she reunited with her long-lost sister, Christy, who had been kidnapped years earlier and turned by demons. Together, Billie and Christy became the Ultimate Power fighting for the side of evil against The Charmed Ones. In the end, Billie saw the truth and came back to the side of good, but her sister died when she refused to give up the fight.

the Elders

Also known as the Founders, they are the highest level of Whitelighter. The Elders control the ranks of the guardian angels and keep track of the good witches they protect. They are not all-knowing but they can aid with their vast wisdom.

Whitelighters

Entrusted with protecting witches and future Whitelighters, these guardian angels guide their charges in the use of their magic. Mortals in life, they are given the choice to become Whitelighters or move on to the afterlife upon their death. Among their many powers, Whitelighters can teleport through a process known as orbing and they possess a healing touch.

Angels of Destiny

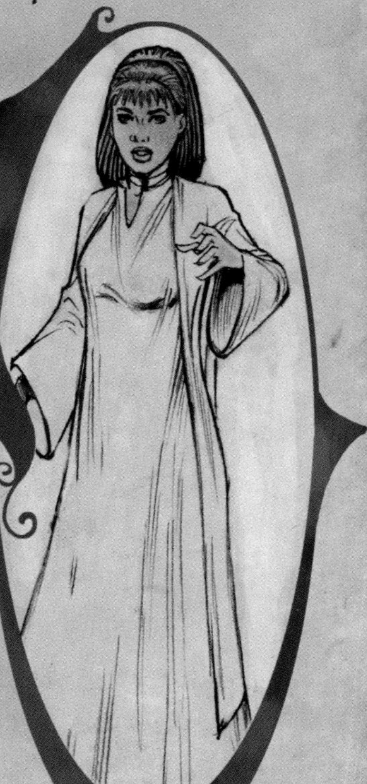

Magical beings that possess the knowledge of all things. They serve as keepers of the Grand Design and bear the responsibility of maintaining that the future plays out as it is destined.

Halliwell Manor

This San Francisco Victorian house has been the residence of the Halliwell family for generations. The Manor was built on land containing a Spiritual Nexus that can be used for either good or evil. The Halliwell family moved into the Manor to claim the Nexus for good and made it their home.

Magic School

The Elders established Magic School as a training ground for young magic users. Set apart in a separate realm, hidden portals all over the Earth allow access to the school for those who have permission to enter. The school was set up as a safe environment for learning and protective wards were created to keep the students safe from death during their studies. Those wards were breached when The Charmed Ones went into hiding, allowing Magic School to fall under demon domain until it could be reclaimed.

The Upper Regions

Known in the vernacular as "Up There," this is the location from which the Elders watch over the world. Only Whitelighters possess the ability to orb into The Upper Regions, though the forces of evil have, at times, stolen those powers to infiltrate the heavens.

To Call a Lost Witch

Put following Ingredients in a Silver Mortar:

A pinch of rosemary
a sprig of cypress
A yarrow root

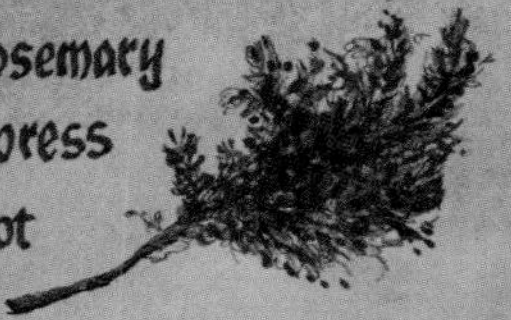

Grind with a Pestle while Chanting:

Power of the witches rise
course unseen across the skies
come to us who call you near
Come to us and settle here

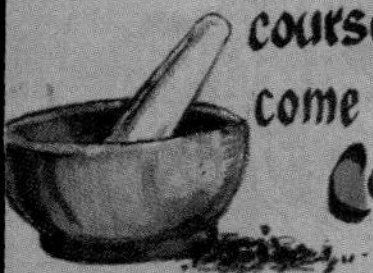

Spill the blood of the Caller into Mortar
and continue Chanting:

Blood to blood, I summon Thee
Blood to blood, return to Me

How to Perform a Seance

A Ceremony to Contact the Dead

To perform this ritual, you will need six candles, White and Purple in color and a White cloth. In addition, you will need to sweeten the air by burning Cinnamon, Frankincense and sandle wood. As the fire burns, concentrate on contacting the Spirit and Chant the Spell that follows. If you know the mortal name of the deceased, adjust the Chant accordingly.

Beloved Unknown Spirit.
We Seek Your Guidance.
We ask that You Commune
with Us and move among Us.

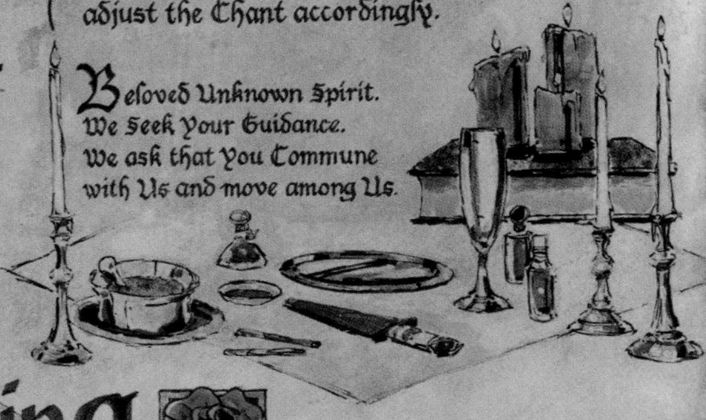

Handfasting

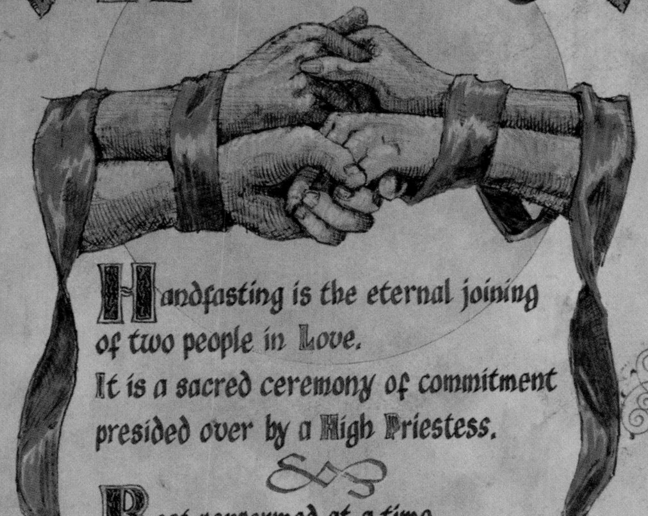

Handfasting is the eternal joining of two people in Love.
It is a sacred ceremony of commitment presided over by a High Priestess.

Best performed at a time of sunrise or sunset where both the Sun and the Moon are present in the joining of the two Lovers.

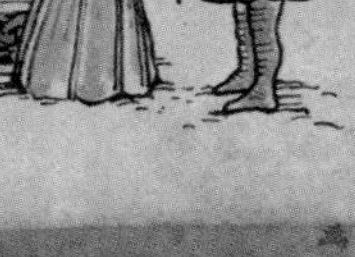

Scrying for something lost

Over a map
a crystal on thread
should flow
Name what is sought
and the point will show.

To call upon our Ancestors

Prudence, Penelope
Patricia, Melinda...
Astrid, Helena,
Laura and Grace,

Halliwell Witches,
stand strong beside us
vanquish this evil
from time and space

To Summon a Darklighter
Uxo Mende Layto Sempar

The Hollow

... To Contain The Hollow ...
aboleo extum cavium du eternias

... To Summon The Hollow ...
nos dico super inconcessus vox
bonus quod malum.
ultir usque a profugus
addo is hic, addo is iam.

... To Return The Hollow ...
iam is addo, hic is addo
malum quod bonus.
vox inconcessus super dico nos

Vanishing Spell

Let the Object
of Objection
Become but
a Dream
As I cause
the Seen
To be Unseen

To Find Your True Love's Name

Fill your heart with only thoughts of love.
Slice the skin from an apple in one continuous peel.
Close your eyes and blow on the apple peel.
Drop the peel into water and
Watch it form the initial of your true love's first name.

Warlocks

Warlocks have one goal: To kill good witches so they can obtain the witches' powers. They are witches that have chosen to follow the dark path by performing an irrevocable act of evil in killing another witch or by marrying a warlock in a Dark Binding. Most Warlocks have the power to teleport, known as blinking, though some lesser Warlocks are too weak to perform that act.

Darklighters

Darklighters are on a mission to kill Whitelighters, which leaves their charges vulnerable to attack by the forces of evil. They can orb through a process known as black orbing, and some can inflict a touch of death, in contrast to a Whitelighter's healing power. A Darklighter's crossbow is armed with arrows covered in a poison lethal to Whitelighters.

Underworld

The dark realm beneath the Earth where evil resides.

Demons

Observations upon the Nature, the Number, and the Operations of the Devils.

The Source of All Evil

The ruler of the Underworld, The Source of All Evil is the most powerful demon in existence. The Charmed Ones first encountered the Source in the body of a demon bearing the scars of an ancient battle, but the Evil essence has possessed the bodies of numerous demons over the centuries. The Charmed Ones succeeded in vanquishing that initial demon body, but its essence was transferred into other evil entities before being banished to the Wasteland. The Source returned, briefly, years later in his earlier, scarred demon form that was ultimately vanquished.

Zankou

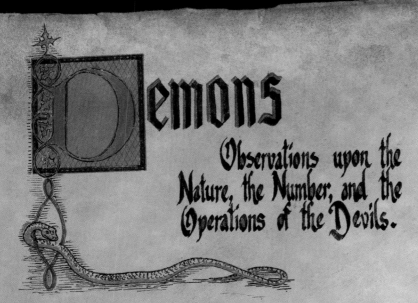

One of the most powerful Demons of the Underworld, Zankou is a threat to all that is good and feared even by his own kind. So great were his abilities and ambitions, he once contested The Source for control of the Underworld and was banished as punishment. After teaming with The Charmed Ones to defeat the Avatars, Zankou continued his evil ways and was vanquished when he united with the Spiritual Nexus located under the Halliwell Manor.

The Triad

The Triad is a collective of powerful upper-level demons. Virtual Emperors of the Underworld, when together, the powers of this evil cabal increase exponentially and there is no known method of vanquishing them. Though unconfirmed, rumors persist of splinter groups seeking to carry out their own agendas.

Avatars

are neither good nor evil. They possess immense power and exist outside time and space. The Avatars viewed the constant battle between good and evil as pointless and enlisted Leo to convince The Charmed Ones to assist them in creating a perfect world. When the price for that perfect world proved too high, The Charmed Ones allied with the demon Zankou to undo the false paradise they had helped create.

Guardians of the Hollow

Thirty five hundred years ago,
The Hollow was unleashed on the world.
The Hollow is a force that has the power
to consume all magical powers, good or
evil and is impossible to destroy.

While roaming the earth, The Hollow
nearly decimated all magic. Good and
Evil had to join forces and combine
their strongest magic to contain it.
It was placed in an ancient crypt and
is guarded by a representative from
both sides, an Angel and a Devil, for all
eternity.

The Ancient Burial Ground

A realm that exists in infinity, outside of time and space, where the crypt that houses the Hollow is located.

Year One

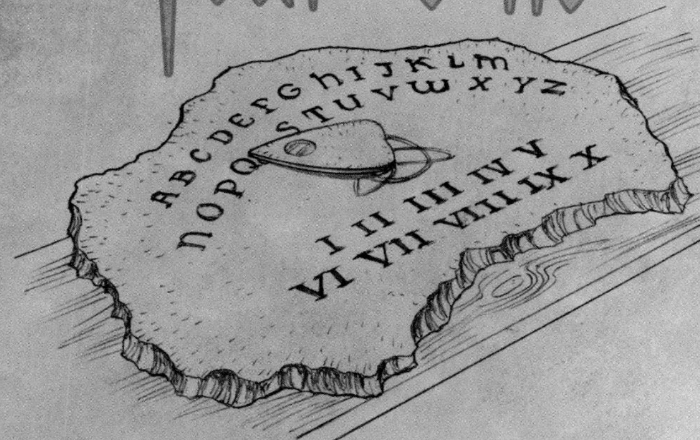
ABCDEFGHIJKLM
NOPQRSTUVWXYZ
I II III IV V
VI VII VIII IX X

In the wake of Grams' death, Phoebe returned home from New York and her failed effort to reunite with our father. Her tense reunion with Prue was cut short when a ghostly hand used the spirit board our mother left us to send a message directing us to the attic in the Halliwell Manor. The previously locked room opened for Phoebe and inside she found this Book of Shadows in an old trunk. Reciting the incantation found on these opening pages she tapped into the magical gifts that had been bound within us as children and awakened the power of The Charmed Ones.

Old flames returned and new relationships were forged over the course of our first year as witches. Prue reunited with her former love, Andy Trudeau, who introduced us to a new friend in his partner, Darryl Morris. The Elders sent us our own guardian angel in Leo Wyatt, a Whitelighter who would eventually become family.

We made some mistakes learning to control our powers, but grew stronger as we studied the magical tenets. We were visited by our ancestor, Melinda Warren, traveled back in time ourselves, and fought many evil beings, including some that had been sent to us by the most powerful demon in the Underworld, The Source of All Evil.

In spite of our triumphs, we also suffered deeply during that first year as The Charmed Ones. Prue's relationship with Andy was challenged when she revealed our secret to him and he was forced to cover up our supernatural mysteries. But nothing caused more pain than when Andy gave his life to protect us.

Year Two

In our second year embracing our Wiccan heritage, we were visited by the spirit of Grams for the first time and learned that it was her ghostly hand that had been guiding us through the Book of Shadows. Though we had gained much insight since our powers were reawakened, it was during this second year that we had one of our most painful lessons to date. A visit to the future forced us to bear witness to Phoebe's death as a possible path we could follow if we made the wrong choices with our magical gifts in the present.

Piper was juggling a lot in both her personal and professional lives. She had finally grown tired of working at the restaurant, Quake, and opened her own club. She named it P3 in honor of The Power of Three as well as for the initials of we three sisters who became partners in the endeavor. Meanwhile, she was bouncing back and forth in relationships with Leo and a new next-door neighbor.

While Prue came to terms with Andy's death, we also discovered that she often visited the lake that was the site of our mother's death. This led to us meeting mom's Whitelighter, Sam, and the discovery that they had a forbidden affair that paralleled Leo's and Piper's love. Sam gave his life to save us from the demon that killed our mother and joined her in the spirit realm. Phoebe also learned to open her heart in time to prepare her to meet a man that would affect her deeply.

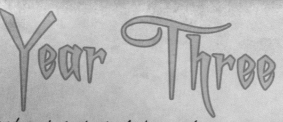

Year Three

Family played an important role for us this year as our father, Victor, returned in the hope that he could be a part of our lives again. We journeyed back in time to ensure that Melinda Warren was born and the Warren line of witches could develop. And Piper and Leo took an important step in their relationship. Word came down from "Up There" that Piper and Leo were to break up or he would be reassigned as our Whitelighter. Tired of Elder interference, they hurriedly prepared a secret wedding that didn't happen. But persistence paid off and Piper and Leo eventually married.

Phoebe had her own relationship issues of a darker sort. Though her powers started to expand with the introduction of levitation, it was a meeting with a half-demon named Cole Turner that was the bigger change in her life. Their relationship started out an endless debate of whether Cole was good or evil, going so far as to get Phoebe to lie to our family and convince us that Cole was dead after he revealed his human side to her.

It was the loss of our sister Prue that stands out as our most tragic event, not only since acquiring our powers, but in our entire lives. In spite of a deal Phoebe made to side with evil to protect her, we were unable to save Prue from an energy blast from the Source's assassin, Shax. The Power of Three was no more, which was an insignificant loss compared to that anguish of Prue being gone.

Year Four

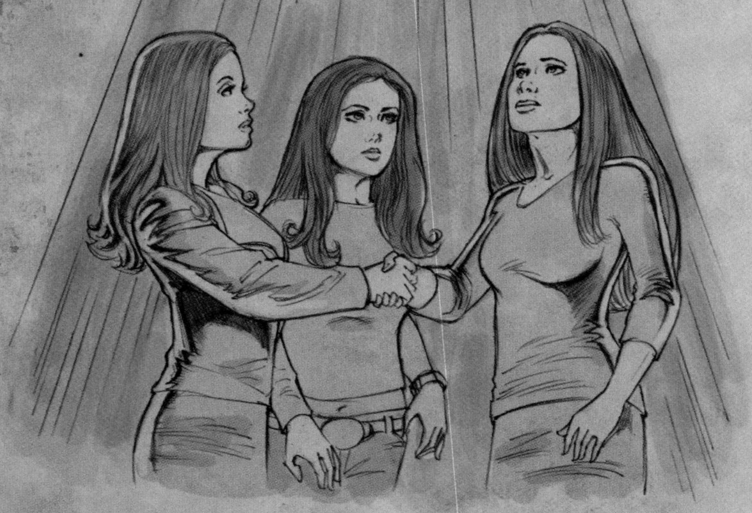

Mourning Prue's death carried us into a year full of darkness and light. Piper was especially affected by the loss of our sister. Her spell To Call a Lost Witch had the unexpected and fortuitous consequence of uniting us with Paige, the sister we never knew we had. The Power of Three was reborn and we were able to vanquish the demon that had taken Prue from us.

After years of battling The Source's demons, we finally defeated the ruler of the Underworld. Or so we thought. As it turned out, we only vanquished The Source's demon form. The Source's essence went into Cole's body, which started off a chain reaction in the Underworld as he battled for power, culminating in a dark marriage to Phoebe that sealed their lives together in evil and conceived a demon child.

We were forced to vanquish Cole, which sent the spirit of the Source into the Seer orchestrating many of the Underworld's recent power plays. Ultimately Phoebe's unborn demon child was transferred to the Seer as well, allowing us to destroy both the new Source and its spawn together. As a reward for what we believed was finally vanquishing The Source of All Evil once and for all, an Angel of Destiny gave us the choice to abandon our role as The Charmed Ones and lead normal lives. One more battle with evil and the return of Cole helped us reignite our belief in the fight for good. We chose to continue to follow our calling.

Year Five

Leo and Piper prepared for the birth of their first child, who was growing more and more powerful in the womb. The arrival of their son, Wyatt, did not ease the constant strain that the Elders' rules had inflicted on Piper and Leo's relationship. The final straw for the couple came when Leo accepted a position as an Elder in order to save the world from the Titans, but he used his powers to help Piper ignore the pain of losing him.

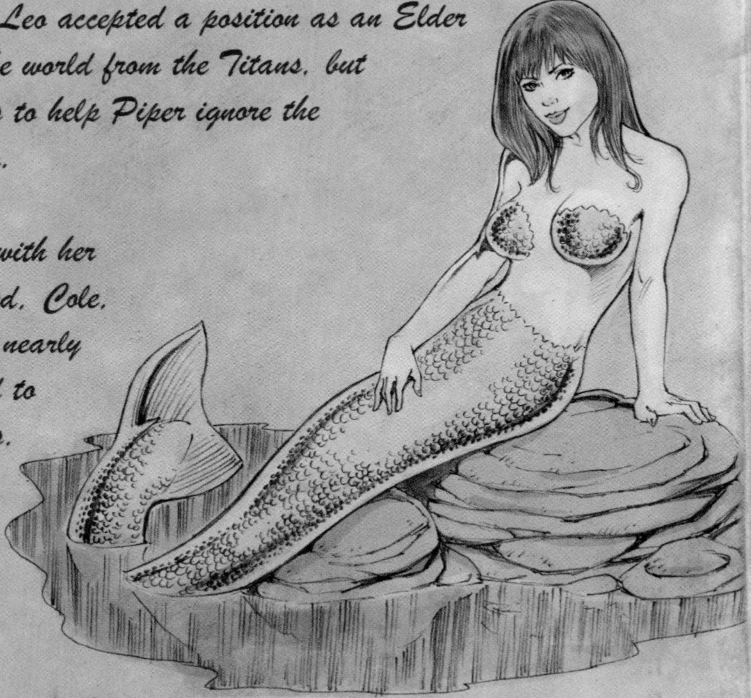

Phoebe's troubles with her resurrected husband, Cole, continued and she nearly became a mermaid to escape the travails. Eventually, Cole came to regret his evil life and tried to kill himself at the hands of The Charmed Ones only to find that he was unvanquishable. He embraced his inner evil again and devised a new plan to win back Phoebe. In an unexpected turn, his evil machinations allowed him to be vanquished for good.

Paige quit her job to become a full time Charmed One, continuing to grow into her powers, which were especially necessary to us when the Titans took over The Upper Regions. Once the battle ended with Leo deciding to reside "Up There", he entrusted us into the care of a Whitelighter from the future named Chris ... who immediately sent Leo mysteriously away.

Year Six

After a month under the impression that Leo was "Up There" ignoring his family, Piper learned that some unknown being had secretly trapped the father of her child in Valhalla. The mystery person turned out to be our new Whitelighter, Chris, who we were even more surprised to learn was the future version of Piper's and Leo's yet-to-be-born second child.

Chris had come to us from a future steeped in darkness because his brother, Wyatt, had turned to evil. We spent much of this next year protecting our littlest one from the forces of the Underworld out to turn him. Being the firstborn son of a Whitelighter and a Charmed One, Wyatt had already displayed some of his impressive powers as a baby, even calling the famed sword Excalibur to him as part of his destiny. Phoebe also gained more magical strength with the power of empathy, while Paige was feeling confident enough with her own power over magic that she decided to return to the workforce.

Leo's Elder mentor, Gideon, introduced us to Magic School, which was created to instruct a new generation of magic users. Another surprise came when Gideon proved to be the one working behind the scenes to turn Wyatt. As a family, we fought off his evil plan in a battle that left adult Chris dying in his father's arms while baby Chris was being born.

Year Seven

The Elders threatened to close Magic School until Paige offered to become headmistress. But even the next generation of witches could not help us against our newest threat. Leo, who was deeply affected by Gideon's betrayal, teamed with the Avatars in their plan to remake the world in their vision of peace.

Paige's latest paramour, Agent Kyle Brody, had some experience with the Avatars and tried to convince her that they were not the salvation Leo considered them. But when a seer showed Phoebe a Utopian future where the fight against evil had ended and she lived happily with a daughter, we began to suspect that the Avatars might be right. We misguidedly joined the Avatars to rewrite the world in their vision: a vision in which free will no longer existed and the most minor bad acts were met with a harsh punishment.

With the idea that the enemy of our enemy is our friend, we teamed with a new foe, Zankou, to take down the Avatars. Kyle was lost in the battle, but the Elders rewarded him by making him a Whitelighter. Leo, however, still needed to be punished for siding with the Avatars and was forced to choose between his family and the Elders. He ultimately decided to remain at home, stripped of his powers so that he was mortal once more.

While Leo took over as Headmaster of Magic School, our friend, Darryl Morris, was feeling the pressure of years of covering for us, especially with his new partner, Inspector Sheridan. Zankou's latest actions forced our secret to be revealed, putting us all in danger. In vanquishing Zankou, we had to "vanquish" ourselves as well, going into hiding from both the mortal world and the magical one.

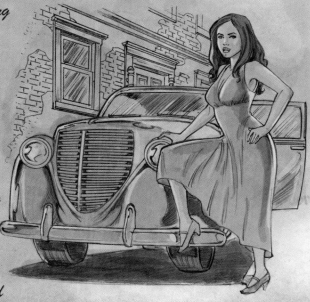

143

Year Eight

Our eighth year in magic began with another loss when our friend, Darryl, moved his family to the east coast to protect them from a danger the world no longer believed existed: Us. The Charmed Ones were gone, though we still lived in the Manor under the glamour of our fictional cousins. We didn't stay in that guise for long as the government came calling and a Homeland Security agent helped us reveal that we lived—and were mortal—so long as we promised to continue the battle against evil.

We did this with the help of a young witch named Billie Jenkins. Paige's latest charge had her own personal demons to fight. While Billie helped us take on evil—including the return of an old enemy in The Source of All Evil—she was also searching for her sister who was kidnapped years earlier by demons.

An Angel of Death came for Leo, but an agreement with The Angel of Destiny allowed us to put him on ice while we made sure that the Grand Design played out as envisioned. We were warned to expect a battle with the Ultimate Power that would shape the future and that Leo's loss would be the motivation for us to wage that war. Little did we expect that Billie would be the key to that Ultimate Power.

Billie teamed with her newly found sister, Christy, who had been brainwashed after years with her demon captors. The Triad, along with Christy's mentor, Dumain, used the Jenkins sisters to call the Hollow in an attempt to destroy us. The fight was intense. Lives were lost and regained. In the end, we dealt a crushing blow to evil, though Billie was forced to sacrifice her sister in the process.

Forever Charmed

So much has happened over the last eight years. So much has been gained and lost. Still, in some ways I feel like my life is really just beginning ... And it was. For, though I had loved before, I'd never really known love until I met Coop; a man who I shared the special little girl I had long ago foreseen, but feared I might never have ... Along with two other special little girls I had not foreseen. I was suddenly so blessed to have a new family of my own and old friends to share it with. And though I kept working and giving advice to those who asked, I was more interested in helping them find love. Since, finally, having been loved...

... Phoebe had become somewhat of an expert on the subject. As for me, life without demons opened up similar avenues. Henry, of course, continued to look after his parolees, even if they didn't want to be looked after, while still making time to help me with his kids and the twins ... Which allowed me time to finally embrace my inner Whitelighter and to help the next generation of witches come into their own...

...So that Paige could pass on all that she'd learned not just to her own children, or to mine, or to Phoebe's, but to other future witches and Whitelighters as well. Which meant that my sisters and I could stop living the fighting and demons life we were all enough to take over ... Allowing me time to get back to my roots and cook something other than potions for once and open the restaurant I'd always dreamed of owning. As for Leo, after we reclaimed Magic School, he went back to teaching, which he continued to do until it was time to retire. And although we've certainly had our struggles and heartaches over the years, we're a family of survivors and we will always be ... Which is why we've truly been Charmed.

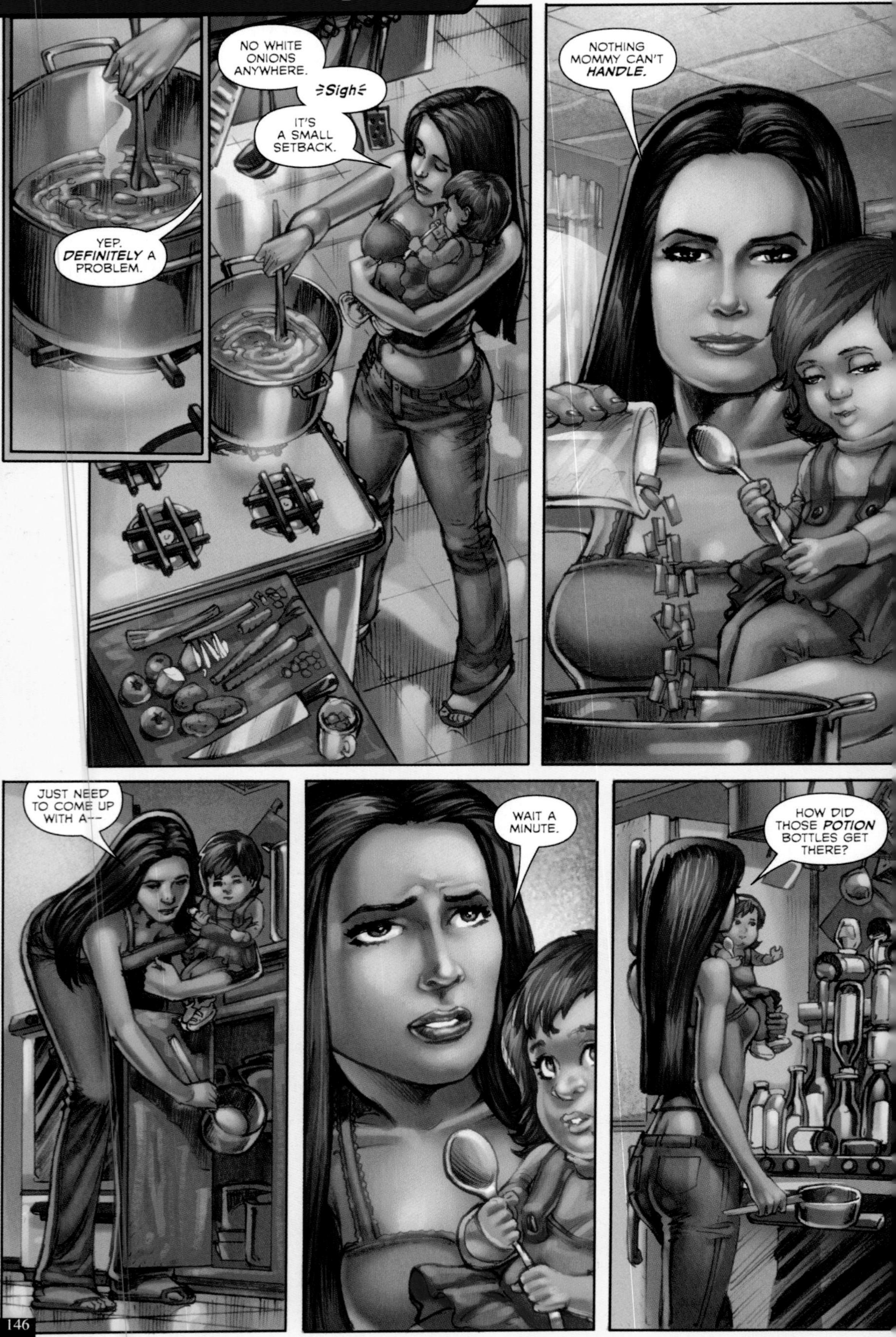
YEP. DEFINITELY A PROBLEM.
NO WHITE ONIONS ANYWHERE.
Sigh
IT'S A SMALL SETBACK.
NOTHING MOMMY CAN'T HANDLE.
JUST NEED TO COME UP WITH A--
WAIT A MINUTE.
HOW DID THOSE POTION BOTTLES GET THERE?

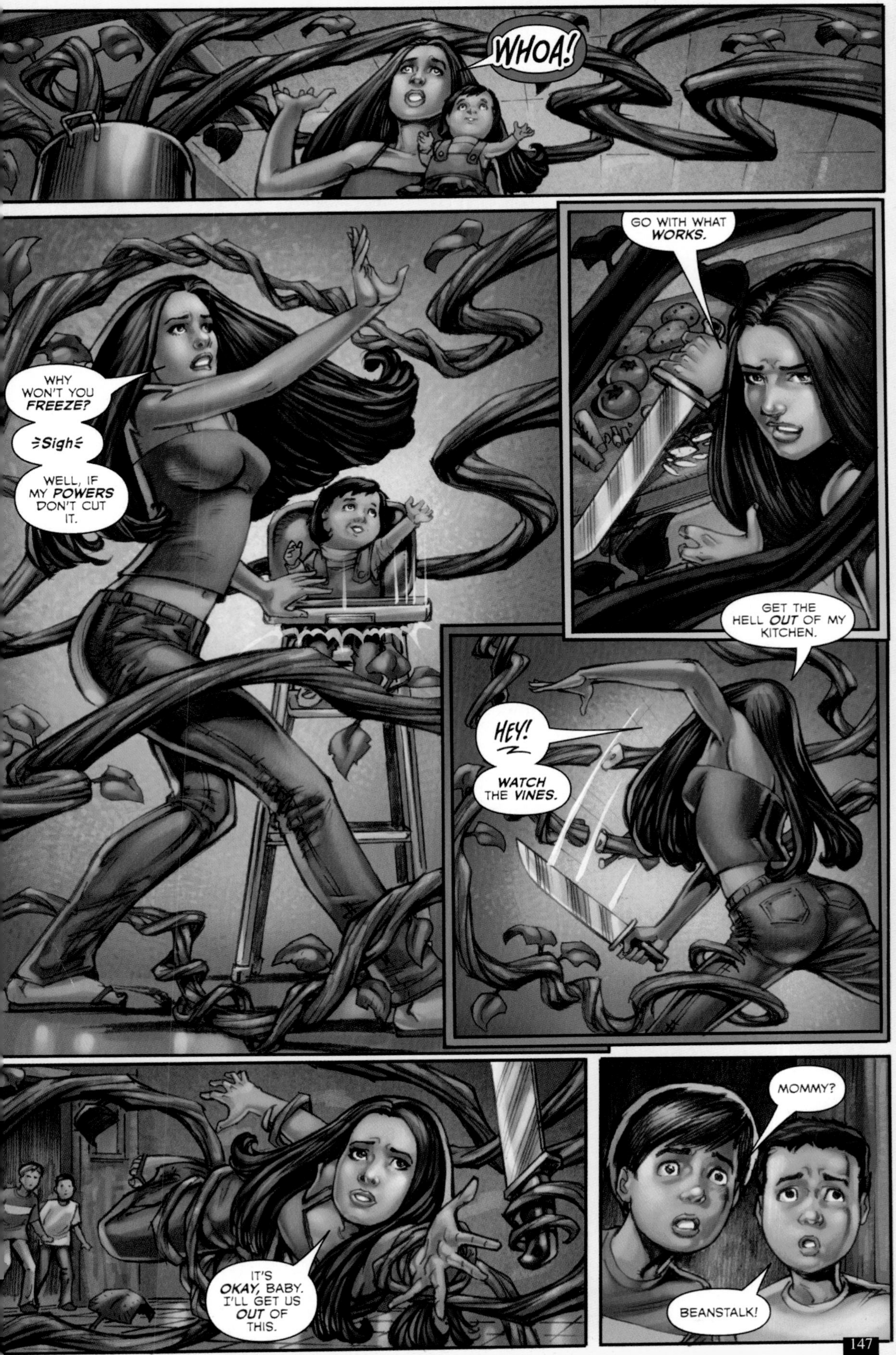
WHOA!
WHY WON'T YOU FREEZE?
⁼Sigh⁼
WELL, IF MY POWERS DON'T CUT IT.
GO WITH WHAT WORKS.
GET THE HELL OUT OF MY KITCHEN.
HEY!
WATCH THE VINES.
IT'S OKAY, BABY. I'LL GET US OUT OF THIS.
MOMMY?
BEANSTALK!

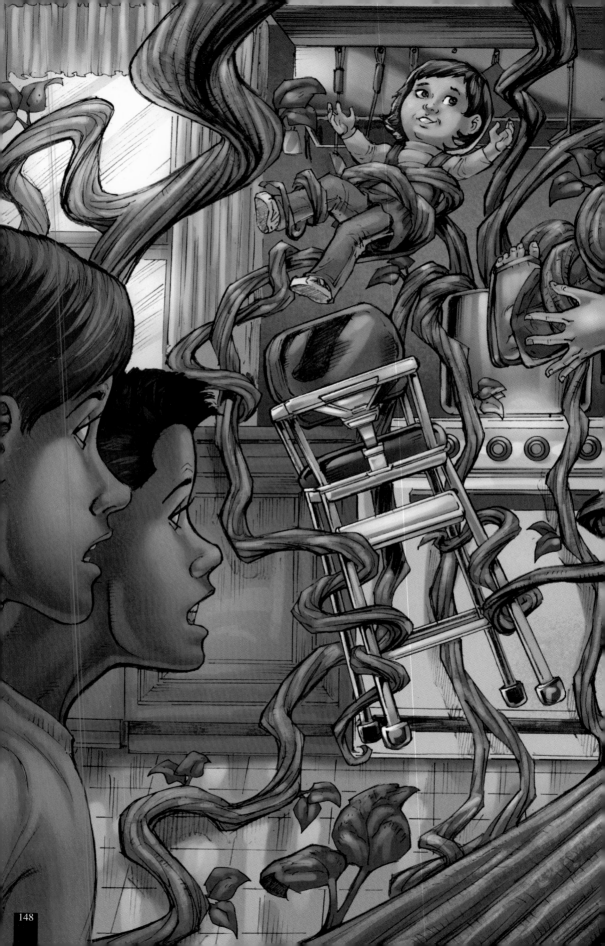

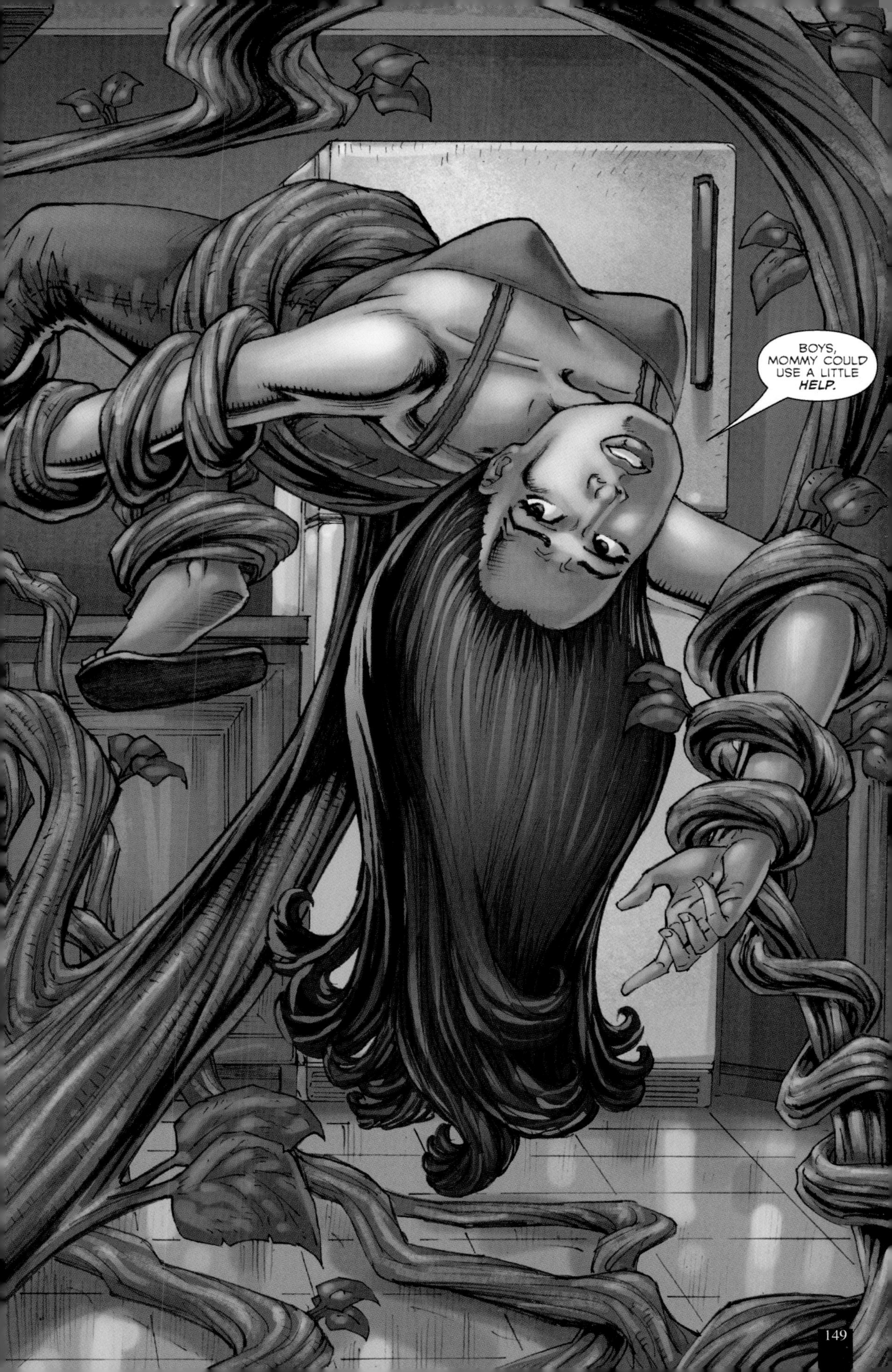
BOYS,
MOMMY COULD
USE A LITTLE
HELP.

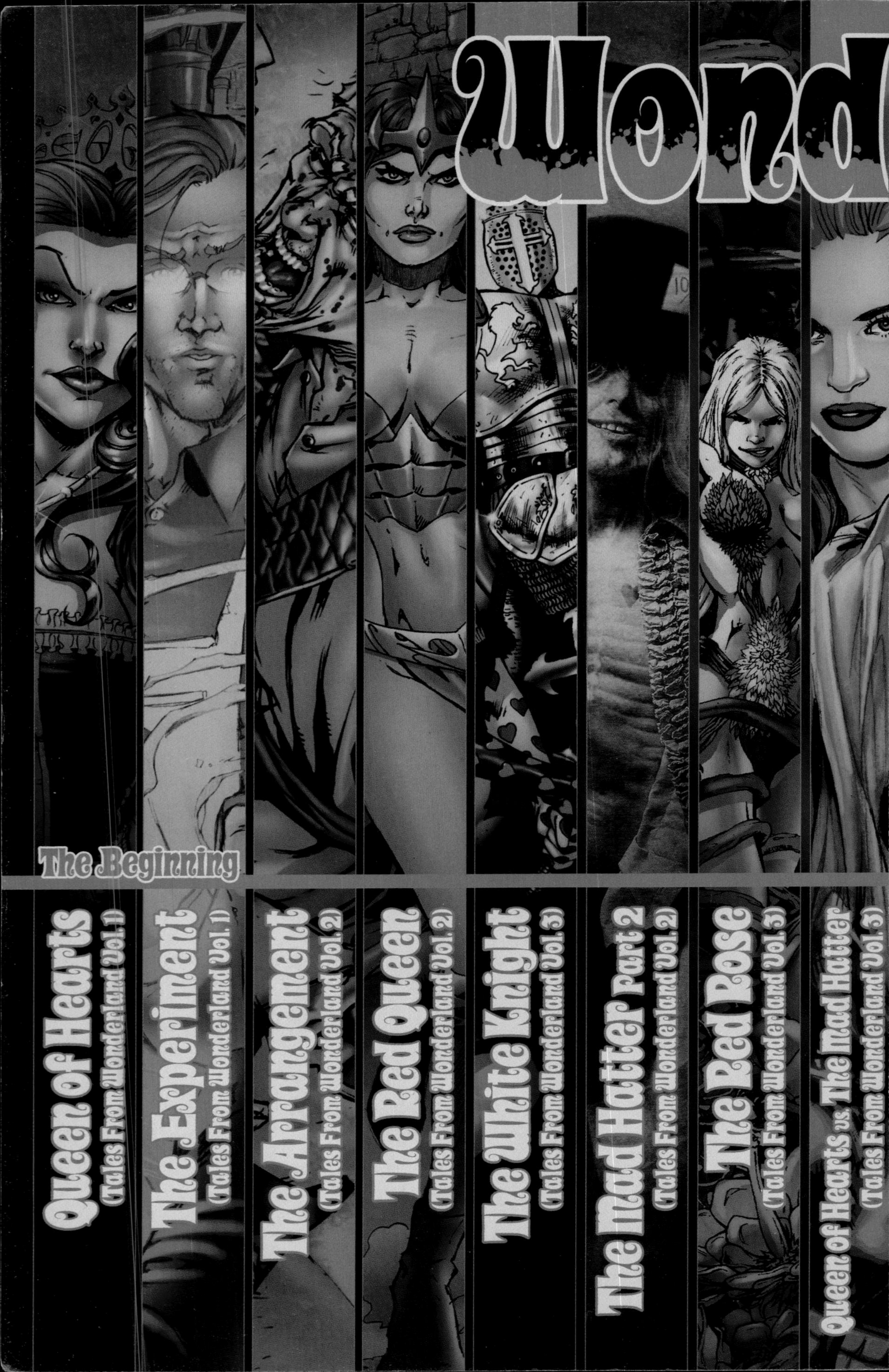
Wond
The Beginning
Queen of Hearts (Tales From Wonderland Vol. 1)
The Experiment (Tales From Wonderland Vol. 1)
The Arrangement (Tales From Wonderland Vol. 2)
The Red Queen (Tales From Wonderland Vol. 2)
The White Knight (Tales From Wonderland Vol. 3)
The Mad Hatter Part 2 (Tales From Wonderland Vol. 2)
The Red Rose (Tales From Wonderland Vol. 3)
Queen of Hearts vs. The Mad Hatter (Tales From Wonderland Vol. 3)

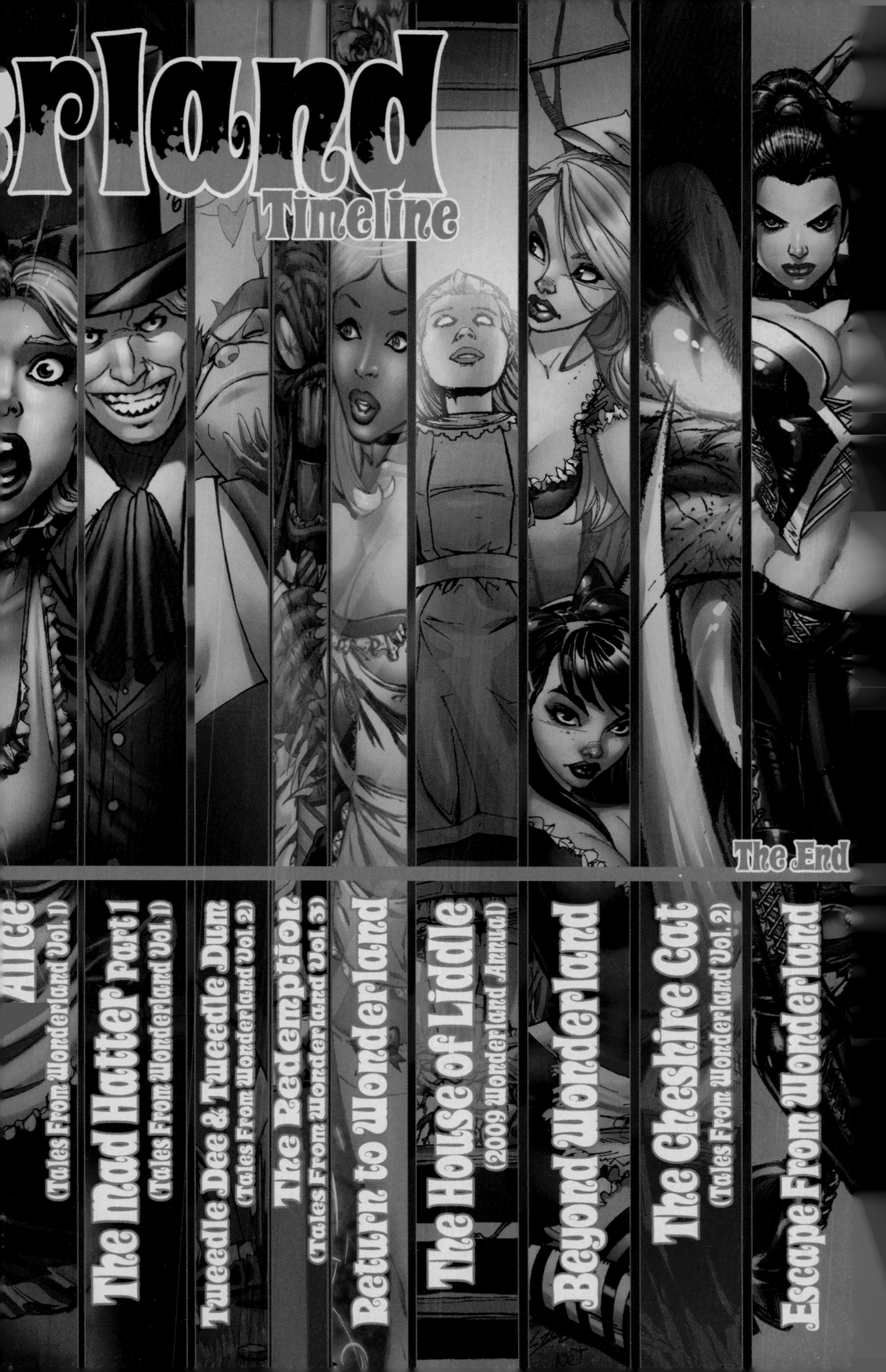
rland
Timeline
Alice
(Tales From Wonderland Vol. 1)
The Mad Hatter part 1
(Tales From Wonderland Vol. 1)
Tweedle Dee & Tweedle Dum
(Tales From Wonderland Vol. 2)
The Redemption
(Tales From Wonderland Vol. 3)
Return to Wonderland
The House of Liddle
(2009 Wonderland Annual)
Beyond Wonderland
The Cheshire Cat
(Tales From Wonderland Vol. 2)
Escape From Wonderland
The End

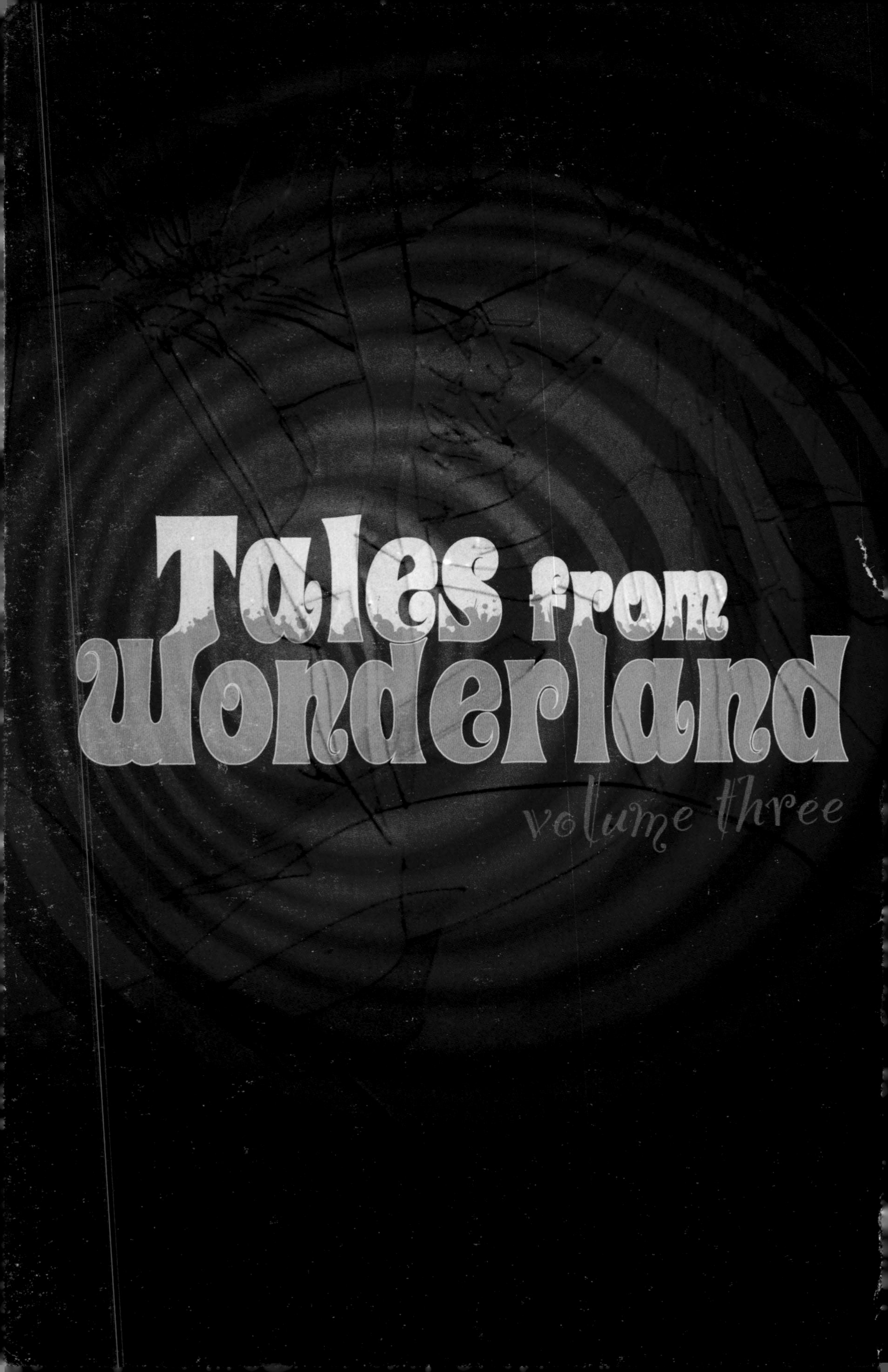
Tales from
Wonderland
volume three